D 7-

SIGNS OF LIFE

WORSHIP FOR A JUST AND LOVING PEOPLE

A TREATISE IN ELEVEN PARTS

RICK FABIAN

CHURCH
PUBLISHING
INCORPORATED

Church Publishing
19 East 34th Street
New York, NY 10016
www.churchpublishing.org

Front cover: Wedding Icon in St. Gregory's Church apse, by Mark Dukes (photo by David Sanger); used by permission

Cover design by Jennifer Kopec, 2Pug Design
Typeset by Rose Design

A record of this book is available from the Library of Congress.

ISBN-13: 978-1-64065-218-7 (pbk.)

ISBN-13: 978-1-64065-219-4 (ebook)

For Donald and Ellen
And for Leesy

Without deviation from the norm, progress is not possible.

—Frank Zappa

Contents

ɔᗡᑫ

Komodo Island Dragon, or the Author at work

INTRODUCTION

cs

What is truth? said jesting Pilate, and would not stay for an answer.
—FRANCIS BACON, "OF TRUTH," 1625[1]

How does it matter what Christians do in church? What harbor do they voyage for, and why in this company? How might more fellows journey there, and why should they choose to? After six decades plotting one course through Anglican waters, I cruised parish ports seeking such answers. Yet even at friendly coffee hours, not many layfolk volunteered reasons. Worshippers told me how they chose this ship or ship line above others, but seldom why they sailed on a church craft at all, or would impress unchurched friends to come aboard. None claiming family tradition explained how that loyalty withstood the waves washing others off decks. Today conventional church charts seem to guide fewer journeymakers over life's undersea mountains and trenches. Therefore this exploration will re-draw those routes, so that a wider spread of passengers and crew can talk and plan together. And here, as in much church life, lay people's voices will have the last words.

The lay teacher Origen of Alexandria (d. 290 CE) was the most influential Christian writer after Paul of Tarsus, and his theological map quickened nearly all later guides, orthodox or not. As the late Richard Norris taught, Origen set our course thirteen centuries before Luther rediscovered it: Christian theology *is* commentary upon scripture. The present book joins two nautical charts lately folded apart, hoping that our ships can sail together again before fresh breezes. Fifty years back, explorers like Benedict Green, CR,[2] navigated both scriptural and liturgical criticism at once, while scouts brought fresh evidence aboard. But more recent Bible scholars steer off liturgical practice as a devotional morass, while liturgical writers row apart from shifting biblical swells. Some captain ritual renewal, and others, missionary innovation. Yet

---

1. Francis Bacon, "Of Truth," *Essays or Counsels Civil and Moral*, ed. Richard Foster Jones (New York: Odyssey, 1937), 4.

2. CR: The Anglican monastic Community of the Resurrection at Mirfield, Yorkshire, UK, includes several eminent scholars and a theological college seminary.

both navies must pilot among the currents of world faiths now, which no longer flow safely far away.

Our flotilla can follow fresh pilot charts from Gregory of Nyssa, a creative Kurdish thinker. Bishop Gregory Nyssen led debates at fourth-century church councils, but for medieval ages his humanism and universalism made mystics his chief followers. Today those very virtues—and Gregory's deep biblical learning—draw admirers inside church and out. He saw every created life as an endless ethical progress. Gregory's final plea to put away rewards and punishments, and only become God's friend, resonates in our era honoring personal expression free from social conformity.

The Episcopal Diocese of California organized St. Gregory of Nyssa Church at San Francisco in 1978, to press further the liturgical renewal that had produced a new Book of Common Prayer. St. Gregory's Church worship and government stress congregational participation, employing insights from modern social research as well as traditions rediscovered. Eastern Christianity has much to teach us from an unbroken history of vernacular popular worship. Indeed, learning from the East has been our Anglican tradition since medieval times. Critical scholarship is also essential for our task, and informs sermons and study groups. Through four decades Donald Schell, Paul Fromberg, and I have served as St. Gregory's parish rectors, testing the innovations recommended on these pages.

Scripture fills them. This book began as an invited response to a journal article opposing Open Communion before Baptism (there mislabeled "without" Baptism), which St. Gregory of Nyssa Church has practiced for forty years, since our founding. Perhaps typically, that article recruited liturgical and philosophical writings without once quoting a Bible text. Another longtime friend sporting the label "conservative" protested against my appeal to Jesus's example, "But Jesus is gone; he's not here; we have Christ now." I replied: then he must jettison the gospels altogether, since they were written to tell us *who it is that is here*. Even the growing body of Open Table congregations too rarely offer scripture for their rationale. Nevertheless, the Bible reveals what our worship is for. That basic question confronts worshippers today over many issues beyond the Eucharist. It calls for fresh reflection on what we do together in church, and on all those rites classically called signs of grace.

Consulting the Bible today requires historical learning and language skill. Readers will encounter here the important name "Septuagint" marking an ancient Alexandrian translation of Hebrew scripture by Greek-speaking

Jews. All New Testament writers knew the Septuagint, although Jesus and his Aramaic hearers likely did not. The name is Latin for "seventy," so abbreviated by the Latin numeral LXX. It springs from a legend that seventy Hebrew translators emerged from seventy locked rooms with seventy identical Greek texts, proving divine guidance. Jewish scripture scholar Nahum Sarna quips, "It would have been a greater miracle if seventy rabbis meeting in the *same* room had come up with one translation!" This book will draw from four English versions sharing a critical approach.[3] For simplicity, God's Hebrew name will appear here in consonants *YHWH* as received, without adding conjectured vowels.

These chapters will also touch upon Christian apologetic among world religions, as parishioners increasingly require. Ecumenical dialog has influenced our ritual talk before now. Church discourse tracked ancient Hellenistic philosophers for centuries through Renaissance schisms, but now it lacks a missionary future without engaging other faiths as broadly. Christians want allies in today's secular world, and may have more allies than our forebears knew.

Today the very text reshapes our troop lines on land. A century's critics have striven over what sayings prove Jesus's "authentic" authorship and on what grounds, like an old battlefield where new-cut paths pass live buried materiel. Other scholarly terrains have also been lumbered and charted anew during the past century. Rehearsing so many campaigns would treble this book's length. Instead let me adapt the Komodo dragon's hunting strategy to worship renewal. Earth's grandest reptile (see illustration), the Komodo dragon bites just one limb; then she waits for her prey to succumb to the spreading infection. I hope that instead of corrupting readers' faith, my single bites will spread desire to explore further so many island jungles of knowledge.

Where my opinion counters others longer or more widely held, I revere the faithful intent that shaped those. Revisionism diverges by definition; nevertheless my predecessors' devotion toward the Bible and our classical Christian conversation matches any today. And their industry so far surpasses my own that I must end this Introduction with my thanks.

Richard Fabian
Rounding Cape Horn, Patagonia, southern spring 2017

---

3. New Revised Standard Version (NRSV), New English Bible (NEB), New American Bible (NAB) and New Jerusalem Bible (NJB), and rarely my own renderings.

CHAPTER ONE

JESUS'S SIGN:
THE WELCOMING TABLE

The Lord's supper takes place on the basis of an invitation which is as open as the outstretched arms of Christ on the cross. Because he died for the reconciliation of "the world," the world is invited to reconciliation in the supper. It is not the openness of this invitation, it is the restrictive measures of the church which have to be justified before the face of the crucified Jesus. But which of us can justify them in his sight? The openness of the crucified Lord's invitation to his supper and his fellowship reaches beyond the frontiers of the different denominations. It even reaches beyond the frontiers of Christianity; for it is addressed to "all nations" and to "tax-collectors and sinners" first of all. Consequently we understand Christ's invitation as being open, not merely to the churches but to the whole world.[1]

—JÜRGEN MOLTMANN

The practice of Open Communion or "Open Table" spreads among churches today amid debate. Opponents criticize its defection from millennia of tradition, or object that instead of theological reasoning, proponents appeal to modern social fashion. Here we will seek to ground an Open Table theology upon modern critical study of Jesus's teaching in the New Testament gospels, and its deeper Hebrew Old Testament foundation. In crucial ways, Jesus's own voice was conservative, against ascendant sectarian fashion. By practicing an Open Welcoming Table like his, we moderns actually imitate classic Christian writers, who sought above all to follow Jesus faithfully. Happily for us, Jesus's Open Table meets the evangelical challenges of our own day, as my own urban parish has found.

---

1. Jürgen Moltmann, *The Church in the Power of the Spirit: A Contribution to Messianic Ecclesiology* (London: SCM, 1975), 246.

St. Gregory of Nyssa Church Altar & Font

Upon first entering St. Gregory Nyssen Episcopal Church in San Francisco, you will see a sanctuary distinctively arranged. Immediately before you stands an altar table in an open space, and rising beyond it in a bright courtyard, a rocky baptismal font. Nave seating for worshippers stretches off to the right.

St. Gregory's altar table before you bears two inscriptions. One pedestal facing the entry doors reads in Greek from Luke's gospel, "This guy welcomes sinners and eats with them."[2]

Not former sinners, not repentant sinners; *sinners*. Gospel critics agree that such insults and scandalous charges, especially those embarrassing to the church, are our most reliable evidence about Jesus. Mainline Christian tradition has always upheld Jesus on this point. The Christian Eucharist may be the world's only religious meal where all the diners are officially declared unworthy to eat, every time they eat. Nor does eucharistic sharing set Christians apart as unlike others. The opposite altar table pedestal facing our font quotes Isaac of Nineveh:

> Did not the Lord share the table of tax collectors and harlots? So then—do
> not distinguish between the worthy and unworthy. All must be equal in your
> eyes to love and to serve.

2. See Luke 15:2. "*Houtos hamartolous prosdekhetai kai synsethêei autois.*" *Houtos* (this one) used alone is dismissive.

Our architectural plan expresses our sacramental custom, and both reverse widespread Christian order: we welcome all to Communion at Jesus's table, and invite any unbaptized to Baptism afterward. Our rationale at St. Gregory's rises from a revised reading of Jesus's teaching ministry and death, to which we intend the same faithfulness that ancient Christians always intended. We express that same faithfulness in a modern way, just as all churches without exception must do today.

Modern History and Jesus

The religious sociologist Peter Berger distinguished "modern" from traditional societies. In modern societies all is done by rational choice, not taken as given: therefore every choice demands explaining. (Let me sidestep the term "post-modern," which suggests faster intellectual change than human society can demonstrably achieve. On Berger's terms the modern world began at the European Renaissance, and is still going on.)[3]

Moderns must criticize the past, not merely purge the past. Our Western sixteenth-century Reformers preached faithfully against superstition; yet they mistakenly destroyed much that was beautiful, truthful, and indeed primitively Christian. We must allow that in every age Christians have intended faithfulness to Jesus's teaching and example. The architects of conventional sacramental policy built for no other purpose. Nevertheless, our knowledge of Jesus has shifted sharply today, and faithfulness to Jesus compels us to shift our practice too. Otherwise we launch something that would truly shock our forebears: an anti-Jesus counterrevolution.

Over a century ago, scripture critics began distinguishing the "historical Jesus" from the "Christ of faith" our written gospels portray. At first, the critics' goal was "positive history." As the German historian Leopold von Ranke (1795–1886) labeled it, *wie es eigentlich gewesen ist:* telling the past as it really was. That project produced a remote and puzzling Jesus, however, variously imaged from conflicting details. In fact, ancient writers prove poor sources for positive history, not only from limits to their own knowledge, but also from their evangelical intention to tell their contemporaries what they believe matters most. Then as now, each interpreter chooses colors for a portrait, and every portrait—from painters calling themselves "scripturally

---

3. *Pyramids of Sacrifice: Political Ethic and Social Change* (New York: Basic Books, 1974), 170.

conservative" to the most hypothetical—must be viewed and appraised for the modern artifact it is.

It seems each new publication about Jesus's time throws fresh darkness on the subject. Said gospel critic H. Benedict Green, CR: the more we learn, the more we must admit Jesus is a man we know very little about.[4]

Trained historians keep clear sight of how little we know. The Jesus Seminar in the United States has usefully publicized historical criticism of the gospels. Yet I recall a presentation where one member proclaimed, "I think I know who the historical Jesus was; I just don't like him very much." That critic was touted as radical, but he was merely out of date. No trained modern historian would claim both to know and dislike Napoleon, let alone a figure two thousand years dead who left only second-hand evidence behind. Many thousands loved Napoleon, and many thousands hated him; but whether *you* and Napoleon would have liked each other is unavailable information, pure conjecture. The historical Jesus is no different.

Even more challenging, the past is a country none today can visit. True modern history-writing began when the Dutch art historian Johan Huizinga (1872–1945) studied the fifteenth-century brothers Van Eyck, and the more he researched them, the farther away their world seemed, and stranger. Huizinga's revolutionary opening deserves quoting fully:

> To the world when it was half a thousand years younger, the outlines of all things seemed more clearly marked than to us. The contrast between suffering and joy, between adversity and happiness, appeared more striking. All experience had yet to the minds of men the directness and absoluteness of the pleasure and pain of child-life. Every event, every action, was still embodied in expressive and solemn forms, which raised them to the dignity of a ritual. For it was not merely the great facts of birth, marriage and death which, by the sacredness of the sacrament, were raised to the rank of mysteries; incidents of less importance, like a journey, a task, a visit, were equally attended by a thousand formalities: benedictions, ceremonies, formulae.
>
> Calamities and indigence were more afflicting than at present; it was more difficult to guard against them, and to find solace. Illness and health presented a more striking contrast; the cold and darkness of winter were more real evils. Honours and riches were relished with greater avidity and

4. H. Benedict Green, *The Gospel According to Matthew*, New Clarendon Bible (Oxford: Oxford University Press, 1987).

contrasted more vividly with surrounding misery. We, at the present day, can hardly understand the keenness with which a fur coat, a good fire on the hearth, a soft bed, a glass of wine, were formerly enjoyed.[5]

That kills "positive history." If even sensory experience cannot build us a bridge into past peoples' lives, a historian must work with what they choose to tell us and past peoples have no thought of talking with us—what can they know of the future? Instead, they talk of their own past. Human thought and behavior change slower than journalists propose, and our continuities typically outweigh our revolutions. So, first of all, a modern historian searches for what ancient peoples say connects them with their own past.

The past is far away from all writers, so all must give reasons for their choices. No proponent claims that the second-century Apologist Justin Martyr or his successors favored the Open Table. Evidence abounds that churches since the age of Apologists have required Baptism before Communion, at least normatively. Nevertheless we claim a stronger continuity with the ancients: our common loyalty to Jesus as our age knows him, and to theology based on scripture study first of all. It was Origen, long before Luther, who established that Christian theology *is* commentary upon scripture.

Jesus's Bible

Scripture looks ever backward. The gospel writers write much the way Chinese painters paint landscapes and Western composers write chorales: with allusions to treasured past words and works, which they mean their public to recognize. Gospel writers present Jesus's sayings and his career in the light of his crucifixion, which was an unknown future for him, but well past for their readers; and they use the yet more distant written past to tell readers what Jesus meant. We must look to Hebrew scripture first of all, in order to understand what the gospels say Jesus is saying.

Today some critics argue that because his parables refer regularly to agrarian life, Jesus must have been a peasant, and so illiterate. Yet others point a few miles from Nazareth to the Galilean city of Sepphoris, a cosmopolitan center where a boy of peasant stock could readily have learned to read the Bible. Synagogues even in small towns like Nazareth and Capernaum were places for study

---

5. Johan Huizinga, *The Waning of the Middle Ages*, F. Hopman trans. 1919 (New York: Doubleday, 1954, 2013), 1.

before they became places for worship. Jewish historians tell us scripture was their first textbook, and schoolboys memorized long passages, much as boys do there in a Muslim *medrassah* today. We will see how internal gospel evidence supports Jesus's awareness of sacred text. And more than one parable turns on a question of literacy.

For example, the cheating bailiff[6] can read: he helps illiterate peasants to forge new low-rent leases, and so to defraud their landlord, his former employer:

> A rich man heard that his majordomo was spending beyond his salary, and told him: "Turn in your accounts, you're fired." The majordomo thought: "How will I live without a job? I'm too weak to be a farmer, and begging is shameful. But I do know how to make people welcome me into their homes." He returned all the sharecroppers' lease documents, allowing each peasant to sign a new substitute promising only half the rent. [The Master praised the unscrupulous man's astuteness because his kind dealt more sharply with their own low type than the "enlightened" do.]

This parable, perhaps drawn from local events, was ethically disturbing enough to call for an editorial gloss at its end but the original can hardly be a story told by an illiterate for illiterates to hear. Peasant folktales exalt canny locals who outwit the educated by their native wiles; they do not hold up educated models like the bailiff, whom illiterate peasants cannot imitate.

Jesus's parables often draw on well-known events or bear multiple interpretations; nevertheless his relation to scripture is one area where we may hope to catch his own beliefs. That enterprise answers more than historical curiosity. The New Testament assigns Jesus unique authority; and the fifth-century Council of Chalcedon likewise ruled that Jesus was not inspired like biblical authors—he spoke with God's own voice. Thus in Paul's case we may modify or discard talk about slavery, about women in church, about other matters, but overwriting Jesus is out of the question for his church.

The twentieth century opened with agreement among Bible scholars and liturgy reformers, that Jesus preached God's future reign would come soon, so his hearers must prepare to handle it. The New Testament uses the metaphor *parousia* in Greek, or *adventus* in Latin: this was a regular administrative event, when a provincial governor came auditing tax returns, rewarding loyal officers,

---

6. Luke 16:1–7.

punishing treason, hearing appeals, and firming up public order. Here was a ready image for the Hebrew *tsedaqah*, which throughout the Bible means, "God undoes our enemies and puts things right." First-century Palestine abounded with groups preparing for God to come like a touring governor, finish off the corrupt world order they knew, and put things right with the Jewish nation properly back on top. So twentieth-century liturgists reformed our worship to restore this rediscovered eschatological emphasis on the future, assuming they were matching Jesus's teaching.

By 1975, however, Hans Küng's *On Being a Christian* warned: modern Christians must come to terms with the fact that Jesus was wrong about the *parousia*. The world did not end as Jesus had prophesied. On the contrary, Roman imperial power thrived for fourteen centuries more, and embraced Jesus as its new official god. Here was the profoundest challenge scientific research has ever made to Christian orthodoxy, far more threatening than evolution! How could Christians hold faith in an incarnate Lord whose "messianic consciousness" was not only bizarre, but mistaken? What further authority could we give him, seeing his favorite obsession disproved? Assigning authority to an all-knowing Risen Christ (once the mistaken Jesus is gone) would contradict the gospels wholesale. They were written expressly to tell us *Who It Is* That Is Here Now: so abandoning the historical Jesus would mean abandoning scripture, too.

A decade later and to many scholars' surprise, Küng's dilemma dissolved, and with it, a scholarly alliance on which liturgical renewal had relied—though some old allies have not yet noticed. In the 1960s, British critics Norman Perrin and Reginald Fuller overturned five decades of earlier argument by relegating all gospel futurism to editors' and later preachers' commentary, which Jewish tradition calls *midrash*. During the next decades Perrin and Fuller's opinion attained critical consensus. Unlike both Jesus's contemporary teachers and his well-meaning gospel editors, Jesus himself preached God's reign already come here and now, before we could possibly prepare or manage it. We must respond wisely, and just in time—otherwise fools will find it is already too late. Here comes God now, ready or not!

Jesus's Prophetic Sign: A Stumbling Block

For his distinctive message, Jesus chose a sign. The Hebrew word for a sign is *'ôth;* the Greek is *sêmeion;* but setting aside etymology and linguistic philosophy that fill some commentaries, we may observe how Hebrew prophets actually use signs to show people what God is doing, because people are dangerously failing to see it. Jeremiah shatters a pot at the Jerusalem garbage dump, declaring: this is what God will do with our nation unless our leaders change their plans.[7] Jeremiah's sign does not pretend magically to break up the nation; rather it is his urgent gesture to win people's attention, so they will see what God is up to before it is tragically too late.

For a prophetic sign of his teaching that God comes here now, ready or not, Jesus took up an image from the prophet Isaiah, who envisioned a banquet where God's chosen Hebrew people and the unclean heathen would feast together.[8] Jesus began dining publicly with notoriously unqualified sinners, those shunned by other religious reformers: a practice that many modern critics think chiefly led to his condemnation and death.

Paul calls Jesus's life and death a scandal, a term that likewise wants defining from usage. The Hebrew words translated as "scandal" or "stumbling block"[9] denote a snare or trap, but one singular Levitical instance became normative for the New Testament. This was part of the Holiness Code, a text that Judah Goldin says all synagogue schoolboys memorized: "You shall not curse the deaf, nor lay a stumbling block before the blind. I am YHWH."[10] Nearly all references to a stumbling block in Hebrew and Greek scripture imply blindness. When Jeremiah warns, "I will lay a stumbling block before this people,"[11] he is taunting them: My people are *blind!*[12] Terming Jesus's ministry a scandal means that people who fail to see what God is doing, despite Jesus's sign, risk downfall and destruction, just as Jeremiah forewarned his nation they would be destroyed. Jeremiah was ignored, and his people perished. Gospel editors believed that had happened again to the first-century Jewish nation who ignored Jesus's sign, when the Romans invaded and paved Jerusalem, and it will happen wherever people fail to see.

Like Jeremiah, Jesus consciously chose a sign to scandalize his nation. In his day kosher food still lay in the future; ritual purity applied then only to the

---

7. Jeremiah 19.

8. Isaiah 25:6–8.

9. Hebrew *mikshol/makshelah* and Greek *skándalon* or *próskomma*—these occur interchangeably.

10. Leviticus 19:14.

11. Jeremiah 6:21.

12. See 1 Corinthians 1:23, 8:9. Romans 9:32–33, 11:9. Revelation 2:14. New Testament writers use the verb "lay a stumbling block" thirty times, twice as often as the noun, echoing the Levitical commandment and so declaring: those who take offense are tragically blind, and in danger.

diners, not to the food. Palestine abounded in dining fellowships called *cha-buroth*, each restricted by profession and by degrees of contaminating business contacts with impure Gentiles and non-observant Jews. So Jesus chose that scandalous sign of common dining to seize people's attention before it was too late. Today that scandal continues wherever Jesus shows up. As the Lutheran writer Gordon Lathrop puts it: "Draw a line that includes us and excludes many others, and Jesus Christ is always on the other side of the line. At least that is so if we are speaking of the biblical, historic Christ who eats with sinners and outsiders, who is made a curse and sin itself for us, who justifies the ungodly, and who is himself the hole in any system."[13]

Some opponents of the Open Table deride its "mere acceptance" of unbaptized people. Philip Turner sees "a theological chasm . . . between those who hold a theology of divine *acceptance* and those who hold a theology of divine *redemption*."[14] But the presence of genuinely wrong and *unacceptable* people at the table was essential for Jesus's sign. It fit his teaching perfectly. The heroes of his authentic parables include criminals, pre-moral children, and pushy women. Jesus's criminals are real criminals: not to be rehabilitated by our "understanding" how they grew up oppressed or in dysfunctional families; not to be welcomed into our company in hopes they will change their ways. In Jesus's parables they never change their ways.

Jesus's Claim to Orthodoxy

That is not to say Jesus thought himself a revolutionary. One of his most famous parables argues otherwise: the parable of the Pharisee and the Tax Collector, which most "conservative" and "liberal" critics concur that Jesus authored.

> A Pharisee and a tax collector both went to pray in the Temple. The Pharisee stood erect praying: "Thank you, God, that I am not like other folks: grasping, cheating, fashionably adulterous, or anything like that tax collector. I fast twice weekly; I donate ten percent of all I get." The tax collector stood far off with his eyes lowered and struck himself, praying: "God have mercy on me a

---

13. Gordon Lathrop, *Holy Ground: A Liturgical Cosmology* (Minneapolis: Fortress Press, 2003), 64f. Cited also in Thomas O'Loughlin, "The Eucharist as 'The Meal That Should Be,'" *Worship* 80, (no. 1, January 2006).

14. Philip Turner, "An Unworkable Theology," *First Things* 154 (June/July 2005).

sinner." But I tell you this second man went home with his life all fixed; the first man did not."[15]

This parable does not oppose a hypocritical Pharisee against a repentant tax collector as models for our ethical choice. Perhaps unique among the parables, this is a theological story-form comment (*halakah*) on Joel 2:13–14, which lays out the Hebrew Scripture's doctrine of God:

Tear your hearts and not your clothing,

Return to YHWH your God,

For he is gracious and merciful,

Slow to anger and abounding in steadfast love,

And relents from punishing.

Joel's text is commonly misheard as an instruction to sorrow over our sins; but Joel means quite the opposite. In Hebrew imagery the heart (*lëv*) is not the seat of our emotions. *Lëv* is where we make *plans*. Hence the Septuagint and Greek liturgical texts regularly translate *lëv* as *nous*, or "mind." "Tear your hearts, not your clothes" means: "Quit mourning over your misdeeds and your predicament, and instead change your *plans*, and return to YHWH." Editors carved a virtual woodblock from the next verse, "YHWH is gracious and merciful, slow to anger, abounding in steadfast love (*chesed*), and relents from punishing," and stamped it eleven more times around their Bible, sometimes bluntly overruling the earlier revanchist theology preserved alongside.[16] This is the Hebrew editors' theology, which formed the Bible we receive; therefore this is the true Old Testament doctrine of God.

Jesus's parable is ingenious. It says God fixed things for the tax collector—just as the biblical *tsedaqah* means: God undoes our enemies and puts us back on top where we belong—whereas the Pharisee went home all unfixed, which is to say, doomed.

But not because of hypocrisy! Hypocrites pretend to virtues they lack, but the Pharisee reports truthfully that he fasts twice in the week, and gives tithes of all he has. Indeed, both his claims exceed the Torah's commands. By contrast, the tax collector guarantees no change of life as a claim on God's love. However

---

15. Luke 18:10–14. *Dedikaiôménos*, "fixed," from the Hebrew *tsedaqah*, putting things right, as next paragraph explains; see also chapter 5, below.

16. See Exodus 34:6 and Numbers 14:18, where the older theology of God's implacable and endless vengeance follows directly: the editors preserved that earlier material while stamping their revision literally on top.

he might wish, this tax collector may yet have to add his share to taxes as before, if only to make his living. "Lord have mercy on me a sinner"—period.

Nevertheless, in the light of Hebrew scripture's doctrine of God, the tax collector is orthodox, and the Pharisee is not. The tax collector tells the essential two truths that Joel and the Bible's editors teach: he is a sinner; and God has *chesed*, the strong love that sticks with people no matter what. (As in "you'll always be my child, no matter what you do.") By contrast, the Pharisee tells two lies, which he wrongly if earnestly believes: (1) that his virtues make him "not like others" in God's eyes; and (2) that God achieved this difference, for which the Pharisee can give thanks; whereas the true God observes no differences among human beings,[17] and God has *chesed* for all. The tax collector's truth-telling is all God requires, to put things right for him. God will not work with lies, so the Pharisee dooms himself.

The parable of the Pharisee and the Tax Collector represents the core of Old Testament Theology, as quoted twelve times around the Hebrew Bible. So the author knows Hebrew scripture more closely than those scholars who fail to recognize his theological allusion. The parable implies more: like the tax collector, its author is orthodox, and his opponents are not. He is loyal to biblical tradition, and they are not. He is the conservative; his opponents are the wrongheaded innovators. Some scholars wonder if Jesus may have been a Pharisee, though of a different stripe than later Judaism would recognize. In any case, if Jesus is the author of this parable—as today's critics and their opponents styled "conservative" concur—then his dining with impure and unqualified sinners laid his strong claim to biblical orthodoxy. His sign came directly from Hebrew scripture itself, in the prophecy of Isaiah, unlike widespread *chaburah* practice. And it upheld the well-published Old Testament doctrine of God, in contrast with the puristic new movements of Jesus's own time.

Rabbis soon shifted their focus from the purity of the diners to the purity of their dinner foods—and the kosher kitchen was born. Today Jews welcome non-Jews to their tables, while Christians cannot agree formally to eat with each other. Instead, we mimic Jesus's opponents, with their various *chaburoth* for diners variously purified. Then in what sense can we call our official closed-Communion policy traditional? Recent essays deploring the Open Table appeal to ancient theologians who indeed required Baptism before Communion, and a few writers

---

17. At Acts 10:34, Peter congratulates a pagan centurion: *Ep' alêtheias katalambanomai hoti ouk estin prosôpolêmptês o theos.* Popular cult believed riches and power were marks of a god's favor: see similar reproofs at Colossians 3:25, Romans 2:11, Ephesians 6:9, James 2:1, 1 Peter 1:17.

side with those for institutional reasons, against Jesus's radical sign of biblical orthodoxy. Yet not one of those ancient Christian authorities would ever have done so. Their purpose was to follow Jesus fully, and their arguments appeal to scripture first, as every Christian theological argument must.

"Fashionable liberal" values do but support our practice. Welcome, acceptance, and openness are indeed important to the gospel but the current debate about such virtues' rightful place within eucharistic discipline sidesteps the main point. It is as though after Jeremiah broke the pot at the garbage dump, the faithful had debated for twenty-five hundred years How God Wants Us to Recycle Trash. (Who should take the trash where? Who may receive it? Who should say what words?) Like the virtue of hospitality, recycling is important: it shows our respect for the environment and our responsibility toward Mother Earth, and may impact our chances for a human future on this planet, but recycling was hardly the point of Jeremiah's sign. Likewise, welcoming strangers and telling them God loves them, building community, and growing bigger and more effective ministries are all fine things; moreover they yield moving stories about people introduced to Communion for the first time. Sara Miles's book *Take This Bread: A Radical Conversion*[18] recounts her change from atheism upon first Communion at St. Gregory's, and how she founded a famous feeding ministry in response. Yet these noble results were not the chief point of Jesus's sign. His chief point was: God is reconciling people who scarcely imagine how they belong together, and making peace among them—God is doing this everywhere in the world, not just in churches—and if *we* do not recognize what God is doing, we are headed for disaster.

Talk of Jesus's own orthodoxy, and Christian and Jewish inheritance from it, raises the question of faith. Classical theory requires faith for sharing Christian rituals effectually, and both Eucharist and Baptism rites expressly evoke faith. Today's public exhibit religious diversity such as our forebears barely imagined: not only ethnic immigrants, but many Christian youth pursue other world faiths and spiritualities, and criticize church standards. Indeed, Luther's Small Catechism holds that the essential action of Baptism is not the water bath, but the progress in virtuous living that follows it, where faith grows. Might we not say the same of eucharistic sharing? What truer faith can we require than the aggressive desire that Zacchaeus[19] exemplifies and newcomers show as they communicate at St. Gregory's Church for the first time in their lives?

---

18. Sara Miles, *Take This Bread: A Radical Conversion* (New York: Ballantine Books, 2008).
19. Luke 19:1–10. See full exegesis in chapter 3 on Baptism.

Forgive Us as We Have Forgiven

John Patton bases his provocative work *Is Human Forgiveness Possible?* on many years' experience guiding people through forgiveness processes. In practice, he finds forgiveness involves discovering that you *have* forgiven people and given up your desire to be separate from them. From Patton's perspective we may remark the line in the Lord's Prayer: "forgive us our debts as we also *have forgiven* our debtors" (perfect tense in Matthew).[20] More radical than Rowan Williams's well-meant praise for "the meals that Jesus shared with outcasts and sinners to show that God was ready to welcome and forgive them,"[21] Jesus's scandalous meals were signs that God *has forgiven* all humanity and holds no desire to be apart from us. Today when we watch people whom we think unworthy join our eucharistic gathering, instead of our telling ourselves we were mistaken about these folks and should reconsider how they deserve inclusion—we had rather think: these are real, nasty, active sinners, and God sees no difference between them and me. I am just like them. So I hereby quit my desire to separate from them.

It is not sinners we accept, but the world that God has already forgiven and redeemed. We can embrace Turner's preferred "theology of *redemption*" if we recall that biblical redemption means paying off our relatives' or fellow tribesmen's compounded debts without their help because they are fiscally or morally bankrupt and absolutely cannot quit them—not because they have reformed and become a better risk now, and should get a second chance. They are not reformed. Neither are you who read this. Let me list some of my own qualifications for this eucharistic feast, which your lives surely mirror. We are a pack of lying, cheating, thieving, treacherous snobs; we are misogynist, misandric, homophobic, racist, ageist hypocrites. You just like me; no changes. *Psychology Today* magazine says the average North American tells hundreds of lies a day. "Lovely to see you!" "I'm doing just great, thanks!" "I'll be there in a minute!" At Jesus's table we liars eat together, offering nothing. Not our repentance; not our frail New Years' resolutions, which neither God nor Jesus could credit; not our little moral improvements; nothing. God does all that happens there.

---

20. Matthew 6:12, *kai afes . . . hôs kai hêmeis afêkamen tois ofeilétais hêmôn.*

21. Ursula Hashem cites R. Williams, "Lecture delivered by the Archbishop of Canterbury at the Islamic University, Islamabad" *ACNS* 4081 (Lambeth 2005).

Still the Right Scandal for Our Day

Today, as in Jesus's day, the eucharistic table is a sign of what God is doing everywhere, which the world otherwise tragically fails to see. Yet the world offers no other answer, and God's answer is urgent. No option remains but forgiveness. That is our world, the world God has already forgiven and completely reconciled to God's self, through Jesus's sacrificial life and death.

In our liturgy, Jesus's Open Table feeds all the genuinely wrong guests together. This banquet serves for more than making people feel accepted, or building community, or growing churches. It serves for more than sharing gifts that baptized Christians, or faithful Trinitarians, or sanctified and morally improved converts can have. Jesus's Open Table remains today a scandal, a stumbling block thrown down on our path, to teach a blind and reeling world what God is doing everywhere in this world, before it is *too damned late.*

Jesus knew the self-doomed took offense: "blessed is anyone who does not stumble blindly over me."[22] Not that he was an unfeeling man, or a social iconoclast. Rather, Jesus was *importunate.* Importunity means demanding attention boldly at the worst possible time, in order to gain what you cannot gain politely.

In Jesus's parables, importunity always works. A neighbor pounds on your door at night to borrow food, betting correctly you will jump out of bed before he wakes your household;[23] a poor widow screams at a corrupt judge in open court, until he grants her justice without his customary bribe;[24] a hungry child demands bread and gets it;[25] violent people storm into the kingdom.[26] In the gospel *midrash* stories added by Christian preachers, a blind man shouts politically dangerous titles ever louder over the disciples' protests until Jesus heals him;[27] and a bleeding woman successfully grasps her healer's robe, when she knows she is ritually impure.[28] By contrast, in real life prophetic importunity is always risky: Jeremiah was shut up (in every sense) in a dry well.[29] Likewise, Jesus could have expounded his policy

---

22. Matthew 11:6 // (and parallel at) Luke 7:23 in Greek: *makarios estin hos ean mē* skandalisthēi *en emoi.* The mathematical symbol // normally links parallel text citations like these.

23. Luke 11:5–8.

24. Luke 18:1–5.

25. Matthew 7:9.

26. Matthew 11:12.

27. Mark 10:46–52, Luke 18:35–43.

28. Mark 5:25–35.

29. Jeremiah 38:6.

politely—but that would have undone his purpose, which was to seize his nation's attention and show them what God was up to while they remained tragically blind. So Jesus chose to make a scandal: importunate, deliberate, and fatal for himself.

Textual criticism undercuts an alternative interpretation favored by some opponents of the Open Table: that the Last Supper differed from Jesus's suppers with whores and greedy villains. At his Last Supper, that argument runs, Jesus dined with his close disciples only, and the Eucharist is properly celebrated thus, with only the qualified present. (This argument is also raised against the liturgical presidency of women.)

Certainly there was *a last* supper, but New Testament evidence does not tell us what happened there. John describes no eating or drinking ritual. Synoptic gospel accounts merely copy Paul's first Corinthian letter, written years prior to the writing of the gospels. There Paul reports what Christians told him at Antioch when he visited, about what *they* were doing in Jesus's memory.[30]

> You are not eating the Lord's Supper when you meet, because each eats his own meal, and one hungers while another gets drunk. Can't you do that at home, instead of shaming those who have nothing, and the whole church besides? The Lord himself handed on to me what I taught you: on the night before his betrayal, the Lord Jesus took some bread, gave thanks, broke it to share and said, "This is my body, which is for all of you, do this to remember me." And in the same way he shared the cup after supper, saying, "This is the new covenant sealed in my blood, remember me whenever you do this." So eating and drinking shows forth the Lord's death until he comes . . . And any who eat and drink without recognizing the body manifest here eat and drink judgment on themselves.[31]

Scholars have debated Gregory Dix's question[32] whether the Last Supper and our Eucharist derived from the Passover Seder or the *chaburah* friendship meal—both of which we now know only from later sources. Recent Jewish scholarship has stilled that debate. All four documented dinner ceremonies represent stages of one evolving ritual: the Hellenistic symposium banquet, which

---

30. My late friend Thomas Talley thus interpreted Acts 11:26. Nevertheless Talley opposed Open Communion today as endangering ecumenical consensus.

31. 1 Corinthians 11:20–29, NJB translation.

32. Dom Gregory Dix, *The Shape of the Liturgy* (London and Glasgow: Dacre, 1945).

is not Jewish at all.[33] With each successive stage, organized teaching moved earlier into the ritual. Thus today's Passover Seder represents the final stage, with all symbols explained before anything is eaten or drunk.

By Paul's report, Christians at Antioch were keeping that Hellenistic ritual at a stage halfway along the development line, with the bread explained symbolically at dinner's start, and the cup and ethical teaching still given afterward. Thus the Antiochenes imported their memorial of Jesus into a Hellenistic banquet order they already knew. We learn nothing about what ritual Jesus himself followed at any supper, including his last: that might have been Hellenistic, but we have no reason to presume so. Paul is not concerned with ritual anyway. He adduces the Antiochenes' Last Supper story to bolster his demand that Christians should share their food. You stupid Corinthians who will not share are failing to perceive Christ's Body in this company present right here. You are *blind* to the sign right before you, and blindness will mean your ruin. Paul's logic focuses on this company, this meal today; not Jesus's last.

Open Table and Baptismal Font

Entering the doors at St. Gregory Nyssen, San Francisco, every newcomer sees Jesus's table nearby awaiting all, and the baptismal font sunlit beyond it. During the liturgy most people accept our Communion invitation, some for the first time ever, and through thirty years and two successive rectorships, all the unbaptized who return regularly to Communion have asked for Baptism soon.

It is important that newcomers should experience welcome at Jesus's table—yet more important, indeed essential, for Christians to *do* the welcoming that Jesus himself did. Early Apologists emphasize our forebears' actions, quoting pagan observers: "See how these Christians love one another!" Jesus's Open Table was his way of showing the world what divine *chesed* means. So, after welcoming newcomers to dine with us at St. Gregory's, we invite them to recreate Jesus's welcome for friends and neighbors like themselves. Upon embracing Baptism, they advance beyond being blessed recipients, and in Jesus's name they join our mission of welcoming the whole humanity God has redeemed, by holding up Jesus's sign—and a hundred more ministries in his Spirit—for a blind world to see, and change its plans. The Open Table serves

---

33. Paul Bradshaw, *Eucharistic Origins* (London: SPCK, 2004), 43–44. Dennis Smith, *From Symposium to Eucharist: The Banquet in the Early Christian World* (Minneapolis: Fortress, 2003) finds forms too diverse to specify a single Eucharist source.

first for their incorporation; Baptism serves next—and urgently—to enroll them in joyfully welcoming more.

Northern Hemisphere churches can no longer presume outsiders' esteem such as the Apologists once claimed. Our contemporaries dismiss our sincerity, our competence, our relevance to everyday life. Their visit to a Sunday or Baptism or wedding or funeral liturgy is virtually the only time most outsiders will see for themselves what the church is up to, and what we believe God is up to. There above all we must uphold Jesus's sign of God's free welcome to a lost world that God has already forgiven and reconciled. Friedrich Nietzsche, a Lutheran pastor's son, put bluntly today's evangelical charge for the faithful inside church and out:

"Christians should *look* more redeemed."

CHAPTER TWO

⁂

THE PEOPLE'S SIGN:
GIVING AUTHORITY TO CHRIST

The pope! How many divisions has the pope?

—JOSEPH JUGHASHVILI, CALLED STALIN ("STEEL")

First Story: Who Is the Head?

On a fall evening in 1781, farmers bearing axes, pitchforks and torches surrounded a house and barn near Enfield, Connecticut. There lived the United Society of Believers in Christ's Second Appearing, called "Shakers." For three decades after the American Revolution, Calvinist churches still legally governed most New England towns, maintaining a strict hierarchy of preachers and lay officers ordained with civil powers. By contrast, the Society of Believers followed a working class English charismatic called Mother Ann Lee, with men and women elders who shared her ecstatic visions. Their irregular beliefs and dancing rites dismayed established Calvinist divines. Worse yet, the celibate Shaker community grew only with converts, and so alarmed farming families who counted on young labor. Shaker women were routinely thrown into ditches or jailed, and a male elder was publicly flogged in Harvard Square.

Mother Ann traveled among her community houses in constant life danger. When Enfield's citizens learned she had arrived, they saw their chance to strike this invasive weed at its root, and men surrounded the Shaker buildings demanding she come out. Mother Ann left the house and walked into the center of the gathered mob. One man shouted, "Are you the head of this church?" Mother Ann answered simply, "Christ is the head of the Church." The mob fell silent. Then after two short questions they turned away, and carrying their tools walked quietly home.[1]

---

1. Reported by Elizabeth Wood, 1851, in Jean M. Humez, *Mother's First-born Daughters* (Bloomington: Indiana University Press, 1993), 59.

That short history encapsulates one purpose of this book: to turn the focus of modern Western Christian worship aside from ritualized sacrificial violence, toward authority for justice and peace. That shift will echo biblical priorities, and better fit our contemporary missionary context.

For centuries Western writers, whether Catholic or Protestant, have stressed sacrificial atonement by Jesus's death as the core of our Good News. Modern scripture criticism somewhat justifies their emphasis. Our oldest record of Christian eucharistic feasting, in Paul's first letter to the Corinthians, shows how the earliest Christians interpreted Jesus's meals and their own meals kept in his memory. At Antioch they told Paul that at Jesus's Last Supper, the Lord spoke of bread and wine in terms any Jew would have recognized as sacrificial: "This is my body . . . this cup is the new covenant in my blood."[2] Elsewhere Paul likens Jesus's sufferings to those he himself endures for Christ's sake, which make up whatever is missing in Jesus's own: an evocation of self-sacrifice by both leaders.[3] Within two short generations the gospel Passion story editors adapted spoken tradition to portray Jesus as a harmless victim of popular envy, sectarian prejudice, politicians' fecklessness, or disciples' cowardice.

Most New Testament writers viewed Jesus's career through lenses tinted blood-red by their Messiah's death, overlooking logical roadblocks that their King's execution still raised for Jews and Greeks alike.[4] It is small wonder that later centuries read their gospels as biographies of a kindly teacher treading a doomed path toward betrayal by the sinful world he had meant to heal. Exactly how Jesus's unjust death saves our world has filled Western discourse since, where blood atonement became the rampant theological line.

In fact, Jesus's claim to authority more truly centers our New Testament, and occupied centuries of patristic era councils, none of which argued about sacrifice. Conflicts soon retold within the canonical gospels (and some non-canonical gospels too) concern Jesus's authority entirely,[5] showing this question was already chief for the next generation of churches. Eastern Christian worship celebrates Christ's living authority, using symbols that followers can uphold without shame. In fact, Western tradition is equally rich with such imagery, if marginalized in our eucharistic talk heretofore.

2. 1 Corinthians 11:24–6.

3. Colossians 1:24–2:3, Galatians 6:17.

4. 1 Corinthians 1:23.

5. Mark 1:22, 27; 11:28–33.

Biblical Sacrifices

Before joining today's debates about blood sacrifice, we may rehearse the role sacrifice actually plays in the Bible. Within both Hebrew and Greek scriptures, atoning sacrifice is sharply contested. The Book of Genesis's first two covenants accomplish atonement between God, humankind, and earth by no sacrifice whatever. Following Abel's murder, God freely sets a sign of protection upon Cain, whose harvest sacrifices were rejected, lest fellow humans take revenge upon him.[6] Noah's stormy trials end when God lays down his gleaming gilt rainbow in the heavens, like a conquering Babylonian general sealing a treaty.[7] That sign promises that God will never again destroy the world, however evil humans become, and our every sight of it recalls God's free covenant with the whole earth. Thus the Bible's two universal covenants omit sacrifices. Later covenants with Israel alone do involve sacrifice in two forms: harvest fruits and animals eaten thankfully (*todah*) in hope of further natural riches;[8] and animals slain—and with one exception, eaten—to seal God's forgiveness after egregious wrongdoing (*chattath*).[9] Centuries later, Hebrew exiles returning to Palestine added this second ritual to earlier thank offerings, hoping to fend off further banishments. Within the Levitical rubrics we now read, a cake offered along with animal parts is the original sacrifice, made for thanks alone.[10] Yet even under this compromise, the prophets and psalmists protest that no sacrifices, whether for thanks or for sin, accomplish atonement or secure blessing. Only a national ethical conversion toward social justice, sacrificial in another sense, can please God and secure peace and prosperity.

Pagan sacrifice was an exchange that humans offered to gods, summarized in the Latin motto *do ut des*: I give to a god something I prize, asking the god to give me something that I prize yet more. By contrast, the Hebrew prophets and psalmists reasoned the opposite exchange.[11] When added alongside cereal thank offerings (*todah*) at agrarian celebrations, meat offerings (*chattath*) assume that the sinner has already forfeited life by sinning, and so owns nothing any human can offer. God already owns all the life in the world, and wants

---

6. Genesis 4:15.

7. Genesis 9:8–17.

8. Exodus 23; Leviticus 2, 23; Deuteronomy 18, 26.

9. Leviticus 4.

10. Leviticus 2, 7.

11. For this *précis* of biblical sacrifice theory much thanks to the late Robert Dentan, a longtime editor of the Revised Standard Version and Old Testament professor at General Theological Seminary, New York.

nothing less than our ethical conversion. "I will not accept a bull from your house, or goats from your folds. For every wild animal of the forest is mine, the cattle on a thousand hills." And again, "I desire steadfast love and not sacrifice and the knowledge of God rather than burnt offerings."[12]

Therefore to rescue sinners from death they have earned, the Bible's God acts creatively. Instead of pouring back into God's life-pool, as usual, the lifeblood of animals that humans kill for food, God gives that life afresh to all who eat at a proper shrine, provided only they pray for atonement as the Levitical texts instruct.[13] The Levitical cult never implies that sinners receive the victim's life, for there is no such thing. There is only *life*: some in the sinner, and some in the victim, until it runs out in death. So unlike a pagan bargain, biblical sacrifice, whether for thanks or atonement, means: God gives humans new life for free.

Just so, the earliest Christians reckoned that instead of taking back Jesus's life into God's universal life pool, God was giving it away freely to all who shared Jesus's meal sign, thus making each meal eaten in his memory an effectual biblical sacrifice. Paul mentions no *do ut des* bargaining claim upon new life. Paul says rather that God gives us for free the life naturally flowing in Jesus's blood—not on account of Jesus's self-destruction, but through his faith alone.[14]

If later preachers adopted Hellenistic pagan sacrificial thought, that appears nowhere in the Old or New Testament. The Letter to Hebrews describes the Levitical sin offering while insisting that it was actually never efficacious, and is henceforward discarded.[15] Nevertheless, within centuries the Hellenistic flood swamped Western minds. In Anselm's influential *Cur Deus Homo* it bled toward tritheism, as the murdered Son obligated his proud Father to forgive humankind. Most Renaissance debaters swam into that pagan riptide like lifeguards hoping to rescue Catholic or Reformed converts from drowning. Today blood atonement formulae swamp the hearers of self-styled "conservative" teachers and examiners, who throw them a life-buoy that contradicts scripture.

Worse yet, moderns find animal sacrifice disgusting, and human sacrifice insanely cruel. The violence of that tradition dismays recent critics, although most miss the unique biblical idea. Weary now of the sectarian strife that blood atonement doctrine has fostered through fifteen centuries, Westerners may

---

12. Psalm 50:9–10 and Hosea 6:6.

13. Exodus 29–30; Leviticus 2, 4, and 7.

14. Romans 3:25, *hon proethetos ho Theos ilastêrion dia pisteôs en tôi autou haimati*, a crucial verse so Englished in NEB and NRSV.

15. Hebrews 10:11–18.

admire Eastern Christians' preference for preaching Christ's incarnation: that is, for seeing God's salvific life already working in Jesus's mortal flesh. That incarnation happened a full lifetime before the death that ended Jesus's story.[16] Jesus suffered unjustly the way too many virtuous humans suffer in our dark world. Yet in his one human life, the virtues God has created in all human life triumphed and saved the rest, through God's presence among us, as one of us. Like Irenaeus (a Greek theologian elected bishop of Lyon), Eastern and Western Christians can see Jesus's death as the self-emptying completion of his lifelong true faithfulness,[17] rather than a violent self-destruction that bled gore over human sin.

Existential Sacrifice and Authority

A generation after Paul, John's gospel invoked a different sacrificial action, well-known within both Hebrew scripture and worldwide human experience. This sacrifice happens outside ritual and invokes no bargain. We may call it "existential," after a movement Europe fostered after World War II. In a seminal 1945 lecture titled "Existentialism Is a Humanism," Jean-Paul Sartre told of a young man who had sought his advice: whether to join the French Resistance to Nazi German occupation, or to stay home with his aging widowed mother, whose sole support he was. Both ethical paths were sacrificial in an existential sense, since both desired outcomes lay within the sacrificer's reach. Sartre never reported which path the young man took, reckoning that was not pertinent; only his choosing was.[18]

More ordinary examples proliferate: Parents who give up a hard-earned vacation to send their children to summer camp (both the cherished vacation and the cherished children lie within their grasp already). Athletes who undertake a "sacrifice play," raising their team's record rather than their own. Scholars who sidestep celebrity to labor on research that may advance useful knowledge, or yet may not. Artists and musicians creating works that will gain fashion only after their death. Nations who abandon wars for booty and build peaceful partnership with neighbors. Bold heroes who take up a cause and lose the struggle. The existentialist movement left a broad imprint on Bible interpretation through Rudolf

---

16. Modern critics reason that Jesus could not have foreknown his crucifixion, so instead editors attributed many such predictions to him by hindsight: for example at Mark 8:31, 9:12, and parallels. See also John 8:28.

17. Hebrews 5:7–9; John 18:34, 37; Romans 3:25; notes 9 and 15, above.

18. *L'existentialisme est un humanisme*, published 1946, after a lecture that Sartre gave at Club Maintenant in Paris, on October 29, 1945.

Bultmann, among others.[19] The universality of existential sacrifice implies it is commonplace; and yet John's gospel prizes it above all ritual actions. "No one has a greater love than laying down their life for their friends."[20] The Good Shepherd lays down his life for the sheep, while the hireling does not.[21]

We expect existential sacrifice from our leaders, as a condition for their authority among us. Christian clergy were ordained from the first with gestures mimicking the prophetic chrismation of King David, and bishops soon enthroned Christian rulers with consecrated oils, praying always for divine authorization. A millennium later, the secular ascendancy of Italian Renaissance *condottieri* sidelined popes, and finally liquidated British, French, and Russian royals who still claimed divine right. It is a precious anachronism, therefore, when today's churches continue using ritual language whereby authority falls from a Higher Power.

Nineteenth-century political philosophers sought to replace that downward authorization with more "scientific" models. Replacing divine intervention, Hegel, Marx, and Nietzsche substituted historical progress, a belief that still catches the popular mind today. If in sad fact "progressive" governments have evolved everywhere into violent dictatorships, nevertheless our cinema habitually crowns underdog young heroes who leap beyond political conformity, marching to independent drums toward self-realization. Church liturgists seek alternatives to royal talk: Iconic biblical images of kings, of God's realm, and of judgment upon the nations give place to abstract nouns flying on banners: Justice! Freedom! Joy! (What atheist could protest?) Even authoritative language has lost fashion: "Lord" and "Master" become "Friend" and "Example," affirming our moral independence, whichever our gender. Yet resistance to leveling does arise occasionally from surprising sources. Episcopal prayer book revisers at first erased "LORD" from their new Psalter, but restored it after older African American women objected: "The LORD is the One who leads people out of slavery. You white folks may not understand that!"[22]

One might expect Sigmund Freud, the last century's outstanding skeptic, to acclaim the popular decline of divine downward authority, and the ascendancy

---

19. Rudolph Bultmann, *The New Testament and Mythology* [1941] *and Other Basic Writings* (Minneapolis: Augsburg Fortress Publishers, 1984).

20. John 15:13.

21. John 10:11–14.

22. Reported by Charles M. Guilbert, Custodian of the Book of Common Prayer, from deliberations by the Standing Liturgical Commission in 1978.

of secular intellectual freedom, but Freud observed the opposite. Addressing the first psychoanalytic congress at Nuremberg in 1910, he declared:

> I have said that we [psychoanalysts] have much to expect from the increase in authority which must accrue to us as time goes on. I need not say much to you about the importance of authority. Only very few civilized people are capable of existing without reliance on others or are even capable of coming to an independent opinion. **You cannot exaggerate the intensity of people's inner lack of resolution and craving for authority. The extraordinary increase in neuroses since the power of religions has waned may give you a measure of it.** The impoverishment of the ego due to the large expenditure of energy on repression, demanded of every individual by civilization, may be one of the principal causes of this state of things.[23]

Second Story: What Is Authority?

After his rebel victory in 1783, the devout Anglican vestryman, church warden, and general George Washington resigned as commander-in-chief rather than accept the kingship, thereby proving his commitment to American republicanism, and he served two presidential terms instead. Monarchy is an unfashionable polity today, and for good reason. British economist E. F. Schumacher exposed its skeletal vulnerability.[24] Pyramids narrow information at every level upward, where deciders must rely upon second- and third-hand reports from below, whether those are honorable and disinterested or not. That is why corporate executives learn to summon competing arguments, effectual royals declare no constitutional changes by themselves, and why, contrary to legend, a monarch's work is uncommonly wearing. The most successful sovereigns in modern history, China's Kangxi Emperor and his contemporary, France's King Louis XIV, exchanged congratulatory letters and fulfilled outstanding careers for their nations' long-term benefit—but each ended in a decade

---

23. Sigmund Freud, "The future prospects of psycho-analytic therapy," opening address at Nuremberg, 1910. *Complete Psychological Works of Sigmund Freud*, standard edition, vol. x (London: Hogarth, 1957), 146. German ed: 1910, *Zbl. Psychoan*, 1:1–2, 1–9. Boldface type added here for emphasis. Thanks to psychologist Dr. Jonathan Dunn for this quotation.

24. E. F. Schumacher, *Small Is Beautiful: A Study of Economics As If People Mattered* (London: Blond and Briggs, 1973).

of personal depression, now and then bursting into anger he had earlier shown the wisdom to forbear.[25]

Among new scientific schools arising after World War II, Tommy Wilson and Wilfrid Bion's Tavistock movement revised common notions of social group behavior. Accepting Freud's observation that even democratized citizens crave authority, they developed exercises for studying how groups actually operate outside institutional myth.

At first, experimenters aimed to chronicle how authority is created, responsibility is carried, and work is done. Before long, however, their focus turned toward dysfunction: how groups devour their leaders; how enterprises get mired in task conflict; how responsibility vanishes; how covert processes undermine formal goals. Tavistock distinguishes authority from power, which may enforce cooperation but can be resisted openly. Instead, Authority requires a compact, so that resistance remains informal, covert, and typically disguised. From years of strenuous experiment, the Tavistock movement defined authority for all organizations, ranks and political forms: authority is the ability to do work.

When the bishop of California invited me to submit an innovative plan for St. Gregory's Church in 1978, I drew on Tavistock insight into crucial parish issues like group membership, which liberal churches typically avoid stressing. The plan for St. Gregory's became a provisional constitution, which church members worked out over three years, and it still influences congregational decision-making. (Meanwhile, George McCauley, SJ, developed a Tavistock approach to standard Western sacramental theory, requiring that participants explain to each other what they believe their ritual actions mean.[26] In many ways, McCauley's work inspired this book.)

Nineteenth-century entrepreneurs displaced inherited aristocracy, but social thinkers maintained a popular belief that natural leaders are endowed from birth with gifts distinguishing them from natural followers. Hence leadership talent—and talents in general—must appear early. That immemorial belief assigned Jesus and various dynastic founders (for example Nannuk, eighth-century founder of India's Chandela dynasty) a legendary virgin birth. Likewise, Napoleon believed that as a cadet he had already proved his inborn genius, which France's foes would overlook to their destruction.

---

25. See chapter 3, on the royal virtue of steadfast *praüs* forbearance.

26. George McCauley, SJ, *The God of the Group* (Niles, IL: Argus, 1975).

Yet Tolstoy's *War and Peace* unmasked Napoleon on campaign, depicting battles so confused, and communications so slow, that every commander made decisions in ignorance. (Or as boxer Mike Tyson said, "Everyone has plans until you're hit in the face.") Furthermore, narrowing pyramids of command magnify chances of catastrophe as well as success: as when both Napoleon and Hitler invaded Russia. In place of unequal talents, Korean War studies found that leaders and followers share identical characteristics: good followers make good leaders, and bad followers do not. Organizational consultant Bernard Haldane reckoned that most people enjoy repeating success more than failure, thus making satisfaction a talent's best index.

Today organizational studies outline a more crew-like model of groups and leaders. Instead of descending from God or from solo charismatics, as hallowed theories held, authority actually emerges when group members compact to accomplish a common goal—otherwise no structure will work. Leadership emerges when some group members make themselves answerable to the rest, and receive their willingness to follow—otherwise followers will choose other leaders who can do so. Success emerges when most members experience satisfaction—otherwise leaders and followers will abandon the work together. (The contemporary collapse of Roman Catholic sex-teaching authority marks leadership failure by all three criteria.) Dictators alone disturb this universal process by forcing submission to their power.

Watching authority emerge "from the bottom up," Dacher Keltner's provocative treatise, *The Power Paradox*, studies essential leader skills including empathy for others, giving to others, expressing gratitude, and telling stories that unite people. The gospels attribute those behaviors to Jesus in retrospect. In any case, the parable stories, our strongest evidence about Jesus, do demonstrate effectiveness amid powerlessness, as low-class criminals and women respond cannily to crisis.

From Keltner's own subjects' responses and nearly two hundred published studies, he tracks the abuses that predictably corrupt the powerful: empathy deficits and diminished moral sentiments; self-serving impulsivity; incivility and disrespect; and above all, lying narratives of exceptionalism.[27] Matthew's gospel elaborates Mark's story of Jesus's wilderness temptations by outlining those distractions concretely. Read as a hero's career launch, Matthew's story reflects posthumously on the purity of Jesus's whole short ministry.[28] An early death

---

27. Dacher Keltner, *The Power of Paradox: How We Gain and Lose Influence* (New York: Penguin Books, 2016), chap. 4, 101 ff.

28. Mark 1:12–13 // Matthew 4:1–11 // Luke 4:1–13.

likewise preserved unalloyed our memory of lost heroes like Martin Luther King Jr. Meant to stifle such inspiring memories, crucifixion humiliated and shamed its victims, and normally undermined what posthumous authority loyal followers might give their leader's example. The gladiator Spartacus was probably the sole Roman rebel whose repute outlasted his crucifixion, because each lieutenant told the arresting soldiers, "I am Spartacus!" until thousands shared his doom.

Throughout the Bible, humankind affirms God's commands and covenants—then betrays them: God alone keeps promises. Even the patriarchs waver, as rabbis will later note. A rare story of a *faithful* human compact appears in Isaiah's call, where the prophet volunteers for duty before all of YHWH Sabaoth's awesome host. That is the sole biblical instance where a mortal enters the heavenly court and sees God. Even Moses sees only the comet's tail, as it were, never the comet itself.[29] Isaiah's call supplies also the sole hymn that Jewish and Christian services sing every week: not a creed, not the *Shema* or Ten Commandments (historically those are readings), but the hymn styled in Latin masses *Sanctus*:

> In the year that King Uzziah died I saw the Lord sitting upon a throne
> High and lifted up; and his train filled the temple.
> Seraphim stood above him; each had six wings.
> With two he covered his face,
> With two he covered his groin,
> And with two he flew.
> And one called to the other and said:
>> Holy, holy, holy is YHWH Sabaoth,
>> whose glory is the fullness of the whole earth.
> Then the pivots of the doors in the foundation stones shook
> At the voice of him who called,
> And the house was filled with smoke.[30]

---

29. Exodus 33:18–23. Editors also augmented vowels in a Sinai proverb: (*bahar YHWH yireh*) "on the mountain God is seen" becomes "God will see to it *(yira'eh)*." (Genesis 22:14). Thus invisible darkness will become Gregory of Nyssa's image for God in *The Life of Moses*, Gregory's great last work, and Byzantine iconography will skip Isaiah's call.

30. Isaiah 6:1–3. The threefold *Holy* is a Hebrew superlative meaning holy above all other sacred places, persons, and customs (see chapter 4). "Smoke" as at Sinai: Exodus 19:16, 40:34. Trans. Otto Kaiser in *Der Prophet Jesaiah / Kap 1–12, Das Alte Testament Deutsch 17*, Göttingen 1963, Englished by R. A. Wilson (London: SCM and Philadelphia: Westminster, 1972).

This *Sanctus* hymn's ritual placement shifted with congregational practice, as E. C. Ratcliff explained.[31] Many synagogue services opened with it, evoking a temple-like context—although Christian ritual may have preceded this. Mirroring Isaiah's heavenly court, both religions adopted Roman Imperial ceremonial here: for example, carrying crowned Torah scrolls, gospel books, and Roman popes on ministers' shoulders: this was how new Roman emperors rode standing (rather than enthroned) on their electing generals' shouldered shields to meet the troops.[32]

Third Story: *¡Para qué sirve un Rey!*

Spain's fascist dictator Francisco Franco had kept King Alfonso XIII in exile, while Franco ruled nominally in the king's stead, and trained his son Juan Carlos, crown prince of Asturias, to rule as a right-wing monarch. When death approached in 1975, Franco thought it safe to put Juan Carlos on the throne. Soon after Franco's death, however, the prime minister and Cortes (Parliament) began liberal reforms. So in 1981, fascist troops invaded the Cortes with machine guns, holding all delegates hostage, and claiming Queen Sofia's support. During that overnight emergency, the young king heard conflicting appeals from all sides. Then leading his little son Felipe by the hand past protesting generals, he strode unarmed into the Cortes and commanded the reactionary soldiers to surrender. Within moments they laid down their weapons.[33] After fifty years of fascism, Spain swiftly became one of Europe's most progressive states, with free elections and a feisty free press; with divorce and same-sex marriage legalized. The crisis won the young ruler political authority that survived royal missteps since. In popular legend, as they approached the Cortes Juan Carlos told his son: ¡Tu eres el Príncipe de Asturias: Hoy verás para qué sirve un Rey! *"You are the crown prince: today you will see what a king is for!" To this day Spain's monarch does not sign his name, but simply* "Yo, el Rey," *and crowns emblazon those national airliners whose royals withstood fascist regimes.*

---

31. E. C. Ratcliff, "The Sanctus and the Pattern of the Early Anaphora," *Journal of Ecclesiastical History*, 1950, and E. C. Ratcliff, *Liturgical Studies* (London: SPCK, 1976).

32. Tamara Talbot Rice, *Everyday Life in Byzantium* (New York: Dorset Press, 1987), illus. p. 30.

33. Paul Preston, *Juan Carlos: Steering Spain from Dictatorship to Democracy* (New York: Norton, 2004). Preston does not cite the words that legend attributes to the young king.

We moderns can no more escape the emotional need for authority than ancients could. On the other hand, Christian liturgists must translate archaic forms in modern social and political terms. For a figure once universally clear, both Bible and liturgy use the title "King." "Christ" ("anointed" in Greek) and "Son of God" were both titles of Israelite kings,[34] and distinguish royals in Old and New Testament texts alike. And yet biblical "kings" have problems far beyond our contemporary preference for democratic polity. While the earliest psalmody does project royal imagery onto God, human kings fare poorly. The prophet Samuel warns his people of known dangers before agreeing to anoint one.[35] Solomon's courtiers wrote the Bible's histories, so he alone enjoys their approval.[36] Besides him, the histories chronicle a spoilt record of apostates, murderers (including Solomon's heroic father, David), cowards, weaklings, and diplomatic bumblers. Only Queen Jezebel matches Solomon's ken, and she dies defenestrated for her crimes, where dogs devour her flesh and gristle in a single night, leaving bare skull and skeleton behind.[37]

Readers today, accustomed to the royal titles that Christians conferred upon Jesus,[38] must admire the gospels' enduring republicanism on this very point. The only two Jewish kings named there, both called Herod, are blackened for vanity and corruption. More important, Jesus himself consistently repudiates royal titles throughout the canonical gospels, particularly in the Passion stories that preserve our oldest narrative material. John's Passion, perhaps the earliest, has Jesus parry Pilate's question about royalty, countering, "Are you asking that yourself, or did someone else tell you so? . . . You may say 'King,' but I was born to speak up for the truth."[39]

Twentieth-century critics delve unsuccessfully to uncover Jesus's mind. Shoveling away the editors' loamy topsoil of meanings, they pan parables and sayings for nugget clues to Jesus's own intentions. Those nuggets weigh heaviest which might embarrass the church, and yet are preserved, but the resulting payload is too small to support constructions of Jesus's "messianic consciousness" sometimes proposed. All the more notably then, even when composing their

---

34. John 1:49. Geza Vermès, *Jesus the Jew: A Historian's Reading of the Gospels* (New York: MacMillan, 1973).

35. 1 Samuel 8:10–18.

36. 1 Kings 4:29–34.

37. 2 Kings 9.

38. See N. T. Wright, *How God Became King: The Forgotten Story of the Gospels* (New York: Harper Collins, 2011).

39. John 18:34, 37, author's translation.

own royalist ideology, the synoptic writers (Mark, Matthew, Luke) never portray Jesus accepting the commonplace vision of a kingly Messiah. When that image is named, he dismisses it in theological terms: "Get behind me, Satan!"[40] If in fact Jesus was a scriptural traditionalist on this point, as demonstrated earlier, he likely did not share that dream. Then in view of the evangelists' belief that Jesus was indeed the very anointed monarch his countrymen had prayed for, we must heed their loyal reportage of his demurrals. However Jesus saw his work, kingship cannot characterize it.

That textual homophony silences one counterpoint tune voiced by interpreters who champion the story of Jesus "cleansing" the Jerusalem temple as the dramatic turning-point aria in his career opera.[41] They hear a prophetic sign sung here, signaling or causing his martyrdom as a political radical, yet we cannot christen that story as historical on the one hand, and honor Jesus's consistent demurrals of royal office on the other. All Jesus's public knew that governing the cult was a Jewish king's top responsibility, because rainfall, pests, and harvests brought crises at every season, while battles and booty came rarely. That is why Israel's sacral *cohens* obeyed their King's ritual commands even when those were idolatrous. Amos, the earliest written prophet, earns a cult priest's rebuke, "Go away, this is the royal shrine!"[42] The priest means: this shrine has our King's supreme religious sanction, which none dare contest lest our nation suffer God's anger. Had Jesus in fact purged the temple by the violent public demonstration the gospels retail, all Jerusalem would have recognized an open claim upon royalty, superseding the Maccabean high priest. Jesus cannot have both publicly claimed kingship, and everywhere rejected kingship: modern readers must choose which is fact.

Most tellingly, the four Passion stories bear evidence that the temple-cleansing event was an editorial addition. Jesus's accusers omit any usurping action from their indictment before Pilate, when it would have corroborated supremely their charge of sedition. John even has Pilate complete his discussion of kingship—the only discussion in the gospels—declaring, "I find no case against him." Jesus's accusers also object when Pilate titles Jesus a crucified king. With characteristic irony, John's Passion presents that twice as a slander only unwittingly true.[43] "What I have written, I have written."[44]

---

40. Mark 8:33 // Matthew 16:23.
41. Mark 11:15–17 // Matthew 21:12–13 // Luke 19:45–46; compare John 2:14–17.
42. Amos 7:12–13.
43. John 18–19.
44. John 19:22.

Here more critical readers find instead a prophecy-fulfillment story, composed later to justify styling Jesus a king. Handel's *Messiah* has made those royal prophecies familiar: "The Lord whom ye seek shall suddenly come to his Temple . . . even the messenger of the Covenant, whom ye delight in . . . And he shall purify the sons of Levi, that they may offer unto the Lord an offering in righteousness."[45] Such close parody of Hebrew prophecy suggests the temple-cleansing story comes from a Christian sermon. Like a faithful sermon, it breathes the challenging air that fills many of Jesus's own parables. It can hardly be a journalistic report, however, since Jesus thereupon leaves the Temple unrecognized—in contrast to Saul and David, whom crowds acclaim as soon as they seize leadership publicly.[46]

The Christ's Authority

Contrary to Roman penal policy, after Jesus's crucifixion his disciples acclaimed him with the very royal titles he had dismissed in life: Christ, Lord, Master, Son of God.[47] They published their conviction swiftly throughout the Jewish diaspora to places Jesus never knew, winning more followers than he could ever have known. Among these, Saul (also called Paul) of Tarsus expanded Israel's covenant community to include racial non-Jews, whose converts eventually outnumbered Jesus's own nation. Here, unlike Jesus's own more conservative draught upon Hebrew prophecies, Paul made the New Testament's most radical innovation, utterly lacking precedent. Matthew Thiessen writes: "We have no evidence that any author or editor whose work the Hebrew Bible preserves perceived [circumcision] to be a rite of entrance into the Israelite nation, for there was no such rite."[48]

If Paul was not the very first schooled rabbi to welcome Gentile believers, he left us the first written arguments. His letters expound Jesus's importance chiefly for aliens to read, with a long summary written for his fellow Jews at Rome. Paul's toughest apologetic task endures today: proclaiming a royal messiah who had sidestepped that office, to a non-Jewish public who never hoped

45. Malachi 3:1, Zechariah 14:21. King James Version translation.

46. 1 Samuel 10; 2 Samuel 5.

47. Maurice Casey, chap. 4 in *From Jewish Prophet to Gentile God: The Origins and Development of New Testament Christology* (Cambridge: J. Clarke and Louisville: Westminster/JohnKnox, 1991).

48. Matthew Thiessen, *Contesting Conversion: Genealogy, Circumcision, and Identity in Ancient Judaism and Christianity* (New York: Oxford University Press, 2011), 63. See chapter 3 on Baptism.

for one. Notwithstanding, they did enjoy one convenience we moderns lack. Despite three centuries of imperial persecution, Christian peoples from Armenia to Ethiopia could readily adapt royal ceremonies and symbols. Now Christians must mark Jesus's authority with symbols our secular contemporaries can recognize, or both evangelism and worship will waste away.

Today's more fashionable political concept "leader" does appear in a New Testament letter[49] and may fit individual devotions but leading is a corporate action, and the gospel writers acknowledge that unlike other messianic candidates, Jesus acquired no popular leader role. The evangelists' own difficulty at winning converts reflected Jesus's lonely fate, and they blame deliberate resistance. Either the Jewish nation rejected Jesus as their forebears had rejected the prophets,[50] or Jesus himself intentionally obscured his identity and the meaning of his sayings and actions—a bizarre rhetoric unlike any other Hebrew prophet.[51] Under either scheme, willful denial brought national catastrophe, when within four decades the Romans invaded and paved Jerusalem over. Matthew rehabilitates that debacle as God's just punishment upon the chosen nation Jesus might have led. Nevertheless, both apologies stain the evangelists' portraits of Jesus as teacher as well as leader. We may wonder why anyone would offer authority to such an inhibited, self-defeating personage!

The Hidden King Discovered

Fortunately for Bible readers, an earlier New Testament Christology escapes this contradiction. That earlier Christology opens Paul's letter to the Romans, and supports Jesus's authority for heading a religious heritage in crisis, as both Jesus and Paul unquestionably did.[52]

Paul may have known that Rome already boasted more Jewish diasporal residents than Jerusalem had. Being the eccentric Apostle to Gentiles, he presumed his Roman church readers must be Jewish, and would want his Jewish *apologia*. Contemporary Jews knew two figures of messianic hope: a traditional conquering captain like David on the one hand; and on the other, a new

---

49. Hebrews 12:2.

50. Mark 6:4; Matthew 5:12, 23:29–37 (Luke 11:45–52).

51. Mark 4:10–12, 33–34; Matthew 13:10–15.

52. Romans 1:1–7. Just seven crucial verses, nevertheless we listen today for what ancient writers presumed was evident without expounding.

spiritual revival of the whole nation.[53] In six opening verses, Paul tells Roman Jews that Jesus fulfills both agendas. For Davidic heritage, Paul cites Jesus's genealogy: one generation later, Luke's gospel will rehearse this.[54] For spiritual revival, Paul borrows a commonplace political analogy, claiming God declared Jesus King (Christ) at his resurrection from the dead.[55]

Some accuse Paul of adoptionism here, as if God deified the dead Jesus as a reward for playing out his exemplary life story in mortal obscurity. Those readers miss Paul's explicit analogy, as ancient readers could hardly have done. Among modern constitutional states, the few remaining royal successions glide along smoothly enough while in ancient societies those occasioned civil war and dynastic cataclysm. Worse yet, most kings secured polygamous alliances, which multiplied warlord heirs to join the fight. A savvy monarch must seek some mechanism to ensure peace, normally by marking his successor well in advance. Caesar Augustus's failure here was his own greatest disappointment, and until Justinian's reign nearly every Roman emperor took power through bloody strife that massacred thousands of citizens and thousands more of their slaves. The grisly Ottoman alternative was to liquidate each newly chosen sultan's siblings, old and young, however loyal.[56]

As he aged toward this dread pitfall, an astute ruler might announce: "A year hence I will declare who is crown prince." All that year long the king's wives and allied families would blandish him with favors, while his many sons competed at skills to win his confidence—until the day arrived, and the crown prince was declared. After that declaration, court historians might write, "At seven years old the crown prince excelled at archery and horsemanship. At nine the crown prince out-reasoned court philosophers. At twelve the crown prince showed God's favor by healing sufferers," and so forth. Such a court history would truly be the crown prince's life story (exaggerated!) even though no one—not the candidate nor perhaps either parent—knew his eventual identity before the king declared it. His accession came by confirmation, not by adoption; indeed all competing candidates had the natural birthright required.

In this Roman letter, Paul argues crucially that Jesus shared Adam's God-like nature with all our race; meanwhile, his words and actions proved his

53. Casey, *From Jewish Prophet to Gentile God.*

54. Luke 1.

55. Romans 1:4 . . . *tou horisthentos huiou theou en dunamei kata pneuma hagiôsunês ex anastaseôs ek nekrôn.*

56. Garrett Mattingly, *Renaissance Diplomacy* (Hammondsworth, Middlesex, England: Penguin 1955, 1964).

sturdy faith, a virtue God had rightly rewarded throughout Israel's national history. Then by raising Jesus from the dead and pouring out his Spirit on humankind, God declared him to be the royal Messiah, with a life story to match. Resurrecting Jesus, God signed the formal papers, and all our race now share the new Adam's character, just as we had shared the old one.[57] Jesus's identity never changed: the same Jesus had been Messiah all along, if unrecognized even by himself before God's effectual declaration. What did change was the authority his disciples accorded him, and accord him today.

Jesus's own historical self-understanding and his "messianic consciousness" now lie long buried beneath gospel storytellers' beliefs. That is why the failure of his fellow Jews today to accept God's declaration at Jesus's rising wants no apology. The Bible's royal histories even prefigure that.[58] Modern readers will focus on David's adult military successes and family disappointments. Paul's contemporaries awaiting a messiah's appearance more urgently parsed David's own discovery and divine authorization, and the dramatic pattern prefigured there.

According to 1 Samuel, David's messianic identity consistently startled his contemporaries' expectations. The boy shepherd's family had not discerned his kingly potential, nor nominated his candidacy; even the inspired prophet Samuel was surprised when God declared: "God does not see as a man sees. Man looks at appearances, but YHWH looks at the heart."[59] David's boyhood victory over the Philistine giant Goliath spread further amazement through both armies and he survived Saul's plan to murder him thanks to unexpected collaboration from Saul's own children. When at last God withdrew Saul's appointment, Samuel confirmed David's succession ahead of Saul's proper heirs. Thus Paul begins this last letter joining David's messianic surprise together with commonplace succession customs, so both allusions will prepare his Jewish readers for Jesus's lifetime concealment, and for Jesus's eventual superseding the sacred authority that had ignorantly crucified him.[60]

European art history provides us a powerful likeness to the doubly hidden Christology opening Paul's Letter to the Romans. Rembrandt van Rijn painted over forty self-portraits, each showing how the artist saw his world. Most reveal the late effects of time and experience in his face; but one that he painted at

---

57. Romans 5:12–21. See also 1 Corinthians 15:45–49.

58. 1 Samuel 16.

59. 1 Samuel 16:7.

60. See 1 Corinthians 2:8.

barely twenty-three years' age now hangs at Boston's Gardner Museum, with this different central detail.

The look in Rembrandt's youthful eye exposes his inner mind: open, attentive, perceptive, compassionate, unafraid, unjudging, trusting his own vision—and a magnetic personality. What could his contemporaries have thought, who spied this Rembrandt on the Amsterdam streets, or ate and drank with him, or married him, as two women did? Could they have known that here was the greatest painter of inner thoughts in the whole history of *homo sapiens sapiens*? Of course they had no idea. Had he? Probably not at age twenty-three, a short decade younger than Jesus lived. But that is who Rembrandt was, and it took humankind another century to recognize his identity, while he labored in the usual painter's poverty and struggles. Contemporaries meeting either Jesus or Rembrandt barely knew them. Every classical icon of Christ had a living human model: Rembrandt's self-portrait is my own favorite, where I pray and meditate daily.

Rembrandt van Rijn, Self-Portrait (detail), 1629 CE

Isabela Stewart Gardner Museum, Boston

Paul's double-concealed Christology has a further hidden purpose: it puts forward his own apostolic credentials, and ours too. As the first apostle to Gentiles, where his whole ministry has taken him, Paul knows the Jewish immigrant church at Rome was evangelized by others who may have known Jesus in the flesh as he did not. So here he reminds them that their commissioning, just as much as his, comes from witnessing Jesus's resurrection. Hereby Paul claims an equal footing with every apostle,[61] throughout the following sixteen chapters that argue for his novel Gentile mission.

Such slow unrolling of true authority became a Christian trope. Canterbury archbishop Michael Ramsey comments that Jesus's emptying himself in

---

61. Here too is the authorization for Paul's claim "I withstood Peter to his face" (Galatians 2:11).

a life leading finally to the cross revealed—clearest at the last—what it is to be like God as all we humans are, because God empties God's self. Today we may call Jesus's emptying an existential sacrifice.

Fourth Story: *¡Tu eres el Príncipe!*

"Either Christianity is fire, or there is no such thing."[62] *Maria Skobtsova was an ornery woman. Divorced in Russia, writing for a Paris newspaper, and a heavy smoker in an era when proper women never smoked in public, Maria asked her Russian Orthodox bishop to let her try solitary monastic life within the city. After first resisting her requests he consented, yet continued his pastoral concern. Paris's streets were filling with homeless Russian refugees from the Communist takeover following the 1917 Revolution. Mother Maria supported herself by sewing and embroidery while she created a prayer hostel for her stranded countrymen. As the Nazis rose to power in Germany, Jewish refugees joined the Russians in Parisian streets, and she took them in too. In 1939, German armies occupied Paris, and soon began rounding up Jews and French resisters for eventual murder at camps in the east. Hoping to protect her Jewish guests, Mother Maria and a sympathetic priest forged baptismal certificates.*

The Gestapo got word of her hostel, and sent officers to capture the Jews there. "Are you harboring Jews?" "Yes," said Mother Maria. "Show us where they are!" She led the officers to her chapel, where she had embroidered a cloth iconostasis with images of Jesus, Mary, John Baptist, and apostles surrounding the altar doorway. Pointing at these icons, she said, "There they are—they're all Jews!" The Gestapo returned to search until they did find Jews hidden in her basement. They arrested her, and deported her with her refugees and her priest to Ravensbrück concentration camp, where guards gassed Mother Maria on Easter Eve, 1945. Another prisoner reported that she took the place of a Jewish woman in line for liquidation. She could not have known that two days later on Easter Monday, the French army would liberate Ravensbrück and release all French prisoners.

---

62. Amy Frykholm, "True Evangelical Faith: Insights of a Martyred Orthodox Nun," in *The Christian Century*, December 2016, cites *Mother Maria Skobtsova: Essential Writings* (Maryknoll, NY: Orbis Books, 2003). Cf Sergei Hackel, *One of Great Price* (London: Darton, Longman & Todd, 1965). Cf T. Stratton Smith, *The Rebel Nun* (London: Souvenir Press, 1965).

If Jesus holds divine authority, what is it good for? Gregory of Nyssa, a moral philosopher, answered for his own fourth century: it is for leading the virtuous life. Former Episcopal presiding bishop Katharine Jefferts Schori, an ocean biologist, answered: for healing the world; and Salisbury's retired bishop David Stancliffe, a concert musician, echoes ancient Irenaeus: for bringing his human hearers truly alive. All such goals serve us but how does Jesus's Spirit show us to advance them, the way Juan Carlos taught his son? Nutritionist Colleen Kavanagh calls the church her lens for perceiving the world.

> Last year was worst in my life. I discovered local San Francisco schools were illegally serving different food to rich and poor kids; my exposing it got on *New York Times's* front page; my colleagues got angry for re-directing funds they wanted used otherwise, or thought I just wanted to raise my own profile. But I imagined Jesus as my colleague and asked what he would say—and that made it clear what I had to do.[63]

In light of Tavistock's definition that authority is the ability to do work, authority shows up in any effective working group. Dr. Jane McGonigal of the Institute for the Future recounts how leading scientists identified a potential cure for genetic disease that involved folding a protein, a mathematical process so complex that no existing computer could accomplish it during their lifetime. They summoned hundreds of young computer gamers to volunteer exchanging binary thumb signals with one another—and within a few hours the gamers successfully folded the protein.[64] Three centuries after Paul, the conciliar orator and bishop Athanasius of Alexandria made a parallel argument asserting Jesus's resurrection, not on the ground of fulfilling old prophecy, but of Jesus's work done among Athanasius's live contemporaries.

> Let whoever will, see and decide, confessing the truth that is in plain sight. For now that the Savior works so great things among humans, and day by day is invisibly persuading so great a multitude from every side, both in Greece and abroad, to come over to his faith, and all obey his teaching—will anyone still doubt whether the Savior has accomplished a resurrection, and whether Christ is alive, or rather is himself The Life?

---

63. Colleen Kavanagh, "Flunking Lunch: How Segregated Lunch Lines and Misused Subsidies Are Undermining the National School Lunch Program," 2015, original web version, *http://campaignforbetternutrition.org/images/Flunking_Lunch_FINAL2.pdf.*

64. "The Power of Gaming, with Dr. Jane McGonigal," San Francisco City Arts and Lectures, January 31, 2012. Jane McGonigal, *Reality Is Broken: Why Games Make Us Better and How They Can Change the World* (New York: Penguin Books, 2011).

. . . Or how, if he is no longer active (as would be proper to one dead)—how does he stay from their activity those who are active and alive, so that the adulterer no longer commits adultery, and the murderer murders no more, nor is the inflictor of wrong any longer grasping, and the profane is henceforth religious?

. . . For it be true that one dead can exert no power, while the Savior does daily so many works, drawing folk to faith, persuading to virtue, teaching of immortality, leading on to a desire for heavenly things, revealing the knowledge of the Father, inspiring strength to meet death, showing himself to each person, and displacing idolatry—and the gods and spirits of the unbelievers can do none of these things, but rather show themselves dead at the presence of Christ, their pomp being reduced to impotence and vanity—whereas by the sign of the cross all magic is stopped, and all witchcraft brought to naught, and all the idols are being deserted and left, and every addiction is checked, and everyone is looking up from earth to heaven—whom is one to pronounce dead? Christ, that is doing so many works? [65]

Athanasius's argument fits apophatic Cappadocian theology as Richard Norris paraphrased it: "We don't know anything *about* God, we only know what God *does*."[66] Unlike undergraduate all-night debaters, classical monotheists do not hold that God exists, but rather that God's job is filled: somebody *is doing* it. The Psalms pray that God will *act* as scripture teaches. Hence the rhetorical structure of salvation songs completing Psalms of lament: God, you have done great things for us in the past, but not much lately; get back to work now, so we can praise you as our forebears did! [67]

Despite the Western Renaissance focus upon Christ's eucharistic presence, ancient consecration prayers never climax there, but continue to intercession and petition for God's action. Indeed, the whole Byzantine rite opens with the deacon's cry, "It is time for the Lord to act!" and a series of processional litanies. Unlike Cranmer's penitential Rogationtide devotion,[68] these voice abundant

---

65. "*Tina an tis eipei nekron? Ton tosauta ergazomenon christon?*" Athanasius, *On the Word Becoming Human*, xxx, xxxj, Englished in volume 4 of Philip Schaff, *Nicene and Post-Nicene Fathers* (Peabody, MA: Hendrickson, 1892; Grand Rapids, MI: Wm. B. Eerdmans, 1987).

66. See chapter 4. Gregory Nyssen: "God becomes visible only in his operations, and only when he is contemplated in the things that are external to him." Paulos Mar Gregorios, *Cosmic Man . . . The Theology of St. Gregory of Nyssa* (New York: Paragon, 1998), 70. Cited in Paul Fromberg, *The Art of Transformation: Three Things Churches Do That Change Everything* (New York: Church Publishing, 2017), 98.

67. Psalms 22, 40, 44, 71, 74, 77, 80, 89, 90, and 107.

68. By a well-meant but mistaken Byzantinism, the American Book of Common Prayer (p. 148) styles Cranmer's composition "the Great Litany." That traditional title belongs properly to the "Prayers of the People" set forth elsewhere in the Eucharist rite (pp. 383–395) where Forms I and V are Byzantine.

charity for the whole world. Without intercession, worship symbols might lure the ecstatic faithful to imagine living in another era, whereas they must know they cannot live in any other era. The world's past is inaccessible; the world's future lies in God's hands—and so in ours if we take inspiration to act now.

Work All Christians Can Do

Assigning our leaders effectual authority requires we agree upon common goals. Global AIDS Interfaith Alliance, a California charity working in Malawi, has learned that when an African village sheikh tells villagers to use condoms, the Muslim men all queue up at once to buy and wear them. What Roman or Coptic Christian pope can claim such authority today?

Three true stories recounted here tell of God working within modern memory. Two show an armed crowd surprised, and of their free will changing their plans, at the bare words of one unarmed speaker. Violence dissolves into peace when authority is recognized: Christ, the head of the church; or the newly crowned king of Spain. All three lay ministers—Mother Ann Lee, Juan Carlos de Borbón, and Maria Skobtsova—risk their safety for their consciences' sake, offering the very existential sacrifice that followers expect. Tavistock studies find that whether leaders attain goals or not, they can earn more resentful gossip than applause. As California bishop William Swing preached one Passion Week, "Mockery is the sound heard while the Cross is carried." Our newspapers report grimly that for every triumphing hero, scores have given up their lives. For every peaceful solution, scores of conflicts have broken out. For every just reward, scores of wrongs are not put right, or not forgiven. That is why ritual signs of hope still center our common prayer life.

Church structures slowly copy worldly changes in authority. Peacemaking decrees by a conquering monarch at Rome or Karakorum or Versailles yield place to secular coalitions like the United Nations, which can regroup and persevere after disasters, while stubborn royals lose their heads. Now that popular participation has become a widespread political goal, hierarchs adopt more responsible behavior toward members, and toward rival faiths as well. Liturgists assign lay volunteers broader work at common worship. Tradition, like scripture, actually supports such changes. Eastern worship is a resource too long overlooked. Unbroken centuries of vernacular cult in the East offer several reasons to refer there now.

St. Gregory's Church began with an organizational plan reflecting Tavistock research, and experimented for decades realizing popular authority in ministry. This focus highlights two liturgical practices. A conversation follows the sermon, as congregation members stand to share their own experiences—rather than reasoned arguments or replies—which the preacher has brought to mind. And three times the congregation moves as a whole: an entry procession, a procession to the table, and a final dance around it. Though at many other churches those are spectator events, they have participatory beginnings, and they realize shared authority at St. Gregory's. Our volunteer choir executes two or three rehearsed anthems, but the congregation's songs predominate, and lead newcomers to participate along with experienced members.

Nevertheless, improving our work and worship structures can never safeguard the church against controversy, covert opposition, or self-contradiction. Tavistock studies find those ubiquitous within human groups and institutions. Emperor Constantine I took up the Roman pontifex maximus's title and religious chores, and convened a council at Nicaea, meaning to secure cultic peace and empire-wide prosperity. Instead, bishops' serial councils overruled Arian emperors, while Byzantine mobs killed one monarch after another. Medieval Roman popes and royals held many a standoff. England's Henry VIII died a Roman Catholic in full communion with the Vatican, thanks to enforcing Latin ritual throughout his typical Renaissance wrangle over princely succession. By contrast, his daughter Elizabeth I made England safe for religious minorities as nowhere else in Europe, but was excommunicated for her pains. Within a century, exhausted German Protestant and Catholic warlords parceled out a stalemate—*cujus regio ejus religio*, "let each prince's religion set his domain's religion"—that still shapes civil wars across Europe. As Martin Luther wrote, *Ecclesia semper reformanda*, the church will always want reshaping. It is no substitute for the reign of Christ.

Tavistock studies define an institution as a social arrangement built to last, carrying forward the ability to do work. That is why institutional forms endure even while their rationale and personnel change, or change faster. Unlike a hereditary Hebrew tribal priest (*cohen*), the synagogue minister (*sheliakh tsippur*) flexibly became a Jewish cantor or Christian deacon. Such offices grew legends contradicting history, like the supposed "apostolic succession" of bishops from Jesus's own vanished circle. Notwithstanding, during the past century, church historians have discarded that pretense without ecumenical disaster.[69]

---

69. William Telfer, *The Office of a Bishop* (London: Darton, Longman & Todd, 1962). Telfer was the Anglican dean of Clare College, Cambridge. See also Roman Catholic historians Étienne Nodet and Justin Taylor, *The Origins of Christianity: An Exploration* (Collegeville, MN: Liturgical Press, 1998).

Indeed, the classic way to recognize a neighbor church's ministries is not by sifting its legends and history, but by reading its ordination prayers, upon a simple Bible principle: God grants a church what gifts that church prays for.

Mutual recognition among working authorities enables collaboration, whereas recognition withheld raises barriers. Ordained church ministries have done both. Our widest-known Christian ministry, called presbyter (elder, shortened to "priest" in English) or bishop (overseer), arose and spread during the second century to safeguard growing churches' teachings against corruption—such as had tragically flooded out the brief community that left us John's gospel and epistles.[70] Unifying people's prayers was a bishop's first job, and still is.

Upon arriving recently at his Hawaiian parish, one new Episcopal rector accompanied a parishioner to her Buddhist husband's funeral. Around the Pacific, funerals form the Buddhist pastoral core. Often a ceremony ends as family and friends turn respectfully away from the casket, while ordained monks lower it into the grave. Our Anglican priest turned his back with the rest, but then he felt a touch at his shoulder, and saw the yellow sleeve of the presiding abbot, who whispered in his ear, "Turn around! you are worthy!" He did so, and the senior Buddhist abbot of Kauai and the new Episcopal rector of Lihu'e together watched the dead man be buried. By contrast, former American Episcopal presiding bishop Katharine Jefferts Schori was told she dare not wear her miter during a worldwide Lambeth bishops' conference, because the Church of England and some other provinces had no female bishops. She modestly carried her miter in hand, while a hundred male bishops swept fully vested up the aisle.

The Church of England did finally accept Parliament's laws by opening all offices to women and men alike. Yet compared with the orthodox Buddhist teacher's respect for Christian orders described above, Anglican hierarchs threw over their founding purpose. The spectacle of a chastely married and canonically elected prime bishop laicized ceremonially to please prelates from the dictatorships of the dead British Empire, whose own extramarital sex lives are customarily winked at, casts doubt upon what work Anglican bishops actually do, and what gospel they presume to speak for. Perhaps like other reactionary monarchs, these have given up on liberal democracy to pursue an imaginary feudal past. Today their layfolk stumble through a spreading wreckage of rival religious fiefdoms. As in feudal times, after decades warring abroad beneath Canterbury's foolish smiles, schismatics have begun battering British home

---

70. Raymond Brown, *The Community of the Beloved Disciple* (New York: Paulist Press, 1978, 1999).

bishoprics with purist rival missionaries. The Bible commands: "Do not answer a fool according to his folly lest you become like him."[71] So this book will track ordained pathways no further.

Fifth Story: *¡Hoy verás!*

Removing our shoes, we entered St. Mary's Church in Addis Ababa for Timket, the feast of Christ's Baptism. A crowned deacon led us foreigners to a dais clouded with incense, while drumming and chanting outside the church told us the dances there had begun. Upon the hour, curtains parted before the Holy of Holies, and a hundred white-clad Ethiopian women burst out ululating high, like a choir of dark-headed snowy birds. In that opening stood a priest brightly vested, bearing on his head a flat bundle with rich brocade veils draped to his knees on either side. Here brought out for the first time in a year was the tabot, *the symbolic Ark of the Covenant that for sixteen centuries has sanctified every Ethiopian altar table. On Timket all the city's* tabots *leave their altars and process gorgeously swathed among chanting and drumming throngs to the baptismal site.*

    Ululating ever louder, our women crowded close and fell prostrate before the priest's feet as he moved down the red carpets, bearing the tabot *on his head. Barefoot men guided his steps into the courtyard and tied on his shoes and ours. The patriarch and twenty clergy joined us with gorgeous colored umbrellas unfurled, like frigates under full sail, and our flotilla entered the broad boulevard—where an ocean of white-clad youth danced with staffs and sang in roaring billows: "We love the Virgin Mary!" Cascading toward us down every avenue as far as we could see streamed more* tabots *and more bright umbrellas from more churches, led by more rolling choruses of girls and boys. Young Ethiopian hands cordoned a space for us foreigners among the waves, and our tide surged toward the old imperial polo ground. There the tabots presided held aloft at a tent by night and an open-air dais by day. Through forty hours of chants, drums, dances, prayers, and fontwater sprayed from hoses and plastic bottles, a hundred and fifty thousand worshippers surpassed comparison to any sports event. Had a new-crowned*

---

71. Proverbs 26:4 LEB.

emperor or the Virgin Mary or Christ himself in glory appeared that day, they could have met no more jubilant royal welcome.

For a hundred years, Western worship reformers moved in step with gospel scholars, who discovered Christ's future reign awaited also in the second-century Syrian *Didachê* prayers. So twentieth-century reformers heightened futurist talk, composing new affirmations for the people to sing: "Christ has died, Christ is risen, *Christ will come again.*" Anglican editors refocused Book of Common Prayer services using a futurist lens. But as the first chapter in this book retells, most gospel critics shifted 180 degrees away from an apocalyptic Jesus, and further translations of early prayer documents also thinned futurism. Even the *Didachê's* Aramaic *marana-tha*, read at first as "Come, Lord!" may be better translated as "The Lord is come!" It is time liturgists acknowledged this shift, writing prayers that reflect Jesus's own distinctive stress on our response *now*.

In fact, people's prayers focus naturally on the present: as one United States senator quipped during debate about public school prayer, "As long as there are math tests, there will be prayer in the schools!" Only liturgical convention has aimed petitioners' faith toward a mythical future. Latin collect prayers and their reformed offspring open with praise and present-day urgencies; yet many then collapse precipitously toward the Last Judgment, begging glorious payback with Christ returned to reign, or earlier once these petitioners are dead. Such endings rhetorically shape congregational intentions like Maoist reeducation camps. For honesty and spiritual health, prayer-writers would better ask for justice, peace, pardon, healing, and the common good in our own day—full stop. Petitions in the psalms and the gospels plead just that way. Luke's Passion even expressly supersedes futurist formulae with immediate blessing: "Truly I tell you, today you will be with me in Paradise."[72]

Future hope does own a firm place in liturgical use of the whole Bible. Among the teeming Palestinian apocalyptic groups, some shared Christian faith.[73] Nodet and Taylor propose, for example, that Rabbi Akiva, martyred hero of later Judaism, could on his own terms have been counted an apocalyptic Christian. Those groups left us at least one gospel story treasured ever since: Matthew's Great Assize.[74] In a different parable more likely come from

---

72. Luke 23:43.

73. Nodet and Taylor, *The Origins of Christianity*, 74–80 and 205–280.

74. Matthew 25:31–46.

Jesus himself, a judge makes a folk figure of corruption, like Israel's kings.[75] By contrast Matthew's Assize judge champions the poor in literary prophetic style, and so may echo Jesus's mind as a scriptural conservative. Hebrew prophets often declare future promises and warnings. As the prophet Joel put it, "Leave off mourning over your past wrongs, and change your *plans!*"—and thereby your future. Jürgen Moltmann's *The Theology of Hope* (1964) emphasized what power concrete hopes can hold. During the twentieth-century Cold War, Moltmann took part in many Christian-Marxist dialogs. Concluding one dialog, an East German theorist told him, "We Marxists have made a mistake, telling Christians that their visions of God's reign at the world's end wrongly palliate Capitalism's ills, and hinder revolution. Instead we should be urging Christians to *intensify* their hopes and longings."[76] That is one proper purpose of Christian worship.

No worship planner dares ignore political hopes today, when many voters feel a greater responsibility and authority for human welfare than ancient folk contemplated. The late collapse of socialist regimes has left religious preachers hoisting the ensign of social justice and peace in their stead. Otherwise, as Freud darkly predicted, worldwide neuroses will multiply. So rather than merely shave away the future the way gospel text critics must do, liturgy planners can intensify hope by echoing Jesus's message: change your life direction *now* because it is already too late to manage God's reign. The longed-for Messiah has come and *is here*, both in Christ's body as we discern it among us, and in Jesus's Spirit inspiring our daily work. That is how Jesus's parables urge us to respond.

Ritual Welcome for Christ's Authority

Our liturgy boasts a natural place for that response, if not everywhere recognized. Many Western churches renewing their worship have restored a central congregational procession, which centuries of Latin low masses had hidden from view. Those reformers typically take their cue from pagan Roman sacrificial cortèges, which led a victim animal decked in garlands and accompanied by offerers.[77] Hence, many of the hymns sung during a Western "Offertory

---

75. Luke 18:1–8.

76. Jürgen Moltmann, lecture at Lincoln Theological College, 1968.

77. Ramsay MacMullen, *The Second Church: Popular Christianity A.D. 200–400* (Atlanta: Society for Biblical Literature, 2009).

Procession" anticipate the eucharistic memorial of Jesus's sacrificial death, as the Great Thanksgiving Prayer will shortly recall it. Such hymns look backward into the biblical past. As for the present, they mention only the worshippers' misdeeds, and hopes that an apocalyptic King will return one day to put everything right. Unhappily, songs and prayers bidding worshippers leave the present for an imaginary future differ little from removing them to a legendary past. The actual Jesus pointed neither direction.[78]

By an enlightening contrast, Eastern hymns for this procession picture Christ coming *today* in this very liturgy, with power to convert *this* people to live justly and peaceably henceforward. Eastern worship focuses repeatedly upon the present. Visitors may wonder at worshippers prostrating themselves well before the Great Thanksgiving Prayer; at the hushed awesome music sung; and at the eschatological blessing echoing Luke's Passion story, "May the Lord God remember you all in his Kingdom."[79] Why do Eastern Christians so revere bread and wine before they are consecrated to become Christ's Body and Blood? For a partial answer, Easterners do not fix upon any one "moment of consecration" the way medieval Latins did, but rather recognize Christ present throughout all services where two or three are gathered.[80]

Yet more importantly, Eastern worshippers respond here and now as Jesus's parables urge them to do. Their hymnody and prayer voice what New Testament critic C. H. Dodd called "realized" or "immanent eschatology,"[81] recalling Jesus's distinctive emphasis upon "God's reign come among you." To all who long for apocalyptic fulfillment, they promise: Christ's hoped-for Second Coming, with authority to transform sinners' lives and spread justice and peace through the whole world—this happens for real on Sunday morning at ten o'clock in your parish!—*Be there*!

This Eastern devotion exorcises ghosts of violent blood sacrifice haunting Western cult. While Western hymns may evoke Hellenistic sacrificial processions, instead Byzantine chants anticipate the Preface, a formal declaration that anciently opened civil court: "The Magistrate is arriving now, so everyone leave off trivial distractions, and attend to High Business." Christians have long

---

78. See chapter 1. A. Schweitzer, *Geschichte der Leben-Jesu-Forschung von Reimarus zu Wrede*, 1906; Englished as *The Quest of the Historical Jesus*, 1910.

79. Luke 23:42.

80. Matthew 18:19–20 and John 14:13–14.

81. C. H. Dodd, *The Apostolic Preaching and Its Developments: Three Lectures with an Eschatology and History* (London: Hodder & Stoughton, 1936, 1963).

rendered that Preface as "Lift up your hearts."[82] Eastern hymns expand the Preface by urging people to replace base concerns with higher ones, because the just King will honor them now. Robert Taft's magisterial study of that procession, *The Great Entrance* (1975), analyzes the six classic Byzantine hymns introducing the Christian Preface, just before *Sanctus* hymn recalls God appearing to Isaiah enthroned above the temple Ark.[83] Their lyrics appear below in an Appendix, together with hundreds of Western parallels already familiar from general devotion and ready for like use.[84] (One beloved Wesleyan example closes this chapter.) Today the six originals adorn every Byzantine Eucharist: their music may change weekly, while their words do not. All express what the young King Juan Carlos purportedly told his son as they entered the Cortes to command the Fascists lay down their arms: *¡Hoy verás para qué sirve un rey!* "Today you will see what a king is for!"

A Liturgical Sign of Justice

Medieval commentaries explain each worship step by biblical analogy, and the practical gathering of dinner foods, a daily custom for Jesus's disciples, became the dramatic heart of Byzantine common prayer. On grand occasions at Constantinople's Hagia Sophia, it numbered six hundred clergy and could take two hours! Greek commentators evoke awe before a Divine Heavenly Emperor reigning high above the current Roman emperor, who was often present. Western liturgists may object that it distracts from the priestly food-handling they are accustomed to watch dramatized. Indeed Byzantine consecrators leave the bread and wine standing untouched upon the table, where a deacon only points to them.[85]

---

82. Greek Prefaces say "Lift up your *minds*," echoing the Septuagint translation of Hebrew *lëv*, or heart, as *nous*. In Hebrew thought our hearts generate plans rather than feelings. For example, by consistently "hardening his heart" (LXX *kardía*) against freeing his Jewish slaves, Pharaoh becomes tragically obstinate as well as cruel (Exodus 7–8). Hardness of heart earns Pharaoh and his people ruin; whereas at the Eucharist we lift our hearts and minds in order to share limitless blessing.

83. Isaiah 6. In *The Great Entrance*, op. cit., p. 3 and *passim*, Taft styles this ritual action "Transfer of Gifts," a bare stage direction, deferring to the "[Little] Entrance" of clergy earlier in the ritual. But only one hymn lyric mentions eucharistic gifts; all the rest exalt Christ's active authority to change lives. The classic label "The Great Entrance" marks its preeminence among countless symbolic summonings of Jesus's Spirit.

84. The Appendix hymn table may be downloaded from *https://www.churchpublishing.org/signsoflife*.

85. A Russian priest may stand yards apart praying with hands raised throughout. In a like way, small medieval French chancels consigned full trays of bread and wine for the sub-deacons to hold while the presider prayed with one loaf and cup. Dramatic priestly touch upon every vessel was a development by baroque Christians, who ate and drank very little.

Most significant of all, this ceremony answers one challenge today's liturgical planners now face: what natural place does justice have in our worship? For five centuries Christian divines have battled over remitting sins but bypassed justice, as though that owned no place outside the occasional sermon. Recent reforms restoring Hebrew scripture readings have opened Western ears to justice, but by no means weekly. The active Eastern welcome of Christ arriving among us Sunday after Sunday, with authority to do all the transforming work that Athanasius describes, plants our hopes for justice and peace at our ritual core. Whereas Hellenistic pagan processions led to blood sacrifices, Christ's Spirit in the Eucharist brings us authority for sharing his sacrificial work of an existential kind. Third-century Alexandrian catechists Clement and Origen read the gospel tales of Jesus's entry into Jerusalem in that very way. Their appeal speaks to our own era, which prizes just action above handling guilt alone.

Modern America offers a civil model for this procession that our forebears never knew. Not a model of fond hopes, but of concrete realization; not a model of conquest, but of liberation; not a model of rank and power, but of equalization; not a model of demagogue leaders, but of popular authorization. This model arose within popular church life, and so can naturally symbolize justice within worship. Here is a news photograph for that historic event, realizing prophecies that Latin monks long sang from the Bible:

> I look from afar
> And behold, I see the Power of God
> Coming like a cloud to cover the land
> With the host of his People.
>> Go out to meet him, and say,
>> Are you the one who is coming,
>> Or do we look for another
>> Who will rule over God's people Israel?
> All you that dwell in the world,
> High and low, rich and poor, one with another,
>> Go out to meet him, and say,
> Hear us! Shepherd of Israel,
> Leading Joseph like a flock of sheep,
>> Are you the one who is coming
>> Or do we look for another?

Lift up your heads, O ye gates,

And be lifted up, you everlasting doors,

And the King of Glory shall come in

    Who will rule over God's people Israel!

I look from afar

And behold, I see the Power of God

Coming like a cloud to cover the land

With the host of his People.

    Go out to meet him, and say,

    Are you the one who is coming,

    Or do we look for another

    Who will rule over God's people Israel? [86]

Archbishop Iakovos & Dr. Martin Luther King Jr. lead the Civic Procession honoring Pastor James Reeb, martyred for marching with them at Selma Alabama, 1965 CE.

The photograph shows Baptist Dr. Martin Luther King Jr. and New York's Greek Orthodox archbishop Iakovos leading the procession to honor Unitarian pastor James Reeb, martyred for marching with them over the Pettus Bridge at Selma, Alabama. Hundreds of men and women of many faiths set a turning point there for the American Civil Rights Movement. For nine years president of the Word Council of Churches, Iakovos had been raised as a Turkish "third-class citizen," and identified vigorously with the African American struggle. After police

---

86. *Aspiciens a longe*, the first Latin Matins Respond for Advent, compiling Ezekiel 38:9, Matthew 25:6, 11:3, 1 Samuel 9:17, Psalm 8, 24:7.

attacked and beat King's first marchers, Iakovos joined King leading his second march on March 9, 1965.[87]

> On my return, someone called me traitor, some others said I should be ashamed of what I have done, some said that I am not an American, and some that I am not a Christian. I know that human rights and civil rights continue to be the most thorny social issues in our nation. But I will stand for both rights civil and human for as long as I live. I feel it's the Christian duty, and the duty of a man who was born as a slave.[88]

King was assassinated within three years. But for thirty years more, Iakovos relived the justice procession he had helped lead, as he bore the Body and Blood of Christ arriving at God's reconciliation feast.

Singing to Welcome the God of Justice

Sunday after Sunday the six classic Eastern procession lyrics build a symbolic bridge to Isaiah's *Sanctus* vision of God's court, and to conversion of life beyond.[89] Indeed, traffic across both those bridges has moved to an energizing, rather than stabilizing rhythm. Sociologist Peter Berger writes that most humans feel one basic religious need: that somebody should keep the universe stable for them.[90] Instead, the Creator God of Genesis fills Adam with *ruach*, a storm wind: so to be human is to stir things up.[91] Isaiah and Jesus did just that. Unlike pagans bargaining with their gods, the prophet Isaiah receives authority for work to do, and the work God authorizes is explicitly disruptive.[92]

> I hate, I despise your sacrifices, incense is an abomination to me . . . I cannot endure solemnity combined with guilt . . . Cease doing evil, learn to do good, search for Justice.[93]

---

87. Gregory of Nyssa's feast day.

88. Recorded interview posted at *https://usa.greekreporter.com/2017/01/16/archbishop-iakovos-why-i-supported-martin-luther-king-in-selma/*.

89. See downloadable Appendix at *https://www.churchpublishing.org/signsoflife*.

90. Peter Berger, *The Sacred Canopy: Elements of a Sociological Theory of Religion* (New York: Doubleday, 1967).

91. See chapter 4 on mystery.

92. Isaiah 6:9–13. Matthew 13:13–15 quotes this passage.

93. Isaiah 1:11–17, author's translation.

Eastern Christians welcome Christ's arrival here and now with music intensely intimate (in Russia) or triumphant (in Ethiopia), and indeed the Bible depicts both responses. C. H. Dodd found realized eschatology strongest in John's gospel,[94] and it has a home in Western hymnody too. Works by Palestrina, Byrd, Mozart, and other Roman Catholic composers realize God's reign in worshippers' immediate sentient experience, so that Western musicians regularly choose their compositions to accompany communion. Reformed composers Schütz, Buxtehude, and Bach enriched their texts with equal profusion of feeling. Popular British "gallery" hymn lyrics evoked emotion like the Byzantines. Alas, Victorian preachers stressing blood sacrifice for atonement led the Wesleys' "strangely warmed" worshippers safely away toward sober reflection instead. Cathedrals modeled a restrained, even repressed emotional style. Popular rapture was for the Baptist pulpiteer Charles Spurgeon and his fellows on the North American frontier—too dangerous for established worship.

Now following new lectionaries, however, seasonal planners may dispense with outdated color-coded calendars and respond as the day's Bible readings suggest. A table of 222 such Western hymns fills an Appendix to this treatise. Most are familiar and beloved—a ready bridge toward affection in the Kiss of Peace, which best follows at once.

One famed Charles Wesley gallery hymn offers an example. Commonly consigned to "Advent season," its theme is immanent and will suit worship all year round. It can supply beloved music to accompany the arrival of Christ in this church, this congregation, this service. Wesley's threefold Alleluias may even have had Eastern processions in mind. A single word-change (italicized below) replaces apocalyptic wailing with joyous royal welcome much as at Ethiopian Timket, honoring Jesus's sacrificial life and death.[95]

> Lo! He comes with clouds descending,
>
> Once for our salvation slain.
>
> Thousand thousand saints attending
>
> Swell the triumph of his train:
>
> Alleluia, alleluia, alleluia!

---

94. C. H. Dodd, *The Interpretation of the Fourth Gospel* (Cambridge: Cambridge University Press, 1960).

95. Recent Lutheran hymnals omit this problematic stanza, thereby losing Wesley's dramatic table-turning *peirazmos*.

Christ the Lord returns to reign.
   Every eye shall now behold him
   Robed in dreadful majesty.
   Those who set at nought and sold him,
   Pierced, and nailed him to the Tree,
   Now in loving triumph, now in loving triumph
   Shall the true Messiah see.
Those dear tokens of his Passion
Still his dazzling body bears,
Source of endless exultation
To his ransomed worshippers.
With what rapture, with what rapture
Gaze we on those glorious scars!
   Yea, Amen! Let all adore thee
   High on thine eternal throne.
   Savior take the power and glory,
   Rule the kingdom for thine own.
   Alleluia, alleluia, alleluia!
   Thou shalt reign, and thou alone.

CHAPTER THREE

⤸

THE CHURCH'S SIGN:
BAPTIZING THE WORLD

I called through your door,
"The mystics are gathering in the street.
Come out!"
"Leave me alone. I'm sick."
"I don't care if you're dead.
Jesus is here and he wants to resurrect somebody!"

—JALĀL AD-DĪN MUHAMMAD RŪMĪ, D. 1273 CE[1]

Worship reforms normally progress from popular innovation to theoretical winnowing and eventual codification. The turn of our twenty-first century witnesses two such shifts in mainline churches' common life: Open Communion Table practice spreads with or without official sanction; and baptismal bathing, no longer socially automatic, quickens devout Christians' sense of commitment. Though some may fancy these trends opposed, in fact they naturally align, and many leaders are allies. Chapter 1, "Jesus's Sign: The Welcoming Table," offers a Bible-based theological argument for the first shift, and concludes that this must lead to the next. Newcomers welcomed to Jesus's table must soon become active agents in welcoming others there, or Christian mission fails. For that work we baptize, and must give an account why we do so. Our rationale must acknowledge recent decades of scripture study, and address the missionary reality of the modern Christian church. Therefore this Baptism chapter will set aside some long-held accounts that no longer serve our task, and propose a new baptismal rationale from the gospels that answers today's plural religious challenge.

---

1. Coleman Barks, trans., *The Essential Rumi* (San Francisco: HarperCollins, 1995), 202.

Our Common Enterprise

Churches have always baptized for purposes beyond confirming people's faith. While prominent in our baptismal rites, Christian faith and language are no longer presumed as they were in Western culture. Other faiths have moved nearby from exotic distances to fill our schools and neighborhoods. Non-Christians can also live by Jesus's Spirit, risen now and free, however their tradition may welcome him. Martin Luther reckoned that "the ascended Christ fills all things."[2] Baptism sets Christian identity within the broad human world of faith, and not apart.

Ecumenical questions surrounded Baptism early. John the Baptizer receives honor in all four canonical gospel texts. Three portray him baptizing Jesus in the River Jordan,[3] though critics have challenged the historicity of that passage. Some read there an institutional legend devised to explain how two disciple groups later became one. Indeed, John's gospel does predict that Jesus's group will supersede the Baptizer's,[4] much as some later polemic will claim that Christianity superseded Judaism.

New Testament documents confirm neither institutional conjecture. Although Palestine swarmed with religious flight-and-fight groups declaring messianic hopes, no Bible text outside the Jordan story shows Jesus's followers joining with those. Quite the opposite pattern emerges: John's gospel and letters evidence his own community battling gnostic invaders, and losing.[5] Again, Paul never argues that Christianity will supersede Judaism; instead he insists that God's promises to Jews are permanent. Paul likens Jews who reject his Messiah to branches fallen off a tree, that can be grafted back on over time.[6] Supersession partisans today might reflect that in horticulture, a grafted branch continues producing its own distinctive fruit, without conversion.

Our Baptism conversation deserves a fresh start. George McCauley, SJ, observes that Christian ritual talk has been skewed for centuries by focusing on what worshippers *receive*, rather than what the church *does* by Jesus's Spirit and example.[7] Talk about Communion has slid into disputes over diners' fitness to

---

2. This was Luther's rebuttal to Ulrich Zwingli, for whom Christ's body had risen to heaven and could not be found on our altars.

3. Mark 1 // Matthew 3 // Luke 3.

4. John 3:30.

5. Brown, *The Community of the Beloved Disciple*.

6. Romans 11:23–24.

7. McCauley, *The God of the Group*.

receive grace that God actually gives for free; talk about Baptism has slid into disputes over the regenerated life that God alone creates and owns.[8] Such disputes direct attention away from the church's true evangelical task, which is to lift Jesus high in the world's sight.

Unless we still hold with old-timey preachers that baptismal floods chiefly extinguish hellfire, we must tell our world afresh what Christians are up to, and why others should want to join us. Robert Daly, SJ, an authority on concepts of sacrifice, puts succinctly the purpose of our Christian enterprise: "To receive love, and hand it along." Daly's declaration offers a universal appeal resembling the Buddhist purpose: to save all sentient beings from suffering. For Daly, therefore, one task overshadows all contemporary theology: "We must find some way to carry on the classic Christian conversation without the old exclusivism."[9]

Daly echoes the Bible. Amos,[10] the Bible's earliest literary prophet, reproves Israel for banking on God's favoritism. He declares that God has also "brought up" every neighbor nation, including Israel's classic Philistine enemies. Amos warns of disaster awaiting any people so "chosen" who fail to give justice to their own needy—a disaster that had surely happened by the time those late verses entered Amos's pages. To complement Jesus's Table Fellowship today, we must likewise uphold baptism as a prophetic sign of what Christians believe God is doing everywhere in the world. Baptism cannot make Christians "unlike other people," as Luke's Pharisee wrongly believed.[11] In urban centers with growing immigrant populations, that has become a lively pastoral issue, since people of foreign faiths now live next door, purvey our food, heal our sick, teach our children, and visit our pastoral celebrations. No longer an exotic fancy, their faithful communities raise living intellectual challenges among educated children of Christian heritage.[12]

Because One God loves and draws all humankind, inspiring humane virtues everywhere, dialog among faithful peoples will move onward so long as our race does. Despite a bloody history of religious conflicts, other traditions do offer us encouraging examples. The Chinese philosopher Zhu Xi was a contemporary of Thomas Aquinas. Both applied foreign metaphysic (Aristotelian or Indian) to a

---

8. That is much the way Hebrew prophets and psalms winnowed the sacrificial cult: Psalm 50:7–13.

9. In conversation with the author at the Society of Oriental Liturgy, Beirut, 2012, and reaffirmed since.

10. Amos 9:7–8.

11. See exegesis of Luke 18:10–14 in chapter 1 above, in the section on Jesus's claim to orthodoxy.

12. One might say that Episcopal boarding schools turn out Buddhists the way Roman Catholic parochial schools once turned out Episcopalians.

more poetic tradition (Hebrew or Daoist), and so set the course of orthodoxy (Roman Catholic or Confucian) for centuries afterward. Chinese Song Dynasty sages were debating whether education best trains us to perform our present duties aright, and so earn promotion to a nobler reincarnation—a common Buddhist idea then as today—or rather fosters progressive improvement in our single allotted lifetime, as Confucian Zhu Xi taught.[13] Zhu invited his top rival to lecture at his college, and then instead of rebutting the opposing argument, Zhu had it cast in bronze and set up in his courtyard for his students to study. That very action embodied Zhu Xi's teaching in a way no rhetorical rebuke could have done. Christian Baptism must show our teaching just as clearly to our plural religious world.

Revisiting Exclusive Language

In many baptismal rites exclusion emerges early, when formal dialogs with candidates evoke a folk dualism foreign to Hebrew scripture. Modern editions typically smooth out medieval renunciations of "the Devil and all his works" into "forces that war against God." And indeed during the recent century, human tyrants have expressly warred against God. Yet such ritual renunciations quicken a fantasy that we can identify some "outside" evil agency to eradicate. Whatever appeal folk superstition may have in our era of vampire films, most hearers know that paranoia has led to inquisitions, witch hunts, and pogroms. By stark contrast, Hebrew scripture's editors embraced the prophets' doctrine that rival deities were empty illusions.[14] The Bible Jesus knew allowed God only one ally or enemy—namely, ourselves—and for early centuries at least, churches followed suit. Among the Apologists, Aristides writes to the emperor Hadrian, "Adversary our God has none, for there exists not any stronger than he."[15] The Apocalypse paints a rival vision, which seventeenth-century Puritan poet John Milton glamorized, but that book stole into the New Testament canon late, and Eastern Christians never read it in church.[16]

---

13. His Holiness the XIV Dalai Lama advises likewise that Christians not convert to Buddhism; any born as Christians should become the best Christians they can, so in their next life they will be reborn as Buddhists. By contrast, Confucians do not teach reincarnation.

14. Psalms 96:5, 115:4–7, 135:15. Habakkuk 2:18, Zechariah 10:2. See chapter 4, on mystery and "The One and Only God There Is."

15. Nicholas V. Russo, "Athenagoras and Aristides and the Origins of Apophatic Language in Christian Euchology," unpublished paper for the North American Academy of Liturgy, Orlando 2014, quoted by permission. (See chapter 4 on mystery.)

16. See chapter 4 on mystery and "The One and Only God There Is."

The fourth-century bishop Athanasius of Alexandria credits the Roman Empire's conversion to the pagan deities' powerlessness beside the ethical benefits of Christ's Spirit.[17] We baptize people into a lifetime of moral choices, and paranoia wrecks moral choice. Genesis 2 portrays humankind in Eden seduced into grasping after a good we already have—being like God—so the tempter actually offers nothing. As Gregory of Nyssa put it: "Evil does not exist as an object to be chosen."[18] Not that evil cannot happen, of course! Rather as an American proverb says, "There's no such thing as a free lunch." Coined during economic depression, that proverb endures in easier times because fools still choose the free lunch they know well cannot exist.

Half a recent century back, mainline rites overwrote institutional labels for the church with "the People of God": an image both scriptural and humane. Today more Christians ask: are not Hindus, Jains, and Sikhs also People of God? They boast noble theological and ascetical traditions—and their cuisine alone proves divine inspiration. Then what are we doing when we baptize them? Churches have long recognized Baptism by desire, without water or chrism; but why should good people of other faiths desire it? We can no longer presume to sever converts from their cultures, nor to cut away the good values already revealed to them by The One and Only God There Is. Updated prayers for "Abrahamic covenant" peoples, meant as an ecumenical opening toward Judaism and Islam, hardly suffice. Watching the murderous violence among Abraham's heirs in the Middle East and elsewhere, the huge majority of the world's faithful see no advantage in joining up.

Better than Initiation

A modern purpose declaration for Christian baptism will forsake some familiar language we can no longer rely upon, while we study better speech, preferably from scripture. By far the least useful language is "Christian initiation," though this title has lately become a reformers' *shibboleth* which only we Philistines eschew. It is by no means ancient. Pierre-Marie Gy discovers it first in ritual books after the Roman Catholic Council of Trent, befitting a garrison church besieged from the Muslim east and Protestant north: intellectually defensive and closed to gifts from kindred faiths.[19] Nor is "initiation" scriptural. The

---

17. Athanasius, *Peri tês enanthropêseos tou Logou* /on the Word becoming human. See chapter 2 on authority.

18. Likewise, "Everything that exists is created amid good." *The Great Catechism.*

19. Harald Buchinger cites Pierre-Marie Gy, "La notion chrétienne d'initiation," *Le Maison Dieu* 132 (1977) 35–36, reprinted in *La Liturgie dans l'histoire* (Paris: Editions Saint-Paul: Editions du Cerf, 1990), 17–39.

Hebrew Bible recognizes no successful rites for that, as the sorry Shechemites learned, massacred after accepting circumcision.[20] Later Jewish conversion processes offer anachronistic parallels, since those reflect Christian ritual influence. Matthew Thiessen writes: "We have no evidence that any author or editor whose work the Hebrew Bible preserves perceived circumcision to be a rite of entrance into the Israelite nation, for there was no such rite."[21]

Thiessen finds that New Testament Christianity aligned with the rabbinate on this point. Converts were first recognized during Second Temple times, and a few circumcised. Yet though some rabbis welcomed foreigners' faith, nevertheless, together with Luke and Paul, they reckoned ethnic identity permanent. Gentile impurity was not ritual impurity, and so could not be cleansed. (Conversely, rabbis still counted as Jewish those children born of a Jewish woman after her conversion to another religion.) Paul opposes circumcising Gentiles—not as superfluous for any who put their faith in Christ, but as fruitless. Baptized Gentiles can only share Jesus's messianic life and work by adoption.[22] Paul's faithful converts keep the same Gentile status where he found them, only welcomed to live by Christ's Spirit.[23] A full generation later, Matthew's gospel still ridicules Jewish conversion campaigns.[24] In fact, Hebrew religion extended far beyond the reach of rabbis at Sassanian Babylon, and incorporated local tribes around the Caucasus and Red Sea. That is how the Lucan evangelist meets an Ethiopian eunuch studying Isaiah,[25] and how today's Ethiopian Jews in Israel reject rabbinical regulations, to their Israeli hosts' dismay. Above even these flaws, summoning converts to initiation squares poorly with Jesus's teaching that God's reign comes now, *ready or not*—and so just as poorly with Jesus's Table Fellowship practice

It is high time we replaced that Tridentine "initiation" label, which has never fit the historical Christian community. Nineteenth-century sociologists fancied Christianity as one among many Hellenistic initiatory cults yet Hellenistic adepts progressed from cult to cult, as Christians dared not do.[26] Moreover, Maxwell Johnson cites Mark Searle's observation that pagan initiators

---

20. Genesis 34.

21. Thiessen, *Contesting Conversion*, 63.

22. Galatians 4, Romans 8 and 9.

23. Galatians, passim. Romans 9:16 also assumes this divide, which Krister Stendahl underscores. Stendahl reverses centuries of misinterpretation by reading Greek pronouns carefully: *Paul Among Jews and Gentiles* (Philadelphia: Fortress Press, 1976).

24. Matthew 23:15.

25. Acts 8.

26. A. D. Nock, *Conversion* (Oxford: Clarendon Press, 1933).

assumed their candidates already enjoyed group membership—unlike Christian Baptism, which differed further yet by requiring a decisive conversion of life.[27] Nineteenth-century social fraternities did run a fad among American men, who undertook successive initiations as Masons, Oddfellows, Elks, Shriners, and German dueling brothers, rather like Hellenistic cults. And yet within decades those fraternities fell from fashion, or vanished when they delayed racial opening-up after the Civil Rights Movement. Such racist delay also crippled American labor unions, which today initiate fewer than ten percent of workers. In secular ears now, the term "initiation" evokes exclusive club fees or college parties flowing with alcohol, rather than blessed water or lofty social purpose. By contrast, eucharistic participation by newcomers at church is growing wherever welcomed. Churches have good reason now to make the Eucharist our formal Christian incorporation rite, as Nathan Mitchell suggests.[28]

Searching for Language We Can Use

We do better to sound out biblical titles for Baptism. Among those the ancient name "Illumination" (or "Enlightenment") has a fine apologetic ring. New Testament texts suggest it, for example where Jesus is portrayed healing the blind: likely a conscious baptismal allegory.[29] And it chimes in with Buddhists, who may be our natural allies more than rivals in freeing this suffering world. Countless enlightened Christian women and men shine brightly under lenses focused upon human rights: Russian Maria Skobtsova, Swedish Raoul Wallenberg and Dag Hammarskjöld, American Martin Luther King Jr., Brazilian Helder Câmara, British Cecily Saunders, Chinese K. H. Ting, Albanian Teresa of Calcutta, and South African Desmond Tutu for a few recent examples. Those heroes make up what is lacking in the sufferings of Christ[30] and draw human hearts everywhere—whether baptized or not—in Jesus's Spirit. Those honor Baptism, and the church that baptized them. Small wonder the "Illumination" image aroused ritual expression. Ephrem the Syrian's baptismal title "Fire on the Water" recalls early Syrian firelight processions to the river: a participatory action involving all in baptizing.

But alas, the rich liturgical denominations have squandered their birthright to that "Illumination" title. Not one of those has shone like its individual

---

27. M. E. Johnson, *The Rites of Christian Initiation: Their Evolution and Interpretation* (Collegeville: Liturgical Press, 1999), xvi–xvii.

28. N. D. Mitchell, *Eucharist as a Sacrament of Initiation* (Chicago: Liturgy Training Publications, 2003, 2007).

29. John 9.

30. Colossians 1:24.

heroes. Roman clerical pederasty and hierarchical cover-ups spread only the very latest clouds darkening Christian identity in the eyes of a world that perceives no sectarian fences. Enlightened Anglican bishops and Jesuits did welcome Copernicus and the new rational sciences, but for two hundred years England's Lords Spiritual fattened off the slave trade, while Africans tilling their estates in the Caribbean and the Confederacy were worked or whipped to death. Their contemporary Eastern Orthodox hierarchs likewise collaborated in enslaving millions of farmers, as "serfdom" spread anew across Russia and Ukraine just as Western states had junked it. Immediately after the American Civil War, Episcopal bishops sacrificed their black membership (60 percent of freedmen in 1865, today 2 percent) by banning discussion of racial justice out of deference to a single slain slave-owning bishop and Confederate general.

More wars and upheavals did convert American Episcopalians into a progressive church body, with civil rights martyrs honored, birth control encouraged, women and minorities ordained, same-sex unions blessed, and campaigns to save our Mother Earth. Nevertheless for embarrassing centuries all the high liturgical churches abandoned slavery's abolition to ritually impoverished bodies: Quakers, Calvinist sects, and atheist revolutionaries. Even today, many ritualist bodies block one-half the human race (females) from ordained authority. Crossing the religious marketplace now, our ceremonial procession candles reek of oppression that incense cannot cover. Were high-church grandees still to claim Baptism as a sign of corporate "Illumination," the unwashed world could retort on evidence that our sign had lost its effect.

Baptism and Christian Education

Some opponents of the Open Table object: "Baptism is open to everyone, so why do they need to move directly to Eucharist?"[31] The Book of Acts indeed retails immediate Baptism when a candidate expresses desire.[32] By contrast today church educators hope committed Christians will face down secular culture, so they block off the ready water font, erecting a new ladder of preparatory steps before Communion. Labeled "catechumenate," an antique Greek name for ordinary learners, those steps revive long-disused customs found in ancient documents, particularly the *Apostolic Tradition of Hippolytus*, which purports to show

31. M. Tuck, "Who is invited to the feast? A critique of the practice of communion without baptism," *Worship*, November 2012 (Volume 86, Number 6), 505–526.

32. The Ethiopian eunuch demands to know why he should not be baptized at once. Acts 8:36.

Roman Church cult before Constantine. In fact, text critique now re-dates that information later to the fourth century, when catechumenal herbaceous borders bloomed briefly before infant Baptism flooded them away. The document's several authors and churches have become impossible to identify.[33]

Lacking information on ancient curriculum before baptism, today's planners have mined post-baptismal lectures ("mystagogy" in technical jargon) for their ore lode of early teachings. Modern catechumenate programs exemplify well today's education models. These substitute an academic program leading to a baptismal graduation, in place of the ancient mystagogical training given afterward. Mark Searle, a movement founder, voiced surprise that instead of producing knowledgeable workaday parishioners as planned, the top catechumens all hoped to train as catechists in turn: an outcome exactly like graduate education.[34] We may wonder why movement leaders do not restore the early mystagogical format wholesale instead, with instruction given *after* the full ritual welcome.

That mystagogical format has fit real church life for ages. We noted in our first chapter[35] how Martin Luther's Small Catechism declares that the essential core in Baptism is not the water bath, but the lifelong growth in virtue that follows it. Luther is hardly alone. As images for Confirmation, the conscious teenage incorporation experience for Western Christians, poet George McCauley, SJ, calls up vivid actions: "unwrapping a new card deck before an all-night poker game"; "sliding behind the wheel for a cross-country drive"; and—my own favorite!—"meeting the person who will give you the transplant."[36] None of those crucial deeds defines what follows; on the contrary, what follows gives each startup its meaning. Today's liturgists were baptized as infants, learned all their doctrine afterward, and have no reverse experience to share. A teaching scheme that overrules its leaders' life experience casts a shadow of fiction over Christian doctrine, as if it all fit only some bygone era.

Luther's pursuit of moral growth after the water bath treads a long pathway. Gregory of Nyssa, the leading theologian of his age, revered progress above achieved status. Because humans have limits (unlike God) we must move and grow forever: toward or away from eternal goodness; in this life and the next.[37]

---

33. P. F. Bradshaw, M. E. Johnson, L. E. Phillips, *The Apostolic Tradition* (Minneapolis: Fortress Press, 2002).

34. In conversation with the author. Searle's early death in 1992 robbed the church of an astute planner. John Hill, a current leader and friend, assures me that this unexpected effect has lessened since.

35. "Jesus's Sign: The Welcoming Table," above: see the section on Jesus's Claim to Orthodoxy.

36. McCauley, *The God of the Group*, 37.

37. A. Malherbe names this the central theme of Gregory's final work, *The Life of Moses* (New York: Paulist Press, 1978); see also Gregory's *Against Eunomius*.

Ethical constancy requires our steady moral progress upward; to pause for even one moment would be to fall away from God.

A century later, Theodore of Mopsuestia, a favorite resource for modern catechists, grounded his writings upon a presumed Pauline sentence emphasizing lifelong progress and achievement: "The Son of God learned obedience through what he suffered, and when he had been perfected, he became for all who obey him the source of eternal salvation."[38] That text centered Theodore's Christology and his mystagogy together, inspiring new Christians to grow as their incarnate Master had done. In fact, Theodore's sermons supply most of what we know about early Christian education, and he delivered them *after* the water bath, matching practice and doctrine in the very way Luther divined.

Life and Death in Service

Origen and Luther agreed that Christian theology *is* commentary upon scripture; and scripture declares two generous purposes in baptizing: conferring the Holy Spirit, and remitting sins. And yet for enticing converts to embrace these gifts, churches have had to color Baptism outside scripture's somber palette. For like a monumental Chinese landscape in rich varying ink monochrome, the New Testament tints Baptism with Death, and beckons beholders to enter the scene at that very lowest point, and walk with Jesus there.

"A Road into the Mountains away from Human Society" by Wang Yuanqi, 1713 CE

author's collection; used by permission

---

38. Hebrews 5:8. R. A. Greer, *Theodore of Mopsuestia, Exegete and Theologian* (formerly *The Christology of Theodore of Mopsuestia*) (London: Faith Press 1961).

Paul writes of being baptized into Jesus's death. A generation later, all four canonical gospels employ parallel rhetoric, as Jesus depicts a looming future baptism he will undertake, or a bitter cup he will drink—and his disciples must follow suit. Both images evoke mortality lying ahead.[39] Jesus's death shadows other gospel scenes of his ministry too. Behind the foreground narrative, readers can glimpse the evangelists' own challenge of proclaiming a Messiah shamefully executed, and their churches' experience of persecution. Mark has Jesus ask whether disciples James and John are willing to share his dark baptism, and when they agree, Jesus insists he can guarantee no higher reward.[40] Critical examination has discovered like passion imagery in further passages less obvious than these: for example, the birth narratives in Matthew and Luke, explored by Raymond Brown.[41] And most dramatically, the Markan Transfiguration on the Mount,[42] a century ago labeled as a bright resurrection appearance editorially misplaced, is now recognized as a meditation on Christ's looming passion, wherein the mount symbolizes Golgotha, the public crucifixion hill. That is why this gospel lection now precedes the Sunday readings in all three Lenten cycles that Western denominations share.

> Jesus brought Peter, James, and John apart to a high mountain, and he was transfigured before them and his garments became white as the light, and Elijah and Moses appeared talking with Jesus. Afraid and scarcely knowing what to say, Peter said, "It is good for us to be here; let us make three tents for you, for Moses and for Elijah." While he spoke, a cloud overshadowed them, and a voice from the cloud said. "This is my Son, the Beloved: hear [and obey] him!"

A critical review of baptismal preaching is overdue. The synoptic Jordan story has spawned sermons and writings for centuries.[43] Those earliest argue that Christian candidates repeat Jesus's bathing experience, sharing thereby his mystical body's life. And because the Jordan Baptism story opens Mark's gospel with a Trinitarian theophany, preachers conventionally portray it as Jesus's public career launch. A few dissenting interpreters have read there an adoption,

39. Romans 6:3; Mark 10:39 // Matthew 20:23; Luke 12:50; John 17, 18:11.

40. Mark 10:35–45 // Matthew 20:20–28, author's translation.

41. Raymond Brown, *An Adult Christ at Christmas* (Collegeville: Liturgical Press, 1988).

42. Mark 9:2–8 // Matthew 17: 1–8 // Luke 9:28–36, author's translation. Compare Mark 1: 9–11 // Matthew 3:13–17 // Luke 3:21–22.

43. Étienne Nodet and Justin Taylor, *The Origins of Christianity: An Exploration* (Collegeville, MN: Liturgical Press, 1998).

when the young Jesus first became God's Son and took authority; others as Jesus's spiritual calling, for his followers' rites to replicate.

But the Jordan Baptism is probably not what journalists today would call a historical event. John the Evangelist's community has evidently not heard of it; the fourth gospel separates Jesus from water ritual, stipulating that Jesus did not baptize, only his disciples did.[44] More tellingly, Roman Catholic scholars Nodet and Taylor conclude from reading all texts about the Baptizer outside that Jordan passage, that John and Jesus never actually met. Catholic historian Nicholas Russo weighs several scenarios that might connect those leaders with Christian Baptism, the way official catechisms presume. and finds each textually problematic:

> Apart from having to describe how an erstwhile peripheral ritual became a central and arguably defining characteristic of the Christian movement, we are left struggling to account for the wide diversity from and, in some instances, stark dissimilarity with the ritual paradigm allegedly established by the historical Jesus that we encounter in the evidence so shortly after his public ministry.[45]

Occam's Razor favors (as always) the simpler explanation: that the Jordan narrative reflects Jesus's own life and death alone.

> Jesus came from Galilee, for John to baptize him. John would have barred him: "It is you should baptize me, yet you come to me?" But Jesus answered: "Allow this for now, while we fittingly fulfill all righteousness," and he was baptized by John in the Jordan, and as soon as he came up from the water, he saw the heavens open, and the Spirit as a dove descending upon him, and a voice came out of the heavens: "This is my Son, the Beloved, my favor rests on him."[46]

Then let me propose we read the Jordan story as another passion meditation like the Transfiguration. In form the two exactly match. Both are set in locales crucial for Israel's national narrative (Mount Tabor; the Jordan River). Both have Jesus's bystanders express amazement with wrong-headed responses

---

44. John 4:2. Maxwell Johnson (*Rites of Christian Initiation*, pp. 16–19) infers from John 3:22–4:2 that Jesus did baptize. Johnson relies upon another writer's grammar hypothesis too abstruse to sift here: let me follow Zhu Xi by inviting my readers to study that for themselves.

45. Nicholas V. Russo, "Did Jesus Baptize? The Historicity of Jesus's Baptizing Ministry in the Gospel of John and Its Implications for the Origins of Christian Initiation," paper for the North American Academy of Liturgy, 2015. Quoted by permission.

46. Matthew 3:13–17 // Mark 1:9–11 // Luke 3:21–22. Matthew alone has dialog.

(Peter, James, and John; John the Baptizer). Thereupon Jesus assures them that what will soon happen fits a tradition they only partly grasp. (Moses and Elijah represent scriptures presaging the Messiah's death; John Baptizer learns the Messiah's real rank as God's Servant.) God's voice closes both stories with the same punch line: This is my beloved Son. (Mark's Transfiguration text adds: "hear," meaning "obey him.") And finally, Jesus's allies in both scenes head directly for deaths like his own: the Baptizer will be arrested and executed in Mark's next chapter; James and John will taste Jesus's fatal cup, as they have asked; Peter's martyrdom is prophesied at John 21:19. Though lacking a Jordan story, John's gospel has Jesus wash his disciples' feet at dinner while preaching about his coming crucifixion, and bid them serve each other likewise.

Binding the Jordan and Transfiguration stories together this way is not wholly novel. Eastern iconographic convention has Jesus and John Baptizer gleam with light as at the Transfiguration, when they "fulfill all righteousness" together.[47] Indeed, the world's finest surviving Byzantine mosaics, in Roger II's twelfth-century Norman Palatine Chapel at Palermo, set the Jordan and Transfiguration scenes side by side above the altar, inviting worshippers to contemplate both at once.

Other artists have filled the Jordan story brimful of Passion awareness. In Piero della Francesca's haunting fifteenth-century masterwork (now at London's National Gallery) tragedy looms on all faces. Jesus ponders painfully the

Mosaic Joining Christ's Baptism & Transfiguration, Capella Palatina, Palermo, XII Century CE

47. Matthew 3:15.

dark path he must walk; and women bystanders look on with express foreboding. Those bystanders prefigure the women at Jesus's cross and tomb, as well as gospel preachers in Piero's time extolling the Messiah's awesome self-sacrifice.

One short text adds a sunnier glow: the so-called Great Commission that ends Matthew's gospel in a new editorial voice.[48] Critics reckon that Jesus actually preached to his own Jewish people only. Then like the extra endings in Mark and John, editors added this Matthean paragraph implying Christ would have approved Paul's Gentile mission—albeit decades now after Roman soldiers had executed both Jesus and Paul, and had leveled and paved Jerusalem in the year 70 CE. Even so, the link between Baptism and death remained paramount for early Christians. They counted pagans who chose to die with them as among the baptized, whether those had voiced desire for any rite or none. Paul Bradshaw has uncovered the tale of a shipwrecked and dying Egyptian mother who anointed her baby in Baptism using her own blood because no oils were available.[49]

We may remark all the more, then, that a hero's death never attained the Christian standard. Unlike Jewish zealot recruiters, Christian churches ruled out rushing to martyrdom. Even in our own era—numerically the greatest age of martyrs, especially deadly in some countries—Christians have drawn candidates by an appeal to lifelong service instead. John's gospel understands Jesus's own death as a costly action of service: to his chosen mission, to his gathered friends, and hence to God. John's insight became a Christian theological principle: God acts by pouring out God's self in service. Here is one source for common Christian speech, which in many tongues equates "services" with "liturgies." Early twentieth-century renewal argued that "liturgy" (*leitourgia*) meant "the work of the people," and not of their ordained clergy alone. But in Hellenistic Greek *leitourgia* more precisely named the public service of rich donors for the common benefit—like building a symphony hall today. Hence the "Divine Liturgy" is public service Christians all join in, by sharing Christ's service to God and God's world.[50]

Service has long crowned Christian community ideals. For centuries churches and monastic bodies, including contemplatives, have practiced "service outreach" as a mark of authenticity. Hindus too rank it highest among spiritual

---

48. Matthew 28:18–20.

49. Paul Bradshaw and Ruth Meyers, *Essays in Early Christian Initiation*, Alcuin/GROW Liturgical Study 8 (Nottingham: Grove Books, 1988).

50. The Septuagint so names the work of priests serving the worshipping congregation, yet not the congregation members' worship. Compare Luke 1:23, Hebrews 8:6.

values. Military recruitment in many cultures evokes heroic service ahead of self-immolation. Here then is the church's noblest aim in baptizing: not an exclusive shift in relationship with humankind's Creator, but a life of committed service like Jesus's own, growing throughout our future beyond the water bath—and perhaps greater even than martyrdom, which ends earthly future.

What Makes a Real Messiah

Therefore let me propose a fresh biblical ideal for Baptism, if not classically assigned to that ritual, yet well-known and widely beloved. Matthew's Beatitudes[51] offer us evangelical signs drawn from scripture, just as Isaiah's banquet and Jesus's table were. They declare what Christians believe God is already doing everywhere, whether or not the world recognizes God at work. Jesus most likely preached the four blessings that Luke quotes, in simple, universal terms.[52] And while expanding those to nine, Matthew means the same. No wonder Eastern monks recite these Beatitudes before Communion, and Orthodox Slavs open every Eucharist singing them (replacing Greek processional psalms). Non-Christian peoples worldwide hear them warmly; after all, Matthew's healing stories point out salvific faith in unconverted peoples without exclusion. The Episcopal Church has taken up the chant in its hymnal, if not yet in its Eucharist rite.

"Blessed are . . ." The Bible spells out the Semitic concept *baruch* in patriarchal narratives, meaning richness deeper and broader than any possible rational explanation. The gospels' Greek word *makarios* evokes happy results for a human actor. But yet more, Hebrew *baruch* brings richness for all those around as well.

Such a beatific service pattern is distinctly human. Other species, including other great primates, will lay down their lives to protect their own young. But self-sacrifice to rescue unrelated fellows is humanoid, and may help to explain the dominance of *homo sapiens sapiens*—whether for the world's good or ill. Freud coined the word "empathy" for this human racial habit. One US Navy captain told the author that among all his duties through the unpopular Vietnam War, he was proudest to bring his full ship of sailors home unhurt.[53] And the *Saving Private Ryan* screenplay's popular success arose from moviegoers' sharing his motivation.

---

51. Matthew 5:3–11.

52. Luke 6:20–23. Luke's four woes follow in verses 24–26.

53. Captain Dennis Holahan, USN.

The Synoptic Gospel Beatitudes Compared

MATTHEW 5:3–12	JESUS (reconstructed)	LUKE 6:20–26
1. Blessed are the Poor in spirit, for theirs is the kingdom of heaven.	The Poor have The Blessing.	Blessed are you poor, for yours is the kingdom of God. But Woe to you that are rich, for you have received your consolation.
2. Blessed are those that Mourn, for they shall be comforted.	The Mourners have The Blessing.	Blessed are you that weep now, for you shall laugh. But Woe to you that laugh now, for you shall mourn and weep.
3. **Blessed are the *Praeîs*, for they shall inherit the earth.** [Quoting Psalm 37:11, in LXX version]		
4. Blessed are those who Hunger and thirst for righteousness, for they shall be satisfied.	The Hungry have The Blessing.	Blessed are you that hunger now, for you shall be satisfied. But Woe to you that are full now, for you shall hunger.
5. Blessed are the Merciful, for they shall obtain mercy.		
6. Blessed are the Pure in Heart, for they shall see God.		
7. Blessed are the Peacemakers, for they shall be called Sons of God.		
8. Blessed are those who are Persecuted for righteous-ness' sake, for theirs is the kingdom of heaven.	The Persecuted have The Blessing.	
9. Blessed are you when men revile you . . . falsely on my account.		Blessed are you when men hate you and revile you as evil . . . on account of the Son of Man.
Rejoice and be glad, for so they persecuted the prophets who were before you.		Rejoice: your reward is great, for so their fathers did to the prophets. But Woe to you when all men speak well of you, for so their fathers did to the false prophets.

Jesus's original four were conundrums, like Zen *koan* riddles. For exam-ple, his "blessed are the poor" shakes a popular Semitic belief that riches reveal God's favor. (That belief resonates in American civil religion.) Jesus's challeng-ing *koan* hints that the poor cannot be misled by such an error, and so can wel-come God's reign in good time while the rich miss their chance. The evangelist Luke writes for a non-Semitic readership, so to clarify the four *koans* he sets a classic Greek rhetorical *peirazmos*, with a woe opposite each blessing: the tables will turn and impoverish those who are rich now. But rather than threaten woes, Matthew adds blessings. Since Matthew broadens Jesus's first *koan* to read "poor *in spirit*," some readers infer that he spiritualizes the lot. But those miss Matthew's real target, which is Christology: his nine Beatitudes draw an ethical portrait for Jesus's followers to imitate. Matthew often paints Jesus like Moses,[54] whose ancient law taught everyone—not Jews alone—how to be human beings as God has made us. Here Matthew's New Moses teaches every-one: *you* can share Christ's humanity, through which God saves the world, if you follow Jesus's example through life and death.

Among Matthew's five new blessings, the first he added (number three in his full list) ranks highest, because this one alone quotes scripture directly: Psalm 37:11. The original Hebrew psalm reads, "the patient poor (*anawim*) shall possess the land." But to catch Matthew's meaning, we must read that verse in Greek, the way Matthew knew it—not "blessed are the meek," or "humble," as the Hebrew word implies.[55] The Hebrew *anaw* is one of the rare human virtues that scripture never attributes to God, who is always in com-mand, even if longsuffering and quick to forgive (Joel 2:13). By now an embar-rassing history of political repression by pretended Christian governments has put passive humility in poor odor. The church can no longer ask the down-trodden to practice passive self-denial. By stark contrast, Paul often advocates training like a runner or boxer,[56] overcoming pain to follow Jesus's heroic faith leadership through death and beyond. Today's Christian activists urge forgiving our oppressors, never bowing to them.

Most important, Matthew's Greek diction means the very opposite of "meek." The Septuagint was translated long after Hebrew editors shaped their

---

54. H. Benedict Green, *The Gospel According to Matthew in the Revised Standard Version*, New Claren-don Bible (London: Oxford University Press, 1975).

55. *Pace* H. B. Green, *Matthew: Poet of the Beatitudes* (Sheffield: Sheffield Academic Press, 2001). Green pairs the first and third blessings, equating both "poor in spirit" and "meek" with the Hebrew *anaw*.

56. Romans 9:16; 1 Corinthians 9:24–27; Philippians 2:16.

imageBROKER/Alamy Stock Photo

Achaemenid Persian Kings Xerxes I & his father Darius I, V Century BCE

doctrine of God in action: patient and resolute, yet never powerless. Perhaps with an eye to the editors' higher theology, the Greek translators render Psalm 37:11 with *praüs/praeis* (pra-EES).[57] In secular use, this trait means avoiding distraction by one's own anger when facing calumny or opposition. *Praüs* is no passive quality of oppressed peoples, but a royal ideal. Throughout five centuries while the Hebrew scriptures were edited, the great Persian Empire governed the biblical lands of Egypt and Babylon, as well as wide swaths of Asia. Its fourth monarch, Darius I, inscribed a tablet at his early capital Bisutun, reciting his kingly claims. He singled out this virtue as the divine gift that actively forwarded justice.

> By the favor of Ahura Mazda [Wise God] I am of such a sort that I am a friend to right, I am not a friend to wrong. It is not my desire that the weak man should have wrong done to him by the mighty; nor is it my desire that the mighty man should have wrong done to him by the weak. What is right, that is my desire. I am not a friend to the man who is a lie-follower. *I am not hot-tempered. What things develop in my anger, I hold firmly in control by my own thinking power. I am firmly ruling over my own [impulses].*[58]

Apart from horsemanship and archery skill, anger control is the sole inward quality Darius I claims for kingship. Amid conflict, that virtue assured him reigning mastery—although not political security. Like many Achaemenid Persian and Roman emperors, Darius I and his son Xerxes I were both murdered by disloyal rivals.

---

57. This word is marked a bisyllable: both singular and plural sound *pra-EES* today as anciently.

58. Josef Wiesehöfer, *Ancient Persia from 550 BC to 650 AD*, Azizeh Azodi, trans., second edition (London: I. B. Tauris, 2001 and 2011), 33. Italics mine.

The Greek biblical writer Sirach extolled *praüs* monarchs.[59] Gregory of Nyssa's third Beatitude sermon shows that Hellenistic Greeks still wrote *praüs* in the classic sense: an ideal sage or ruler who faces down calumny or opposition with resolute forbearance, never distracted by temptation to wrath, discouragement, or indifference, and acts only to put things right.[60] Joel's prophecy at 2:13 could scarcely want a better one-word summary of God's behavior, and editors repeated that core passage twelve times through the Pentateuch. Rendering Psalm 37 by that word, the Septuagint translators—and so Matthew's gospel—summon readers to do as God does, and thus inherit the earth.

Praüs virtue rises proud in the passion stories, our oldest narratives, where Jesus cuts a regal figure in shameful contrast to pliant Pilate. The few socially radical sayings that do likely come from Jesus himself spell out *praüs* forbearance: do not return evil for evil; turn the other cheek; serve longer than compelled to; and so forth.[61] Roman occupation may have set their historical context but not their meaning. No lowly servility is here, but self-mastery furthering one's main purpose—very like the Zoroastrian king. As Isaiah wrote: "I did not hide my face from insult and spitting; YHWH helps me, so no insult can wound me . . . therefore I have set my face like flint."[62]

Influenced by Isaiah and Sirach, later editors added *anaw* to the Hebrew description of Moses,[63] and accordingly Matthew's gospel alone writes the word *praüs*. He augments Mark's tale of the entry into Jerusalem so that Jesus rides an ass like ancient Akkadian royalty, following Solomon's example and Zechariah's prophecy.[64] Likewise, Matthew's Passion retells the final trials of a regal Peacemaker much like the murdered Darius I: here is a resolute, truthful, and right-dealing hero, Israel's hoped-for King, and all who follow his example will inherit the earth. Drawing upon the Greek Bible his readers knew, Matthew's third Beatitude paints Messiahship in a royal blood crimson that any can wear who resemble Jesus, in any walk of life. Without this regal virtue we could recruit no career military, police, or firefighters; no epidemiologists; no

---

59. Ecclesiasticus 45:4.

60. Hauck et al. in Gerhard Friedrich, *Theologisches Wörterbuch zum Neuen Testament (TWNT)* (Stuttgart: W. Kohlhammer, 1979), vol. VI. See *St. Gregory of Nyssa, The Lord's Prayer; the Beatitudes*, trans. Hilda C. Graef (New York: Newman 1954).

61. Matthew 5:38–42 // Luke 6:29–30.

62. Isaiah 50:6–7.

63. Numbers 12:3, a sole occurrence. G. Friedrich, *TWNT* vol. VI, 647.

64. 1 Kings 1:28–49. Zechariah 9:9, Matthew 21:5.

ill-paid schoolteachers or geriatric nurses; no missionaries or undercover spies. All those will pay the costs without distraction or anger, when the calling they choose requires. Matthew makes Jesus a model for every committed life: "Take up my working yoke and study me, because I am *praüs*, and my plans are not distracted by narcissistic revenge. My yoke will fit you smoothly and lighten your workload."[65]

This resolute forbearance enjoys reverence among other world religions, too: Buddhists for example, with whom Christians have a growing conversation. And Zhu Xi would have recognized here a Confucian ideal: *Liángzhi* means steadfastly treating everyone as good by nature, the way Mencius taught, however contrary they may act.[66] Non-Christians attending a Baptism can pray readily with us that our candidates will grow in a *praüs* life. Our challenge is how best to translate the word! "Meek" will hardly do; "slow to anger" is too narrow; "staunch forbearing" might serve, as it evokes Gandhi, Mandela, Tutu, and a myriad martyrs like Maria Skobtsova, who all took Jesus for their hero. Muslims rank Jesus among the five Possessors of Steadfastness (*ul al-'azm*), and teach that Jesus always speaks the truth.[67] Like patristic sermons that translators consult for variant Bible texts, Islam may conserve meanings from early Christian discourse that later renderings obscure. Bible scholars have only recently begun exploring Islam as a resource.[68]

Above all advantages, the *praüs* quality is redemptive. Dr. Stephen Holtzman teaches anger management at California's San Quentin State Prison to men approaching parole. Throughout prison life, inmates' constant reprisals lead to extended sentences. Holtzman reports his life's most satisfying work is watching the spiritual growth of men often re-imprisoned, who now learn they need not return fellow prisoners' challenges and insults, as entrenched habit has led them to do. Their new *praüs* virtue speeds their own release and cuts overall prison recidivism, which otherwise averages 40 percent.

The church teaches that Baptism washes away sin. Far from making Christians different from others, Baptism into Jesus's *praüs* Spirit washes away the

---

65. Matthew 11:29–30. In the Bible's agricultural talk, "yoke" means farm work, not slavery. And "heart" is where we make plans, not feelings. Author's translation.

66. P. J. Ivanhoe, chap. 4 in *Ethics in the Confucian Tradition* (Atlanta: Scholars Press 1990, rev. 2002).

67. Zeki Saritoprak, "Who Is Jesus for Muslims?" *The Christian Century*, June 2, 2017, 32–34.

68. Kamal Salibi, *The Bible Came from Arabia* (London: Pan Books in association with Jonathan Cape, 1987); *Secrets of the Bible People* (London: Saqi Books, 2004); *Who Was Jesus?: Conspiracy in Jerusalem* (London: Tauris Parke, 2007); *A History of Arabia*, second edition (Beirut: Dar Nelson, 2010).

sexism, racism, ethnic prejudice, and ageism (for example) that enrage humans and distract us from our true calling: to become one with each other and with all creation. Taken together, Matthew's nine Beatitudes spell out how Animists, Buddhists, Condomblés, Daoists, Hindus, Hopis, Jains, Jews, Muslims, Shintoists, Sikhs, and Zoroastrians can live alike in God's eyes. Our heroes have lived alike too. The Buddha Siddhârtha Gautama, who found enlightenment centuries before Jesus or Paul, and spent a longer career teaching humanity to transcend suffering: he was *praüs* clear enough. His virtues reflect the goodness of The One and Only God There Is; and they have spread blessing—fruitfulness beyond all reason—exactly as Matthew's gospel promises. Some centuries after that blond Aryan sage lived and spoke,[69] a duskier Jewish Jesus fulfilled every Matthean Beatitude completely. And now as Luther teaches, the ascended Christ fills all things. Therefore we may baptize all races who revere Jesus's name, praying his Spirit will lead them ever forward into a life more like his, whatever their culture and religious heritage, and so will bless still others. That is why we call Christian Baptism a sign of what God is doing throughout the whole world, inside churches and outside.

The Coin's Darker Side

Luke's fourth and last Beatitude and woe reflect Jesus's light upon all human history of persecution and exclusion. And Matthew preserves Jesus's original stress on existential choice. The sacrifices and sufferings of martyrs are *baruch*, enriching others beyond reasonable calculus. That is how Paul claims his travails fill out "what is lacking in the sufferings of Christ,"[70] spreading richness rather than retributive debt. And Luke's Passion has the dying Jesus absolve persecutors: "Forgive them, Father, for they know not what they do."[71]

John's gospel's final resurrection appearance originally completed the story with Jesus commanding Thomas, "Put your hands into my wounds, and believe!"[72] John's original text does not claim that Jesus's wounds have healed, or that resurrection brings restoration such as the book of Job retails. Instead,

---

69. The Buddha's life dates are now less certain, but his sobriquet *Sakyamuni* means Scythian Wise Man. North India's Scythian invaders were famously blond, so Siddhârtha was too. See Susan Whitfield, chap. 1 in *Life along the Silk Road* (Berkeley: University of California Press, 1999).

70. Colossians 1:24.

71. Luke 23:34.

72. John 20:27. An epilogue retelling two more appearances was added by another author.

John bids us recognize Christ's Spirit at work in all living self-sacrifice just as it happens. By Russian Orthodox nun Maria Skobtsova, who gave out forged baptismal certificates to Jews until the Gestapo sent her to her death at Ravensbrück; by Dag Hammarskjöld, Lutheran General Secretary of the United Nations, who flew peacekeeping missions in Africa until Israeli agents shot him down; by Episcopal seminarian Jonathan Daniels, murdered while registering African American voters at Selma, Alabama; or by Mohandas Gandhi, who was refused church sacraments but consciously followed Jesus's example of nonviolence until his assassination. These martyrdoms do not merely promise some future happy world after resurrection. Already their existential sacrificial lives *are* Christ's resurrection. "Put your hands into my wounds, and believe."

Opposition and death inevitably threaten anyone seeking to transform relations with foes. The baptized need not rush to martyrdom, but only face it resolutely as *praüs* Jesus did. Luke's Passion may offer *peirazmos* reversal, like his earlier Beatitudes: "Today you will be with me in Paradise."[73] But Matthew's "Great is your reward with God" implies an even higher reward than all that the faithful have given up. So Gregory of Nyssa echoes Matthew, closing his *Life of Moses*:

> This is true perfection: not to avoid a wicked life because like slaves we servilely fear punishment, nor to do good because we hope for rewards, as if cashing in on the virtuous life by enforcing some business contract. On the contrary, disregarding all those things for which we do hope and which have indeed been promised us, we regard falling from God's friendship as the only thing dreadful, and we consider becoming God's friend the only thing truly worthwhile. This, as I have said, is the perfection of life.[74]

Everyone moving toward God reflects God's shining virtues, and so guides others forward into God's unfathomable dark. Once started on the Beatitudes' path, the baptized will never stop progressing towards God's goodness and beauty, because they will never stop having ethical steps to take. That progress beyond the ritual gives Baptism its proper meaning: here is Gregory Nyssen's moral vision; Theodore's teaching practice; McCauley's inspiration; Luther's dream.

---

73. Luke 23:43.

74. *Gregory of Nyssa: The Life of Moses*, A. Malherbe and E. Ferguson, trans. (New York: Paulist Press, 1978), 137. See chapter 8 for a longer quotation from this passage.

Then in place of ancient "illumination" or baroque "initiation," let Baptism become our Christian sign of *serving* according to the Beatitudes, with Matthew's third Beatitude in chief. Paul says as many as have been baptized into Christ have put on Christ:[75] just so, we dress the baptized in Jesus's purposeful *praüs* clothing. Of course it is oversized at first, but as his Spirit works upon us we grow daily until we fit it well. Richard Norris drew out Paul's metaphor so, and Theodore and Luther would surely second him. Matthew's nine Beatitudes cut the full Christ-like tailor-pattern to fit each of us: whether we suffer persecution or not; whether we mourn or rejoice, while our plans remain pure and our love steady; when we face indignity steadfast for what is right; and finally when we make peace where justice can no longer be sorted out: thus day by day every Jesus-imitator receives God's love and shares it with the world, the very way Robert Daly summarizes our Christian cause: "To receive love, and hand it along." Our baptismal sign declares that Jesus's devout Hindu admirer Mohandas Gandhi spread Christ's blessing as surely as Gandhi's admirer Mother Teresa of Calcutta did. This ritual touchstone identifies our truest talk, as Daly hopes, "to carry on the classical Christian conversation without the old exclusivism."

Blessing All Peoples of Faith

Matthew's gospel Beatitudes set forth a life pattern for all humankind to follow; and Luther's dictum, that the Ascended Christ now fills all things, has provocative implications for Baptism ritual. Whenever we encounter steadfast faith in the face of opposition or calumny, whether among Jews, Muslims, or Buddhists, for example, our rite should properly acknowledge the Spirit of Christ at work. After all, if we cannot revere their faithfulness, Mark's gospeler might well ask us, why the devil do we baptize them? Mark's editors clearly insert Jesus's temptation stories as expositions upon Baptism.[76] Freedom from fear is the most widely attested fruit of Christian conversion; freedom from envy and hatred follow close. Thus we need hardly separate peoples from their steadfast faithful practice, to earn them the Bible's promise that they will inherit the earth. In place of renunciations, should not a revised baptismal dialog open by acknowledging Christ's Spirit already at work? And spell out the desires felt since birth, that have drawn these candidates to the church's rite?

---

75. Galatians 3:27.

76. Mark 1.

My universalist argument may unsettle some who believe their own church's doctrine alone befits Christian Baptism. On the other hand, it addresses today's plural religious context, which urbanized Christian missionaries know. Some patristic and medieval writers took an exclusive view of church rites, without dialog or cooperation among religions sharing ethical values, but not all ancient authors did so. To defend against pagan accusations that Christians were atheists, early Apologists likened Christian doctrine to the apophatic strain in Greek philosophy.[77] Appeals to non-biblical thought became a fixture of Christian apologetic ever after. A famed Tang Dynasty stele from the Church of the East adopts Daoist concepts, asking renewed Chinese imperial support for Christian mission.

The New Testament writers leave us no way to distinguish Jesus's thoughts about faith from their own. For Paul, our earliest New Testament author, faith means trusting God to fulfill promises despite doubtful appearances, just as Abraham and Jesus have led the way. Paul demands no faith-content beyond God's plan, which Christ's resurrection proves—not even our accepting Paul's own arguments. Rage he may against opposing opinion, but Paul never claims that his words are salvific, only that God's actions are.

Next, faith shows up in gospel *midrash* stories by Christian editors and preachers, where aggressive people grasp for the healing power they believe Jesus has, and unconverted pagans earn God's blessing upon their faith even more than believing Jews. Both the Samaritan leper and the Syrophoenician woman (a Philistine) are traditional rivals of the temple cult; the Roman centurion is purposely distinguished from Jewish believers; yet the gospels reward all expressly for their faith.[78] Simple doctrinal declarations do begin to appear in *midrash* stories reflecting later church life, yet Matthew has Jesus teach that correct belief is wholly a gift from God, not anything humans can provide.[79]

Here the synoptic editors conserve Jesus's singular rhetoric, whose parable protagonists puncture his hearers' moral assumptions. Matthew reports a saying likely by Jesus, "from John the Baptizer until now . . . violent people have taken the Kingdom by force."[80] Luke's Zacchaeus *midrash* represents that teaching by a precisely constructed tale.

---

77. Russo, "Did Jesus Baptize?" *op. cit.*

78. Luke 17:19, Matthew 15:28, Matthew 8:6 // Luke 5:12.

79. Matthew 16:17.

80. Matthew 11:12.

Jesus was going through Jericho. Zacchaeus, a wealthy senior tax collector, was too short to see through the crowd, so to glimpse Jesus passing by he ran ahead and climbed a tree. Jesus looked up and said, "Zacchaeus, hurry down! I must stay at your house today." He came down and welcomed Jesus joyfully. Everyone seeing it complained, "He's gone to stay at a sinner's house!" But Zacchaeus stood his ground, saying "Lord, I give half my property to the poor here and now, and if I've cheated anybody I'll restore it fourfold." Jesus said, "Today salvation has come to this house, for this man too is a son of Abraham. And I have come to seek out and save what was lost."[81]

Thus the loathed tax collector Zacchaeus responds at once to an arriving opportunity, much as Jesus's own parable heroes do; he acts aggressively, as the healing stories teach; Jesus invites Zacchaeus unconditionally, to the crowd's blinded consternation; and Zacchaeus responds as the prophet Joel would have him do—not with tears, but a change of life plans. Here is Luke's portrait of his own church, faithful at once to Jesus's teaching and to the ethical core of Hebrew scripture.

Luke's *midrash* adds a moral nuance further inferred from the prophet. Zacchaeus answers Jesus's dinner invitation as the parables' heroes do not, by an absurdly generous plan that he cannot credibly fulfill. Yet Jesus thereupon declares his salvation, since human shortages cannot measure out God's *chesed*. Luke's church expects a change of plans must result from eucharistic fellowship, though never properly earn it. In like vein, the Lutheran theologian Dietrich Bonhoeffer warns against "cheap grace": a fatal error that consists not in taking salvific gifts like the Eucharist undeservedly (what Lutheran would object to that?) but failing to change one's life direction in faithful response to God's free gift.

Christian hymns and exclamations flowed swiftly into the New Testament, as gospel editors blended Jesus's sayings with sermons and bromides, until this full-stirred brew boiled up didactic formulae like yeast foam. Late patristic churches installed their symbols (most Westerners call them creeds) before Baptism and Communion. But the New Zealand Book of Common Prayer follows some early rites by reversing that order at Baptism. After the water bath and anointing, the newly baptized join the whole community professing faith together, in a biblical summary that non-Christians can understand, and some may even repeat.

---

81. Luke 19:1–10, author's translation.

That New Zealand formula affords moderns our closest likeness to New Testament faith. God's grace surpasses reason, whatever our beliefs. As James 2:19 warns, "The demons believe the same as you do, and they tremble with rage and fear!"[82] Nor can our rites reward Christian prayers above non-Christians, as some propose without biblical support, since Grace (Hebrew *chanan*) by definition does not flow through channels.[83] The more universal our understanding of faith, the more scriptural and traditional we actually become, and the readier to promote Christian Baptism among the world's folk. Judging their faith is beyond our ken. Like heroes in *midrash* healing stories, they must come on their own terms and tell us what they mean by coming. Paul presents Jesus as the New Adam who restores all humankind—not believers alone. And Gregory of Nyssa reasons that since Adam and Eve were created in God's image, and sexually sourced all their descendants, therefore God's image can never be seen in me, or you, or any Christian church, but only in the human race as a whole:

> To say that there are 'many human beings' is a common abuse of language. Granted there is a plurality of those who share in the same human nature . . . but in all of them, humanity is one." "Christ's body, as it is often said, has been united to all human nature.[84]

And so perhaps uniquely among ancient writers, Gregory Nyssen preached against slave markets.

> If [the human race] is in the likeness of God, and rules the whole earth, and has been granted authority over everything on earth from God, who can be one's buyer, tell me? Who can be one's seller? To God alone belongs this power; or rather, not even to God himself. For *his gracious gifts*, it says, *are irrevocable* (Rom 11:29). . . . Whenever a human being is for sale, therefore, nothing less than the owner of the earth is led into the sale-room. Presumably, then, the property belonging to him is up for auction too. That means the earth, the islands, the sea, and all that is in them. What will the buyer pay, and what will the vendor accept, considering how much property is entailed in the deal? If you are equal in all these ways, therefore, in what

---

82. Jerusalem Bible translation.

83. See chapter 4 on mystery.

84. Gregory Nyssen, *That There Are Not Three Gods*; and *Tunc et Ipse Filius*. Quoted in Olivier Clément, *The Roots of Christian Mysticism* (1982; Hyde Park, NY: New City, 1992), chap. 5.

respect have you something extra, tell me, that you who are human think yourself the master of a human being, and say, "I got me slaves and slave-girls," like herds of goats or pigs![85]

Here speaks a Christian identity deeper than any church ritual can define—as well as a patristic judgment upon the worst failure by our rich liturgical traditions (see above). Notwithstanding, Eastern Christianity has long brought Gregory's universal humanism forward, overriding hoary enmities. After an Easter reading about Israelite slaves crossing the Red Sea, which now introduces most Vigil Baptisms, the sixth-century preacher and poet Romanos the Melodist sang at Holy Wisdom Cathedral, in the Roman Empire's final capital:

> Then the Red Sea did not save all,
> only the [Hebrew] people whom the waters revealed.
> but now it is open for each person and all races.
> They are not turned back, nor separated from one another.
> You are not an Egyptian, are you?
> Whoever you are, come,
> for living water has shown your resurrection.[86]

85. Paul Fromberg cites Gregory Nyssen, *Fourth Homily on Ecclesiastes*, in *The Art of Transformation* (New York: Church Publishing, 2018), 74.

86. Walter Ray, *Tasting Heaven on Earth: Worship in Sixth-Century Constantinople* (Grand Rapids, MI: Eerdmans, 2012), 115.

CHAPTER FOUR

⁂

THE SIGN OF THE DIVINES:
DANCING THE MYSTERY

Painting ghosts is easy, because No Body has seen one.
Painting animals is harder.
Painting people is hardest, because Every Body believes
they know what they look like.

—CHINESE CLASSIC LIÈ-ZĪ, FOURTH CENTURY BCE

D ante Alighieri's fourteenth-century *Comedia* introduces famous figures busy at activities symbolizing their fatal crimes or life work or model behavior. In his *Paradiso* Canto X, Beatrice shows the poet a circle of humming lights, and he meets Thomas Aquinas among other divines. Modern literary commentators may puzzle over that symbol,[1] but Dante's contemporaries had seen it in the flesh. Medieval Western theologians lectured in Latin, and only to matriculated university pupils, but they gathered from monasteries and schools and danced publicly around candidates at the granting of doctor of divinity degrees, a celebrated civic event. That doctorate was the ancient universities' most senior award, never conferred honorarily even today. Circle dancing in crimson academic gowns was the medieval divines' single public ceremony, a marvel for common folk to see and remember. German theological faculties made famous dancers. At Cambridge, the custom lasted well into the eighteenth century, inspiring British millenarian groups like the Shakers to carry it to the New World.

This book has sidestepped the Latin label "sacrament" distinguishing some Christian ritual acts, as that has become fraught with counting, which once was

---

1. John Sinclair leaves this symbol singly unexplained. *The Divine Comedy of Dante Alighieri: 3, Paradiso* (London: J. Lane, 1946; New York: Oxford University Press, Galaxy Books, 1961), 157–160. But see Gerardus van der Leeuw, *Sacred and Profane Beauty: The Holy in Art* (Nashville: Abingdon Press, 1963), 32. Curt Sachs, *Eine Weltgeschichte des Tanzes* (*World History of the Dance*) (Berlin, 1938), *The Commonwealth of Art: Style in Fine Arts Music and the Dance* (New York: Norton, 1945).

The United Society of Believers in Christ's Second Appearance (Shakers), 1885

simple. Roman armies recruited soldiers in pairs, who swore an oath *sacramentum* to fight together. Cowardice or desertion by one partner could mean execution for the other. Roman civil lawsuits began with a binding oath named likewise, implying sanctions as costly.[2] Latin Christians expanded that warrant into ritual theory. A quest for certainty dominated church debates, and drew ever more lingo from military strategy. *Validus* (Greek *bebaîos*) meant "firm," certifying that a bridge would carry an army safely over a river; *licitus* and *regularis* guaranteed loyal obedience to higher command. Schoolmen's drive to systematize created concepts no military campaign could endure, however: by marching a battalion over a "partially valid" bridge, safe only for some; or "valid but irregular," meaning no commander survived to captain troops after the crossing. Latin legalists distinguished some prayerful actions (their fond mystic number seven) as "sacraments," hedged about with drastic civil penalties (torture, prison, burning at the stake) while others were not—never mind Matthew's and John's blanket gospel promises:

> If two or three of you on earth agree to ask anything at all, it will be granted to you by my Father in heaven. For where two or three meet in my name, I am there among them.[3]

> Whatever you ask in my name, I will do, so that the Father may be glorified in the Son. Whatever you ask in my name, I will do.[4]

---

2. T. G. Tucker, *Etymological Dictionary of Latin* (Halle [repr. Chicago]: Ares, 1931).

3. Matthew 18:19–20.

4. John 14:13–14.

Eastern Christians see no virtue in numbering rites. Medieval Byzantines were practiced at quelling mob rivalry, and they paraphrased both those gospel promises in one entrance collect. Caroline Anglicans, after a failed Solomonic judgment did not satisfy both Catholic and Reformed parties (1604),[5] adopted the Byzantine solution instead (1637).[6] Notwithstanding, in prayer as in all human talk, "grandeur of ideas is founded on precision of ideas," to quote English poet William Blake.

The book of Genesis makes Adam's first task naming all the creatures[7] and Hellenistic philosophers draw grand rational structures to uphold a world's weight. Yet both taxonomy and logic must fail without living energy, so poets and biblical writers work more like bespoke tailors fitting grand flat stuffs close to a moving human body that is already beautiful in itself. Adam and Eve undertake this work as soon as they taste the fruit of knowledge.[8] They practice an art we all know and see. In London's famous Savile Row, diverse craftsmen may make military or clerical or business or evening or court dress but their prize artist is always the fabric cutter, who creates the fit defining a firm's repute.[9]

For example, the Book of Common Prayer defines: "The sacraments are outward and visible signs of inward and spiritual grace, given by Christ as sure and certain means by which we receive that grace."[10] Tailored chiefly for arguments over Eucharist and Baptism, however, that definition suits other rituals less well, because each phrase is a portmanteau of loose-fit metaphysical cloth. What is "outward and visible" in ritual Reconciliation, for example? And if

---

5. The corpse of Caroline compromise lies a-moldering in Article of Religion XXV. The Puritan Commonwealth had buried the whole Book of Common Prayer until cavalier armies and a new Stuart Parliament exhumed and resuscitated it in 1660. The two "sacraments" then recognized were celebrated only once yearly, or once in a lifetime, before the Victorian ritualist revival. Queen Victoria loathed that, so sacramental rituals crawled for decades through English law courts. American Episcopalians accepted or rejected them regionally like German princelings, until the Catholic *regio* won out with the 1979 prayer book. Yet even today the ghost of Henry VIII still drags his chains through Anglican reforms like Dickens's Jacob Marley.

6. Now prayed morning and evening in most Anglican prayer books: "Almighty God . . . you have promised that when two or three are gathered together. . . ." Restoration prayer books left sacrament numberings mixed (1662), and Anglican arithmetic still varies. See "An Outline of the Faith, commonly called the Catechism," p. 860. The new American prayer book cuts out Caroline compromise by quoting Matthew 18:20 alone, pp. 59 and 102. Marion Hatchett, *Commentary on the American Prayer Book* (New York: Seabury, 1980), 131.

7. Genesis 2:19.

8. Genesis 3:7.

9. Richard Anderson, *Bespoke: Savile Row Ripped and Smoothed* (London: Simon & Schuster, 2009). As cutter, the author won his firm the 2017 award for London's Best Tailor.

10. "Catechism," p. 857.

Jesus did not give us Matrimony, then by what "sure and certain means" does its grace come? Christian thinkers must look first to the Bible, where sound interpretation rewards precise work. Modern scholars divide design trends within the Bible, such as between priestly and prophetic schools.[11] Historians[12] catch dissent and mistakes inside hallowed traditions. (Judah Goldin told his Yale students, "The modern era has no monopoly on idiots, gentlemen.") Hence critics work texts piecemeal like fabric cutters, dividing and trimming words before grand themes.[13]

One swatch of martial uniform stuff does feel a firm scriptural "hand," where Hebrew writers draw warrior images for God's action. The divine title *YHWH Sabaoth*, Lord of Hosts, conjures an army, and prophets envisioned angelic troops amassed before a battle.[14] In the patriarchal narratives, God casts a rainbow into the sky like a Babylonian general laying down his gold-embossed signal bow, and so guarantees peace with all creation.[15] In place of "sacraments," Eastern writers and councils have favored a different secular word found in both Testaments: Mystery. The Roman canon also quotes Jesus calling the chalice of his blood *mysterium fidei*—words missing from our New Testament accounts of the Last Supper.[16] Centuries of wrangling over the metaphysic of Jesus's eucharistic presence may lead weary Westerners to hope "mystery" will paper over systematic contradictions, but those readers misrepresent the term's biblical use.

Picturing God at Work

Across the broad Christian landscape, our theological rootstock sprouts a thriving vine that asserts God cannot be described, and we label it *apophatic*, Greek for "not speaking." It flowered first among the third-century Apologists,[17] and

---

11. For example, rival comprehensive *Old Testament Theologies* by Gerhard von Rad (Munich: Kaiser Verlag, 1957) and Walter Eichrodt (Stuttgart: Ehrenfried Klotz Verlag, 1959).

12. See discussion in chapter 1.

13. For example, Edmond Jacob (1955).

14. As at 1 Kings 22:19. The title *YHWH Sabaoth* (Lord of Hosts) occurs 282 times, almost all in the prophets.

15. Genesis 9:13–17. See chapter 2 on authority, note 7.

16. Textual paraphrase precedes exact quotation, so we honor this variant.

17. Nicholas V. Russo, "Athenagoras and Aristides and the Origins of Apophatic Language in Christian Euchology," unpublished paper for the North American Academy of Liturgy, Orlando 2014, quoted by permission.

soon among the Cappadocian party of Basil, Gregory Nyssen, and Gregory Nazianzen, whose arguments triumphed at fourth-century councils condemning Arianism. Those won it a permanent role limiting Christian speculation. In his study *Silence*, Diarmaid MacCulloch proposes offhandedly that the Cappadocians chose apophatic reasoning from awareness that their opponents understood Hellenistic philosophy better than they did.[18] But closer reading shows Cappadocian silence was selective. Gregory Nyssen wrote: "God becomes visible only in his operations, and only when he is contemplated in the things that are external to him." Or as Richard Norris paraphrased him, "We don't know anything *about* God, we only know what God *does*."[19] That doctrine has tap roots a thousand years deeper than Hellenism.

Hebrew religion and the lineage we call Vedic or Hindu sprang up contemporaneously in the same Eastern Mediterranean region,[20] and both theologies blend conflicting stories of God's doings. Battle scenes in the Pentateuch and Bhagavad-Gita depict divine demands little short of genocidal. "Thus says YHWH Sabaoth . . . Now go and strike down Amalek; put him under the ban with all that he possesses. Do not spare him but kill man and woman, babe and suckling, ox and sheep, camel and donkey."[21] Eventually both religions spiritualized such bloody massacres, thereby reaching toward universal ethic and theology. Some preserved those problematic primary texts alongside their new statements of how God acts. The editors' fresh pigments effectively overpainted their old source material, and gave us the biblical and Hindu orthodoxies we know.

All Bible lineages now show that orthodox revolution, starting from the seventh century BCE: prophetic, priestly, wisdom, royalist, poetic, and patriarchal legends. Their editors' theology is thus the Bible's true theology, even though later polemicists may elide citations to imply otherwise. For a crucial example, the editors' Hebrew grammar includes echoes of Babylonian polytheism, like God's plural name *Elohim*. Babylonian gods met in council, called *Sôd*, which decreed mortals' fate secretly. Human rituals begging for hints might secure success for a royal enterprise. Septuagint translators shunned such polytheist imagery, however, and drew a word from secular urban design instead:

---

18. Diarmaid MacCulloch, chap. 3 in *Silence: A Christian History* (New York: Penguin Viking, 2013).

19. Chapter 2, note 66. Paulos Mar Gregorios, *Cosmic Man . . . The Theology of St. Gregory of Nyssa* (New York: Paragon House, 1998), 70. Cited in Paul Fromberg, *The Art of Transformation*, 98.

20. Liny Srinivasan, *Crete to Egypt: Missing Links of the Rigveda* (Bloomington: AuthorHouse, 2013).

21. 1 Samuel 15:2–3.

mystêrion, the floor plan of a house.[22] In ancient cities, blank walls hid home
interiors from the street, so that thieves or foes could not know where the
women's quarters, treasury, or armory were. Like home architecture, the Bible's
mystêrion is not vague nor unknowable, but on the contrary is a concrete plan
knowingly hidden until safely disclosed. Paul was the first New Testament
writer to borrow this Septuagint image for his Christology.[23] He contends that
even after Christ's appearance, many of his fellow Jews longing for a messiah
fail to recognize God's hidden plan—so in their stead Paul preached to Gentiles about Jesus's faith, offering those adoption into God's household.

In modern mystery novels, a clue in opening chapters eludes the reader at
first, until a sleuth spends hundreds of pages unwinding feints and wrong reckoning to discern it in a final chapter. At mid-twentieth century, the American
Mystery Writers' Guild surveyed their readers. Among respondents, the largest
professional group were clergy, and the largest denominational group, Anglican
clergy. That discovery surprised some crime novel authors who thought their own
worldview brutally secular, but it reflects brutal experience. Pastors who counsel
parishioners over intractable problems like alcoholism, incest trauma, adultery,
and clinical depression find welcome relief in reading about a resolution—even a
tragic resolution—to life's dilemmas. Pastors also recognize their own familiar
ignorance of what game is really afoot until afterward.

Progress Hunting the Truth

Mystery exercises broad appeal. Why else would scientists worry classic para-
doxes despite years of failure to resolve them? Why else would mathematicians
labor to answer famed conundrums? Why else would philosophers rebut arguments that fewer and fewer readers understand? Our universe seems tantaliz-
ingly and inexhaustibly mysterious. The human passion for discovery draws
us onward from one resolution toward the next. Should scientists one day link
quantum mechanics with relativity, as they now cannot do, further mysteries

---

22. For a history of the word "*Sôd*," see Raymond E. Brown, *The Semitic Background of the Term "Mystery" in the New Testament* (Philadelphia: Fortress Press, 1968). Hauck (Kittel and Friedrich, *TWNT*) and
Brown agree: "nowhere does *Sôd* serve as an original translated '*Mystêrion*' in the LXX." Answering Brown,
Hans von Campenhausen and Henry Chadwick find that Greek word used in commonplace domestic architecture. (*Tradition and Life in the Church*, 1972.) In either case, the biblical term *mystêrion* evokes "plans"
and not Hellenistic pagan cults by that name, as some wrongly infer.

23. Colossians 1:26, Romans 16:25. Later, 1 Peter 1:12 likewise describes God's plan held from the
beginning, so secret that even though "angels longed to look into it," they could not know it ahead of Christ's
appearance.

will surely follow. Such fathomless attraction inspired Lutheran scholar Rudolf Otto to identify the Divine with *Mysterium Fascinans et Tremendum*, a mystery that powerfully draws us, and as powerfully shakes us up.[24]

In his *Life of Moses* (395 CE), Gregory of Nyssa writes that our passion for truth is one of many human passions by which God draws our progress, while God truly remains in darkness. To arrest our search for truth or beauty or goodness would be to fall away from God.

> Hope always draws the soul from the beauty which is seen to what is beyond, always kindles the desire for the hidden through what is constantly perceived. Therefore the ardent lover of beauty, although receiving what is always visible, has an image of what he desires, yet longs to be filled with the very stamp of the archetype. And the bold request which goes up the mountains of desire asks this: to enjoy the beauty not in mirrors and reflections, but face to face.[25]

Progress requires a former state to surpass, of course, so despite inquisitors' obsessions with error, an earlier faith profession cannot be simply "wrong." Progress offers the plainest sense for the blessing that originally ended John's gospel, when the disciple Thomas's skeptical doubts about Jesus's resurrection meet palpable proof. There the risen Christ declares, "You believe because you have seen; blessed are those who have not seen, and yet believe."[26] John's text does not mean that faith outweighs doubt—that would invite folly—but that moving forward with risk, rather than demanding surety, brings richness (*baruch, berakah*) beyond rational explanation. Long before biblical prayers projected "blessing" upon God, that primal concept described wondrously lucky human beings, and the Bible fills with oddly lucky human choices. Isaiah and Amos override their quite reasonable misgivings when they answer their prophetic call.[27] They echo Abraham's obedience,[28] which Paul declares the prime example of God's secret plan at work.[29] In like manner, today's

---

24. Rudolf Otto, *Das Heilige*, 1923, trans. by J. W. Harvey as *The Idea of the Holy: An Inquiry into the Non-Rational Factor in the Idea of the Divine and Its Relation to the Rational* (New York: Oxford, 1958). Otto names this quality "numinous," after the Latin *numen* for an unreasoning primal power.

25. Gregory of Nyssa, *The Life of Moses*, p. 114, cited in Richard Harries, *Art and the Beauty of God: A Christian Understanding* (London: Mowbray, 1993), 94.

26. John 20:29, author's translation.

27. Isaiah 6:5–7, Amos 7:14–16.

28. Genesis 12:4–5, 15:2–6, 22:1–19, et al.

29. Galatians 3:6.

parish wedding couples embrace ritually before knowing those matrimonial joys which grow only over a lifetime together. And some modern atheists, like Sara Miles venturing her first Communion,[30] become converts, while others seek truth by different paths.

Liturgical Mysteries Serve Seekers

The Divine Liturgy appeals naturally to seekers like Sara Miles. Western visitors may be surprised to hear a Byzantine preacher hope that this Eucharist (though often in a foreign tongue) has increased their understanding, rather than salved their guilt.[31] But in a fourth-century urban society like our own, churches filled up newly with worshippers so diverse that clergy could no longer presume why they were there. Preachers conceived the liturgy as an educational machine, whose every ritual act disclosed a discrete event or doctrine. Eastern Christians still uphold that educational purpose, and it can serve religious seekers among our mixed public as well as theirs. In the synoptic gospels, the aggressive seeker always wins. John's gospel likewise promises greater rewards for seekers than any received so far: "I have many things to say to you, but they would be too much for you now. But when the Spirit of Truth comes, he will lead you to the whole truth."[32]

Classic Christian theory declares all diners equal at Jesus's Table, whatever their faith condition. As Paul writes, "No distinction is made: all have sinned and lack God's glory, and all are justified by the free gift of his grace through being set free in Christ Jesus. . . . God has imprisoned all human beings in their own disobedience only to show mercy to them all."[33]

Diverse progress in faith argues against one ritual block that has "let and hindered" Christian worshipers for nearly two millennia: a creedal confession before the Eucharistic Thanksgiving Prayer. Any hurdle that people must leap before praying together impedes the gospel. Indeed, the customary text from the Second Council of Constantinople (not Nicaea) was never written for worship. A defiant schismatic bishop cemented it to his liturgical Preface[34] as

---

30. Miles, *Take this Bread*.

31. Hugh Wybrew, chaps. 3–4 in *The Orthodox Liturgy: The Development of the Eucharistic Liturgy in the Byzantine Rite* (London: SPCK, 1989).

32. John 16:12–13a.

33. Romans 3:23, 11:32, NJB.

34. See chapter 2 on authority.

a hurdle to trip up any who accepted the orthodox Council of Chalcedon in 475.[35] Medieval Anglicans would not recite it in church until the fifteenth century. Today's renewed Eucharistic Thanksgiving Prayers retell a biblical story that most people can grasp. There seems no virtue in rehearsing that narrative twice. Church of England parishes increasingly drop the Creed, as St. Gregory's parish does, and other Americans should do for our mission's sake.

Truth's landscape outruns system maps, much as earth's round globe outruns flat projections at every point. Gregory of Nyssa graphed the last systematic projection until Thomas Aquinas, eight centuries later, and newer charts by Barth and Tillich recognized how disruptive historical experience has exploded two common presumptions. Some liturgical writers would conserve fragments of these, like postwar Pacific Islanders unearthing buried shrapnel, but we do better to quicken church life with biblical hope instead, although that may systematize only very roughly.

The first exploded presumption, that the universe obeys coherent rules for humankind to discover, and so to thrive and escape tragedy: this arose in the ancient Egyptian "wisdom movement" and spread across our northern hemisphere. The Bible's books of Proverbs and Ecclesiastes voice it, and the Enlightenment mathematician Leibniz condensed it logically: God, omnipotent and good, has created "the best of all possible worlds."[36] That premise collapsed in the Lisbon earthquake, triple tsunami, and five-day fires of November 1755, which claimed a hundred thousand lives and 85 percent of homes and churches. At 9 on the Richter scale, that catastrophe remains the worst on human record. It set a new moral calculus by which bad things do naturally happen to good people, and good things to bad people. Popular superstition may yet insist that our past actions decree our present and future fortunes; but that premise has vanished from serious discourse (as in orthodox Buddhist *karma* teaching, whose aim is to end the suffering of sentient beings, not to justify it). One American fundamentalist[37] politician recently dismissed ecological legislation on the grounds that Christ will return soon and end this world

---

35. Dom Gregory Dix, a journalist before entering Anglican Benedictine monasticism, retells the story best in *The Shape of the Liturgy* (London: Dacre Press, 1945). Eastern ritual books never christen this creed Nicene, but only "Symbol of the Faith."

36. Gottfried Leibniz, *Essais de Théodicée sur la bonté de Dieu, la liberté de l'homme et l'origine du mal* (Amsterdam: Troyel, 1710).

37. Like "catholic" or "orthodox," this label properly identifies the movement that coined it. Rebuking "modernist" scripture study, the Niagara Bible Conference of 1876–1897 defined conventional Calvinist Bible-readings as "fundamentals" of Christian faith, and adherents styled themselves "fundamentalists."

anyhow. By contrast, the true biblical hope focuses on how God already acts among us, and inspires us to act.

The second exploded presumption is ideological, and arguably racist. For three millennia, "Abrahamic tradition" speakers prophesied that God would empower one tribal bloodline above all the rest. Christian chauvinism applied that promise to the church and to "orthodox" imperial polities. Alas, that ideology falsely obscures many contrary biblical statements,[38] and its baleful political results fill history. Yet even after World Wars and failed totalitarian states have exposed its dangers, some Christian worship leaders continue to pray that Christ will vanquish intellectual doubts and non-Christian faiths alike. They might better focus their congregation's hopes on justice and peace among all people now living on earth, the way Jesus's chosen Table sign plainly points. One virtue of today's United Religions Initiative and Global AIDS Interfaith Alliance is gathering local groups from different faiths to collaborate devoutly for peace and human health—without contesting their religious allegiances. These modern enterprises model how the Bible tells us God already acts everywhere in the world.

Like the distinction *sacrament*, or a creedal *shibboleth* required before prayer, much debate about Christian rituals is juridical, or magical, or both. In harmony with Hellenistic cults it focuses on what human rituals do to govern life's trials, and how many those may rightly be, whereas the Bible focuses on what *God* does. In the earliest prophetic stories, people do only ordinary things—God does all that matters. The Syrian Naaman protests at first when Elisha tells him to have an easy wash in a nearby river, an everyday act—but then when he does so, God heals him.[39] The chorused priests of Baal deploy their gory magical arts to no effect; then God's fire descends from heaven and consumes Elijah's sacrifice alone—though this had no magical preparation.[40] Even the priestly instructions in the Levitical material are not potent ritual cookbooks. They focus on distributing foods after God has done God's part: who shall eat what. Jesus answered that question much to his own cost: every human alike shall eat with him.[41]

---

38. See chapters 3 and 7, citing the exemplary prophets Amos and Isaiah.
39. 2 Kings 5:1–19. See note 71.
40. 1 Kings 18.
41. See chapter 1, "Jesus's Sign: The Welcoming Table."

God Acts Freely and Faithfully

In place of our accustomed martial lingo, then, let homelier images guide our ritual theology. Long evolved through Hebrew scripture, they shape Christian belief the way a skeleton defines body movement. British philosopher Alfred North Whitehead advised that when asked to agree with some premise, we wisely refrain until we hear what we will be expected to assent to *next*. Then what mystery does our worship proclaim, if not a list of fixed definitions or cultic taboos? What mystery once revealed lets God remain in unfathomable darkness?

There were no atheists in biblical times, and the Psalmist's "The fool has said in his heart 'There is no God'" properly means: "God is *not here* and cannot see what I do, so I may do any evil I choose, and God *will do nothing*."[42] Unlike abstractions that philosophers might prefer, the Bible borrows familiar human life experience to convey *how God acts*. Two principles balance biblical revelation: *God is free*; and *God is faithful*. Both impact our ritual practice, so we will balance their images here.

For example, God's deeds demonstrate God's *chanan*. Translated as "grace," *chanan* means a gift made beyond necessity, obligation, or fairness. The everyday Greek word *charis* and Latin *gratia* do not denote such absolute freedom. But a British monarch creates high office and noble rank by "royal grace and favor" alone. A meritorious hero may desire those rewards, and yet has no claim. Nor can disappointed aspirants sue when an expected prize goes unawarded—as Nobel and Pulitzer committees have sometimes omitted to do. Handbooks labeling Christian rituals "channels of grace" distort them, since *chanan* by definition does not go through channels, and no church can legislate its limits. Church canons only prepare people to enjoy what blessings God will give for free. Moreover, Eastern Christian tradition equates grace with the Holy Spirit, and the Holy Spirit with the Spirit of Christ. Such theological simplicity renders moot later Latin proposals for a novel "created grace" that the church might govern.

Yet for all God's freedom, both Old and New Testaments declare that God keeps promises. Translated as "true," the Hebrew *emeth* (or *emunah*) might describe a chair that holds your weight whenever you sit upon it, so you quit overturning it to inspect each time you sit down. The worship response "*Amen*" comes from this root, and means "we count on what you say." By contrast,

---

42. Psalm 14:1, 53:1. Common English idiom renders the Hebrew *naval* as "a *damn* fool," whose folly costs us all plenty.

Israel's neighbor gods often changed their minds, abandoning their devotees. Homeric and Hesiodic deities, unknown in Palestine, were too busy betraying and fighting each other to keep promises toward anyone. The contrasting biblical concept of *Berith*, Covenant, declared God's willing faithfulness even when humanity showed none: first toward murderous Cain,[43] then toward creation purged by drowning,[44] then toward wayward Israel and other nations beyond.[45] God makes free covenants, not *despite* human unworthiness, but *because* of it. The prophet Malachi put it bluntly: "I YHWH do not change: therefore you, O Israel, are not consumed."[46] "Unchanging" is properly one of the Hebrew Torah's names for God. By the clearest translation, God instructs Moses to tell the enslaved Israelites, *Ayeh Asher Ayeh*—"Unchanging has sent me to you."[47]

Classical pagans struck hopeful contracts with their slippery gods, making gifts so that gods would return even bigger gifts: as the Latin phrase has it, *do ut des*, "I give to you, O God, so that you will give me something else I want more." Without the expected sacrifice or libation, hungry Homeric deities cherished grudges: the *Iliad* and *Odyssey* retell doomed struggles to pay off some god's accounts receivable. By contrast, the lopsided covenants in Jewish, Christian, and Muslim theologies focus on God's restoration and human progress thereafter. Indian thought is similar. Although karmic retribution may haunt Hindu and Buddhist popular cult, inspired Indian teachers focus upon extinguishing karma and rebirth altogether. The *Great Parinibbana Sūtra* insists the Buddha Siddhârtha Gautama did so, and urged his followers to work out their own salvation likewise. In Mahāyāna teaching, Amitabha Buddha will grant that to the faithful who ask it. Therefore the Buddhist cure for pernicious attachments is compassion, not ascetic purgation. Gregory Nyssen would surely agree.[48]

Alas, beginning with third-century baptismal debates, Christians inferred that God's *emeth* waits upon correct human thoughts and deeds. Chaos has resulted: conventicles wrangle over whether Russians and Greeks, or Latins and Ethiopians, or Mormons and Episcopalians can worship together. Is their Baptism effectual? Are they in communion with one another? No one knows, no one agrees. Rather than modeling a renewed human race at peace, church

---

43. Genesis 4:15.

44. Genesis 9:9–11.

45. Amos 9:7.

46. Malachi 3:6.

47. Exodus 3:14.

48. See "Parenting" in chapter 6.

authorities tinker with definitions at conflicting councils, and bypass God's changelessness to worry about such questions. Today a nautical model christened "baptismal ecclesiology" happily reduces clericalism on board, but for navigating life's stormy seas the church needs a more inclusive ship design. Our next chapter will offer Matrimony as a better biblical candidate.

One Lover, Two Loves

The Bible values love above all values, and presents another free and faithful counterpoise of human experiences of love, projected upon God's work. The common Hebrew *chesed* means "strong" at its root. God shows faithful love, like a parent's "I'll always be your mother, no matter what you do." The Greek Bible renders this word *eleos*, from *eleia*, a healing balm. The Latin *misericordia*, "have a heart for the poor," gives us the English word "mercy." These connotations overlap, together evoking reliable kindness.

Less happily, faithful *chesed's* free partner *ahavah* has sprung a flood of Christian misunderstanding. Among commonplace Greek love-words, the Septuagint translators chose *agapê* to render *ahavah* using a convenient homophone. Indeed, *agapê* extends throughout stratified Hellenistic social relations, while other words may not. Yet despite later sermons extolling *agapê* as uniquely virtuous, Hebrew *ahavah* is neither spiritual nor ethical, but names the wild love that drove Samson fatally into Delilah's arms: passionate, unreasonable, compulsive, even tragic. "I don't know what she sees in him." "How odd of God to choose the Jews." Or as the Prussian chancellor Otto von Bismarck mused, "Divine Providence shows special protective care for fools, drunkards, and the United States of America." Country and western singers voice it, and laments outnumber happy love songs in most cultures. Secular literature first painted *agapê* in nobler colors during the fourth century, presumably echoing Christian sermons about God. By contrast, living Greek still uses *agapê/agapein* for all love in general even today. So Snaith more precisely renders Biblical *ahavah* "election love," and *chesed* "covenant love."[49] Romantic couples who fall into *ahavah* pledge *chesed* at their wedding. The French Enlightenment skeptic Voltaire was once challenged, "Do you believe in God?" and answered wittily, "We have a nodding acquaintance." But Voltaire died declaring his "love for God and for human kindness." His last words bound *ahavah* and *chesed* together.

---

49. Norman Snaith, *The Distinctive Ideas of the Old Testament* (London: Epworth Press, 1944).

Inspiring and Promising

Like *ahavah*, Christian preachers have domesticated Biblical *ruach* beyond recognition. Greek *pneuma* and Latin *spiritus* suggest calm respiration, whereas
Hebrew *ruach* names a *violent* wind, more a hurricane than a breeze. At Genesis
1:1, God begins working upon a lifeless desert mass awash in a dark sea-storm.
There *ruach elohim* is an expletive: *"and a wind—God what a wind it was!—
whipped up the waters."* In the earlier creation story at Genesis 2:7, the same
violent wind blows Adam up quick like a balloon, making humanity uncontrollable as God is uncontrollable, until that wild *ruach* leaves us at death.
Throughout the Bible's historical books, that blast drives leaders into battle,
and blows prophets where they do not expect, anointing surprising replace-
ments for upset authorities.[50]

Yet for all *ruach's* wildness, scripture says God faithfully keeps a promise,
the divine *davar*. This verb means not only speaking a word, but *giving* your
word, and *keeping* your word in English idiom. The Septuagint renders *davar* as
logos: an open door toward Hellenic metaphysic, where Renaissance Reformers
and Counter-Reformers would later do battle. A more faithfully Bible-minded
short rhyme attributed to England's Queen Elizabeth I expressed her faith
in Christ's eucharistic presence without favoring either Catholic or Calvinist
metaphysic: "His was the word that spake it, and for what His Word can make
it, that I believe and take it."

The Bible's conceptual counterbalances make Jewish and Christian rites
proof against magic. Paired thus, for example, free *ruach* and faithful *davar*
distance biblical worship from the laws of doom which gods and humans elsewhere obey. Anthropologist Claude Lévi-Strauss found two such laws at the
heart of magical religion: (1) things once together are always together; and (2)
things that are alike are the same. So African Hottentot pygmies do actually
sicken and die upon hearing that some enemy has cursed them from very far
away and "pointed the bone" burned in a campfire in their direction. But no
human ritual can force our God's hand, whether by black or white magic or
formulae of words. An aged Navajo medicine man, converted to Christianity
and baptized by Episcopal bishop Kilmer Myers, was summoned to a council of
peers who solemnly called down upon him the curses of the Hopi gods, most
lethal of all. He replied, "Those have no effect on me; I belong to Jesus now."

---

50. 1 Samuel 15–16; 1 Kings 19:11–18; Jeremiah 1:10.

God's free will undergirds biblical faith. Unlike the gods scrapping atop Mount Olympus, yet powerless before *chthonic* ("underground") Furies, the Bible's God is free to promise forgiveness everywhere no matter what the sacrilege, as Joel 2:13 asserts. Forgiveness by God and humans alike accomplishes a new creation. Indeed, all Christian ritual mysteries are creative, just as new human songs or art works are.

After a long history of promises, the New Testament says Jesus revealed God's full loving plan. Early Apologists claimed that Christ's Incarnation at once fulfilled all earlier hopes by a lifetime ministry leading to his death and resurrection. Anglican John Austin Baker summarizes their teaching: "Love does not send others to suffer in its place. Love comes itself."[51] This generosity properly rules Christian worship discipline. Episcopal bishop William Swing counseled his clergy, "You must obey the prayer book rubrics—unless you find a good missionary reason not to, in which case you must disobey the rubrics." The new Armenian Catholicos from Holy Etchmiadzin invited a hundred Protestants and Catholics gathered to welcome him at Grace Episcopal Cathedral to Communion with his thousand Armenian Apostolic faithful. He was not breaking or bending Armenian Church order: *that is* Armenian Church order.

Holy Character and Right Action

Here are the closest conceptual pair that the Bible often links: "holy" and "righteous."[52] Each word describes a distinctive trait of God's work, projected from common experience of life, and well known beyond Judeo-Christian cult.

Hebrew *qadosh* strictly means set apart from ordinary use.[53] The feminine noun form *Qedeshah* names a prostitute—a woman devoutly, but by no means exclusively, set apart for shrine fertility rites. At first, like Polynesian *taboo/kapu*, Hebrew *qadosh* had no ethical content, and could be lethal as lightning. King David brings the Ark toward Jerusalem by oxcart, and dances naked before it to God's approval. When the oxen slip and his lieutenant Uzzah reaches out to steady the Ark, God strikes Uzzah dead in a flash. With horror and anger, David diverts the Ark away from Jerusalem.[54]

---

51. John Austin Baker, *The Foolishness of God* (London: Darton, Longman & Todd, 1970), 407.

52. For example, at Isaiah 5:16.

53. Hence LXX *hagios* and Latin *sacer/sanctus*, "set apart." Tucker, *Etymological Dictionary of Latin*.

54. 2 Samuel 6:6–10.

Contemporary with literary prophecy arising in the sixth century BCE, however, a Priestly revolution introduced moral content into this word: "Be holy, for I the Lord your God am holy."[55] Leviticus 19 spells out this new ethic in a "holiness code." Never take all you can claim, but share with the poor and with foreigners. Judge impartially, weigh and measure fairly, and pay workers on time. Respect the aged, deaf, and blind; do no revenge; spread no slanders. Love God with all that you are, and love both compatriot and foreign neighbors as yourself.[56] (Today's populist politicians exalt opposite behavior, showing what greedy quicksand still lurks alongside holiness's path.) The Priestly creation story that opens the book of Genesis was actually one of the last texts composed within Hebrew scripture.[57] There each day God sees fresh reality and declares it good. Like an architect rebuilding a collapsed Babylonian dualist edifice, Genesis's monotheist author lays a new foundation of goodness undergirding all life. Not to worry that we encounter good mixed everywhere with suffering, conflict, and tragedy. In Hebrew Priestly eyes, God's holiness secures created goodness as no logical proof could do.

Applied to humans, *qadosh* means having God's stamp on you—a mark permanent, indelible, and translated as "character." The Greek word *charactêr* is a sovereign's face stamped on a coin, assuring its value despite rough usage. Impurity or faulty behavior by a holy person cannot efface character. So holiness differs from blessing (*berakah*), which can fade or be recalled (see below). In keeping with Hebrew Priestly tradition, Paul rebukes his Corinthian converts: you *are holy*, so clean up your act![58] Western liturgical creeds wrongly translate it "I believe in the communion of saints," as if distinguishing believers or some believers above others. Those mistake the original Latin: the noun is a neuter plural (nominative *sancta*), meaning the "holy *things*" that all the faithful can share, whether they count themselves saintly or sinful.[59]

Indeed, the medieval distinction of saints (*Sancti*) from sinners is not biblical, nor is the Latin juridical process for determining who is an "official saint"— and who is not. Local churches have always had their heroes, and legends have grown about them, which scholars sensibly sift. The Roman Catholic focus on legend and miracle tests evidence that no modern historiographer would seek,

55. Leviticus 19:2.

56. Leviticus 19 expressly names non-Jewish neighbors as well as Jews of a different tribe.

57. Genesis 1:1–2:3.

58. 1 Thessalonians 3:13, 4:3–7; 2 Corinthians 7:1; 2 Timothy 2:21; Romans 6:19–22.

59. Stephen Benko, *The Meaning of "Sanctorum Communio"* (Naperville, IL: A. R. Allenson, 1964).

however. So Renaissance reformers, abhorring "superstition," stopped identifying "saints" for annual commemoration. That was a reform reasonable enough: all of St. Paul's saints including ourselves have had moral problems. Our heroes display exemplary progress, and yet never pure or completed virtue. On a parish retreat, therefore, St. Gregory's Church members identified heroes from every era, walk of life, ethnicity, and faith tradition who showed God's holiness stamped upon them in ways Gregory's teaching emphasizes. Progressing toward God's goodness, their lives overcame natural and moral boundaries that their times took for granted. Eighty such saints now dance life-size on the walls above our altar, where worshippers dance below during services. Here is our most celebrated parish icon: saints above dancing with saints below. Thus St. Gregory's Church embraces the New Testament idea of sainthood. Although some critics may demur, our "dancing saints" are as "real saints" as you are, dear reader!

Since the third-century African Donatists, sectarians have impugned the church's holy character and separated, seeking purer community membership. Being no sectarian but an internal reformer, Martin Luther authored a formula that Protestants and many Catholics have honored too: *Ecclesia semper reformanda*: the church will always need reforming. Meanwhile like a minted gold sovereign, the Spirit's character holds and keeps its battered currency, redeeming Christian relationships daily: Baptism, Matrimony, Absolution, and Ordained Ministry. Opponents may impugn or oppress these, but cannot erase them until death. When the Japanese navy took Hong Kong in 1942, Anglican bishop Ronald Hall ordained Li Tim-Oi to be the first woman priest since patristic times, so she might provide Anglicans their sacraments after the male colonial clergy were imprisoned or shot. For decades until 1971, Li was forbidden public ministry by the Japanese invaders, by China's Communists, and by the restored British governors. Then at Hong Kong and Toronto, Li Tim-Oi took up open eucharistic presidency without further ceremony, because her priestly character was reckoned indelible.

God alone owns and rules holiness. "Sanctify my name"[60] means that we *acclaim* God's holiness, not that we manage it. The earliest Christian process for sanctifying a liturgical object is simply to *use* it in worship, expecting God's holiness will stick to it ever after. Nor does the Bible allow for removing holiness, so that a sanctified thing or place might return to a supposed "secular"

---

60. Isaiah 29:23.

realm. Ceremonies drafted for that purpose are what the Reformers called superstition. The church has no business pretending to de-sanctify any creature in God's world.

Humans revere holy character outside biblical rituals, just as inside. Some sacred native Pueblo ceremonies of the American Southwest are announced by rumor only, so that urban friends must drive many miles overnight to attend. On Epiphany, the traditional government changeover day since Spanish times, Pueblo leaders attend Roman Catholic mass; then all process to the plaza where thronging choruses—from full-grown to tiny athletes—dance and chant the day long in feathers, dyed leathers, and body paint representing eagles, owls, deer, buffalo, and other creatures of their semi-arid world. Watchers are welcomed into nearby houses to feast with the dancers. During one such ceremony, a Caucasian woman in furs demanded of the pueblo's Franciscan missionary, "What do these people think they are doing?" The Franciscan answered, "They're creating the universe." "Oh!" she exclaimed in pleased surprise, and attended devotedly until the dances ended at nightfall.

How Things Ought to Be Done

Whereas *qadosh* describes a fixed quality, *yashar* describes current behavior by God and humankind. Translated more accurately as "rightness" rather than "righteousness," *yashar* identifies normative behavior, if not normal. A chair that holds your weight no matter how old or thin the wood; a promise kept; an evergreen tree whose needles may fall but never fail. In the Jordan Baptism story, the Baptizer protests that Jesus's holy character blocks baptizing him; but Jesus replies that they must do together all that is "supposed to be done."[61] Isaiah prophesies that his people will become *yashar* trees: like evergreens forever flourishing and growing ethically, while other species or mores wither with seasons and fashions.[62] The Bible's priests and prophets teach that human *yashar* brings God's *baruch* blessing: incalculable fruitfulness. If on the other hand we do not respond "the way it's supposed to be done," we can lose far more. In the Genesis story of lost paradise, all three wrongdoers—the serpent, Eve, and Adam—forfeit their original gifts for harmonious living.[63] Later, when God

---

61. Matthew 3:15.

62. Isaiah 61:3. The botanical misreading "oaks of righteousness" obscures his livelier image.

63. Genesis 2–3.

withdraws King Saul's royal appointment, Saul is doomed.[64] Just so, Israel's prophets warn: if our kings rely on military treaties for safety while our merchants oppress the poor, our nation will be punished for sure. Oppressing the poor is not "how it's supposed to be."

Thus unlike *qadosh*/holiness, but like a poet's inspiration, a seer's vision, or a royal election, *yashar*/rightness and *baruch*/blessing are passing things. God freely creates them and may as freely withdraw them—that is, unless God's free *davar*/promise secures them anyhow. Here is what classical Western theory originally meant by the label "sacrament": a promise God freely makes and freely keeps, however right or wrong we act in return.

God also creates an inexhaustible capacity for rightness within human nature: here is one way our race images God. Right action can be quickened at any time, place, or state of life. No former error can block our turning to YHWH as the prophet Joel bids his people do.[65] That is why Christian rituals cannot be invalidated except by frivolous or deceitful intent. Church authority may control their performance, yet never their impact. For example, weddings solemnized by a fraudulent priest endure firmly and blessedly anyhow. Here the Bible's *yashar* parallels a Buddhist teaching that all sentient beings are already enlightened, only we humans become distracted and lose track. Like enlightenment, we can catch rightness instantly from exposure to another human doing what is supposed to be done. That faculty for perceiving right action afresh with a change of heart, Christians call conscience; and we rank it our prime moral judge, reigning above every church or secular authority.

Indeed, a celebrated Buddhist tale tells exactly what the Hebrew Bible means by *yashar*. During civil wars attending the fall of China's Yuan Dynasty, rival armies overran the great Chan (Zen) foundation at Shaolin, and the monks fled into the nearby forest—all but the abbot, who remained sitting alone in the meditation hall. Suddenly a warrior rushed into the hall brandishing his bloody sword, stopped before the abbot, and shouted, "Fool! Do you not see that a man stands before you who can kill you without batting an eyelash?" Unmoving, the abbot replied, "Fool! Do you not see that a man sits before you who can *die* without batting an eyelash?" Sheathing his sword, the warrior departed. Both men were *yashar*: the abbot did as an enlightened agent is supposed to do; and the soldier caught *yashar* behavior like a virus from the

---

64. 1 Samuel 28.

65. Joel 2:13–14. See chapter 1 on Jesus's sign.

abbot's example. Indeed, the warrior's change of heart is the story's true point. In the same way, from her first taste of eucharistic communion at St. Gregory's, lifelong atheist Sara Miles went out to launch scores of church food pantries for feeding the poor.[66] Here is why Christian rituals require company, and are never solitary. Their purpose is not merely to exercise right behavior, but to spread it. Hence the proper meaning of the Latin creed's *sanctorum communio*: "I believe in the sharing of holy things."[67]

The One and Only God There Is

At the apex of these paired insights, one biblical trait distinguishes God's action with no counterbalance: *el qanna'*, the jealous God. Named after the hard human experience of jealousy, this doctrine can guide our worship choices as we encounter other faith customs nearby in modern cities.

At its earliest biblical appearance, the Hebrew *Shema'* was not monotheist but *henotheist:* among all YHWH's manifestations, one God is worshipped. On the other hand, later biblical editors have left us a vigorously monotheistic text. For example, psalms and prophets parody Canaanite worshippers bowing to animal idols without life or power.[68] Recovered Canaanite documents tell us that those statues represented a deity's strength in the form of a beast that the god rode upon. Worshippers actually bowed to the empty space above the carved animal, where a local shrine god heard prayers unseen. Hebrew temple cult was no different: *YHWH Sabaoth* was enthroned in the empty space above the Ark.[69] Isaiah saw God there; and sacrificial blood was sprinkled there.[70]

If Israel's temple ritual was a close Canaanite fit, its theology was not—or not for long. Outside Egypt, Middle Eastern shrines worshiped local divinities and their consorts in couplings that ensured the fertility crucial for farmers and herders. Yet no archaeological trace of YHWH's consort has ever been found. On the contrary, the Bible's histories show monotheism spreading among early prophets. One carefully crafted miracle storytells of the leprous Syrian general Naaman, whose mighty suzerain has sent him to tiny Israel for healing. Israel's frightened king protests that the local shrines he governs cannot work wonders

---

66. Miles, *Take This Bread.*

67. Benko, *The Meaning of "Sanctorum Communio,"* and note 59, above.

68. Psalms 96:5, 115:4–7, 135:15; Habakkuk 2:18; Zechariah 10:2.

69. Exodus 25:17–22, 30:6. Hebrew *kaporeth*, LXX *hilasterion*, AV "mercy seat."

70. Isaiah 6, Leviticus 16:14.

but the prophet Elisha, using no rite whatever, simply instructs Naaman to bathe in the Jordan. At first, the Syrian scoffs that his rivers back home carry local numens as powerful as any Jordan river god could be, and with more impressive rituals. Naaman's servant urges him to try such an easy medicine; and when it works, Naaman declares, "Now I know that there is no god in all the earth except in Israel." He asks to take some Hebrew soil home so he can worship there the god who healed him, and none other. "And when my master, leaning on my arm, goes to worship at the house of Rimmon, and I bow down in the house of Rimmon, may YHWH pardon me on this one count." Elisha sends him away in peace, because Hebrew authors are replacing local cults with a universal monotheism that will identify their later heirs: Jewish, Christian, Muslim.[71]

El qanna', the jealous God, admits no alternative powers anywhere. The Pentateuch's first commandment ends, "You will have no gods before me," meaning: My temple's forecourt will have no lesser altars dedicated to allied local numens, as Canaanite shrines have. Hence, Hebrew scripture never allowed for demons. Those are a heterodox shadow of folk superstition falling across the gospels. The Bible's YHWH knows only one ally or enemy: our human race. All earthly power and triumph, all virtuous thoughts and deeds, in all traditions and lands, come from The One and Only God There Is.[72] On this point, Jesus was likely a scriptural conservative as usual. Although gospel healing stories banish demons dramatically, the grammar of Jesus's own sayings cites his hearers' beliefs rather than his own, and redirects their focus onto here and now: "*If* (as you see it) by God's finger I am casting out demons, that proves God's reign has come among you."[73]

Earlier monotheist prophets were hardly so open-minded, alas! Elijah challenges his people to choose which god they will worship: Baal, a familiar local numen among many; or YHWH, the new universal god of the whole world.[74] After seeing a miracle, the crowd acclaims YHWH. Elijah thereupon murders Baal's shrine clergy, adding religious slaughter to Israel's savage ethnic license. And for century after bloody century, through crusades, pogroms, and warfare, leaders flying YHWH's banner have effectively chosen to march for their own Baal. Today we can only hope that interfaith collaboration for peace can

---

71. 2 Kings 5:1–19.

72. Or as modern skeptics jest: there is *At Most* One God.

73. Luke 11:20. The New Testament Apocalypse alone affirms a tough fight between rival spiritual powers: one likely reason why the Eastern Orthodox never read that book in church.

74. 1 Kings 18:21.

turn those armies to serve the universal *el qanna'* before it is too late. Luckily, grassroots ecumenism can proceed where hierarchs falter. Cappadocian ruins conserve Christian and Muslim cult buildings side by side, showing that Seljuk villagers once worshipped in both traditions on different weekdays. In some Syrian villages today, local Muslims still spread their prayer rugs inside churches at their five appointed hours, pray, and then depart as the Christian deacon begins censing. The United Religions Initiative, with nine hundred interfaith cell groups working for peace in a long alphabet of states and countries (California, Canada, Indonesia, Italy, Myanmar, Pakistan, Saudi Arabia, Yemen) make a hopeful sign for our shared human future.

God's mystery realizes far more than intellectual truth. People enter a church hoping to sense awesome union with the whole universe. That is the classic description of mystical experience. Beautiful music and art can draw worshippers beyond rational thought into a space where inspiring moments transform their vision and life direction. Above these, mystery's most powerful liturgical moment is silence, especially silence worshippers keep together. Services at St. Gregory's Church include shared silences after each reading and sermon. These are a gift from Mirfield Monastery prayer. We start each silence with a resonant deep bell, focusing and energizing, and sit a minute or two until another bell summons us to speech and song. Monastic congregations often share silence following Communion, with like mystic effect.

Mystical Dancing

Congregational dance and bodily worship gestures also arouse mystical feeling.[75] Biblical psalms are rich with dancing;[76] prophets were famous for dancing, often naked, with King David a champion messiah among them;[77] and the synoptic gospels report Jesus likening his opponents to children who won't dance.[78] Ramsay McMullen identifies popular dancing among the ties linking pagan and early Christian worship.[79] That bond was strong: Christian peoples carried it forward for centuries despite serial conciliar disapprovals—which of

---

75. William McNeill, chap. 1 in *Keeping Together in Time: Dance and Drill in Human History* (Cambridge: Harvard University Press, 1993).

76. For example, Psalms 149, 150, and the Song of Miriam at Exodus 15:1–21.

77. 2 Samuel 6:14–23, cf 1 Chronicles 15:25–29.

78. Matthew 11:17 // Luke 7:32.

79. MacMullen, *The Second Church*.

course evidence its hardy endurance. A full century before those bans began, Gregory Nazianzen extolled Easter dancers "trampling down death,"[80] and Gregory Nyssen wrote:

> Once there was a time when the whole rational creation formed a single danc-ing chorus, looking upward to the Leader of this dance. And the harmony of motion which they learned from His law made its way into their dancing.[81]

Perhaps congregational custom explains why Gregory Nyssen chose *peri-chôrêsis*, circle-dancing, as his monotheist image for the Holy Trinity. Any

David Sanger

St. Gregory's Congregation Dancing with the Saints

who have not danced Greek style may miss Gregory's point: Mediterranean circle dancers do not execute separate fig-ures, but all as one follow a leader, until another takes the lead with another step. That image distinguishes Cappado-cian doctrine from cruder Trin-itarian models popular today, which divide God's works among three Persons—as if one were Creator; another, Redeemer; another, Sanctifier. In sermons and prayers that cleavage slides swiftly into tritheism. For the Cappadocians, all three Divine Persons are Creator, Redeemer, and Sanctifier in turn—a col-laborative union like common folkdance. (Hindu monotheism

---

80. Gregory Nazianzen quotes the "Resurrection Troparion" from Jerusalem worship, as in Book of Common Prayer, p. 500, *Wonder, Love, and Praise: A Supplement to The Hymnal 1982* (New York: Church Publishing, 1997), 816–817.

81. Gregory of Nyssa, Homily on Psalm 6, in Hugo Rahner, *Man at Play* (New York: Herder & Herder, 1972), 89. Ronald Gagne, Thomas Kane, and Robert VerEecke, *Introducing Dance in Christian Worship* (Washington, DC: Pastoral Press, 1984), 49. See also Doug Adams, *Congregational Dancing in Christian Worship* (North Aurora, IL: Sharing Company, 1977) and *Dance as Religious Studies* [with Diane Apostolos-Cappadona] (New York: Crossroad, 1990); J. G. Davies, *Liturgical Dance: A Historical, Theological and Practical Handbook* (London: SCM, 1984).

argues likewise: whichever divine person you follow with full devotion will supply all your needs and blessings.) By contrast, classical Greek and Roman heroes suffered the dire favoritism of competing gods, which destroyed mortals except when a very few were elevated to join the querulous Olympian ranks.

Eastern worship reflects Cappadocian theology concretely. Russian rite Jesuit Stephen Armstrong observes that Westerners worship like an orchestra under a single conductor, whereas Easterners worship like a jazz jam session, where one instrument leads awhile, then another, and all follow whoever leads now. This style lends liturgy constant flowing energy. It requires only that ministers arrive ready in place to speak or sing, as theatre actors must do, rather than walking disruptively through silences while others sit to pray.

Younger North Americans dance happily in restaurants and public streets, and many are ready to try this ancient custom in worship.[82] When launching St. Gregory of Nyssa Church at San Francisco, I attended University of California dance classes in several European traditions, and chose the circular style that Greek, Slav, Turk, and Arab villagers share. With a hand placed simply on the next dancer's shoulder, sidewise steps enable each dancer to feel the whole company moving as one. These movements are as old as Indo-European tongues: mosaics show Alexander the Great's soldiers dancing recognizable figures before and after battles. At St. Gregory's our whole congregation dances twice. Led by drums, we step together in a sung Procession to circle the altar, welcoming Christ's coming to us before the Kiss of Peace and Great Thanksgiving Prayer. This dance joins two of Paul's Christological images: the Body of Christ moving in harmonious company; and Jesus arriving now with authority to transform worshippers' lives. Then again, after we eat and drink new life in Communion with Christ, the whole congregation dances around Jesus's table, where food will be distributed to the needy this week. A hymn envisioning Christian hope fulfilled realizes a palpable sense of God's reign, as dancers physically feel all the races and classes present "keeping together in time."[83] Thus Jesus's own immanent eschatological sign of the table opens up our vision of God's universal mystery, which

---

82. Donald Schell reports from pastoral experience that the parishioners readiest to try are older women attending midweek services, who love to dance, and are too rarely invited.

83. McNeill, *Keeping Together in Time*, i.

St. Gregory's congregation dancing around the Altar at Easter

all humankind can serve daily together. Our nighttime Easter celebrations expand into a full half hour of dances, songs, and blessings.

So like a proper Cappadocian *perichórēsis*, this chapter on biblical mystery theory circles back to the Shakers, who danced round and round with celibate affection until their communities died out mere decades ago. Here is a dance lyric by Mother Sally Eads, set to a sprightly tune in a minor key:

> The Israelites, when they got free,
> From Pharaoh's land in haste did flee,
> And on the shore of the Red Sea
> A joyful scene commencèd:
>> An elder sister led the band
>> With sounding timbrel in her hand,
>> While women moved at her command,
>> And after her they dancèd.
> At Shiloh was a yearly feast
> Where women met from West to East:
> These women were a type at least

Of those that follow Jesus:
    If they went forth in dances then,
    Why should our dancing now offend?
    Since from the alluring power of sin
    Our blessed Savior frees us.
Salvation to the Woman's seed!
From bondage and corruption freed,
They shall possess the earth indeed,
And every gift recover:
    Cemented in the purest love,
    They on their way to Canaan move
    And soon will join the host above
    And praise the Lord forever.[84]

---

84. Adapted from *Millennial Praises*, 1813. *Music for Liturgy: A Book for All God's Friends*, second edition (San Francisco: St. Gregory of Nyssa Episcopal Church, 1999).

CHAPTER FIVE

⁂

THE SPOUSE'S SIGN:
LOVE BEYOND DEATH

Yet, when I recall this life, I have to think that it was rather strange for us both! We could not lead it as we wished, and have had to endure a heart-rending separation. May at least in all our future lives the slightest separation be spared us! May fatal destiny spare us, after this life that has treated us so cruelly, so repeatedly without respite! . . . May Lady Pen be my wife in my future lives . . . following me in each existence! I ask to see her if I am reborn in heaven. May she be with me if I return to this world![1]

—HINDU EPITAPH AT ANGKOR WAT, CAMBODIA, XVI CENTURY

I f churches today seek a sign to gather Christian ritual and theory around a standard model, the institution of Matrimony would serve us best. Contrary to the current rising fashion for baptismal ecclesiology, from long Korean experience Anglican liturgist Nak-Hyon Joseph Joo observes there a serious drawback. Throughout Asia, Baptism appears as a foreign rite, implying repudiation of native cultural values, however fine and beloved. Apology for such cultural arrogance is hopeless. By contrast, marriage is the central concern of traditional Asian societies, which rank the union of families and friends in top place, and individual choice in a supportive role. Today's growing acceptance of divorce has hardly weakened matrimonial solidity. Despite shifts and dislocations throughout industrial societies, the successful endurance rate of first marriages remains steady at 80 percent. (Only serial remarriages halve that figure downward.)

Contemporary matrimony has changed in other ways, however. Mutual commitment within one gender, labeled "homosexual marriage" and important

---

1. Madeleine Giteau, *The Civilization of Angkor*, Katherine Watson trans. (Fribourg: Office du Livre, and New York: Rizzoli, 1976), 246–247.

for a tenth of our world population, is increasingly reckoned part of the natural order; whereas subjugation of one gender to another is no longer widely reckoned so. Matrimony's broad support helps explain why educated Indian youth may still ask their parents to arrange marriages for them. Tolstoy's *Anna Karenina* opens declaring, "Happy marriages are all alike; every unhappy marriage is unhappy in its own way." If so, arranged marriages populate both categories. This chapter opens with a moving epitaph carved near Angkor Wat by a sixteenth-century Hindu aristocrat, surely married by arrangement, now widowed. His prayer says all that the world might hope to hear from any faithful Christian husband.

Love is, after all, the New Testament's favorite topic, for which Hebrew scripture supplies our Christian theological vocabulary. The previous chapter pairs biblical ideas of how a loving God acts both freely and faithfully. Christian marriage learns its terms there too, as couples who have fallen into *ahavah* (blind, unreasoning love) promise *chesed* (strong, enduring love) to one another. Cementing those loves, couples begin a life of incalculable blessing together, growing beyond whatever they expect and enriching those beyond their own household.

Marriage can center our ritual signs of life because in two qualities it surpasses the rest. Words for salvation in Greek and Latin (*sotéria, salus*) conjure physical health and well-being. Indeed, married life does generate emotional and spiritual health for many people, which their families and friends share and enjoy. Often those feelings emerge with the wedding celebrations, and then with awaiting a first child. The Hebrew Bible's salvation imagery is more vivid yet. *Yasha'* (literally, broadness) implies freedom from confinement, as in Psalms 31:8 and 18:20, "you have rescued me and set my feet in a large room." In happy marriages such opening experiences are ubiquitous, and even in stressed marriages, a potential endures that suffering cannot cancel. The familiar greeting *shalom* evokes peace—not of a quiet graveyard, but of a wheat field growing and alive. All our rituals serve these ideals, so Matrimony naturally takes their center.

Married life also exhibits—repeatedly in most couples' lives—the Hebrew Bible's chief salvific concept: *tsedaqah*, putting things right. Unlike modern civil courts, where judges supervise correct process, the Bible's judges ferret out wrong and intervene to fix it, exacting amends where needed. The prophets and psalmists phrase God's *tsedaqah* as "judging the nations," which means: God confounds our enemies and puts Israel back on top, where she should be.[2]

---

2. Among countless examples, Isaiah 2:4 and 11:4. Psalms 9:8 and 110:6.

Pacifying that warrior image for Greek readers, the Septuagint chose *dikaio-synê*, the Homeric goddess Dikê's work restoring broken boundaries between gods and mortals. Hence the Latin translation *justificatio*, perhaps misleadingly translated as "justification," meaning the way your printer justifies the margins on a page. Modern Jews call *tsedaqah* doing good for its own sake: for example, devout Jews donating to rebuild an earthquake-damaged Christian cathedral. Most marriages are rich with *tsedaqah*, and with forgiveness and repair on a daily basis. Creativity and newness come alive there just as they do in Genesis's opening verses. Of course, ritual signs of Reconciliation, discussed in chapter 8, are Matrimony's close cousins—though those ceremonies happen more rarely, whereas the occasions for *tsedaqah* are frequent in a healthy relationship, and are often joyful for both sides.

Second, as the previous chapter observes, Christian rituals require community—what our Creeds call *sanctorum communio*, translated aright as the "sharing of holy things."[3] Growing within marriage excels other life-long human relations that are set permanently from their start. For example, the Latin word *pietas* means "faithfulness to our teachers," and so to our past; the intense friendships of youth hold over decades despite drastic alteration in our personal lives.[4] By contrast, marriage is expected to shift with life changes that might close off another commitment. The Book of Common Prayer vow "forsaking all others" means not foreswearing romantic affairs, but yielding up other sacred duties to keep this one. Hence, the steadfast honor given marriages when one spouse converts to a different faith or national allegiance.[5] Hence the legal protection from testifying against one's spouse in court. Hence, Anglican missionary Roland Allen persuaded polygamous South African converts not to put away their junior wives, lest those starve.[6]

Daphne de Marneffe's book *The Rough Patch*[7] recounts her experiences counseling couples in midlife crises. From infancy we form our identity by

---

3. See chapter 4.

4. In Robert Musil's lapidary German, "*Denn im Grunde ist Jugendfreundschaft um so sonderbarer, je älter man wird. Man ändert sich im Laufe solche Jahre vom Scheitel bis zur Sohle und von den Härchen der Haut bis ins Herz, aber das Verhältnis zueinander bleibt merkwürdigerweise das gleiche und ändert sich sowenig wie die Beziehungen, die jeder einzelne Mensch zu den verschiedenen Herren pflegt, die er der Reihe nach mit Ich anspricht.*"—*Die Amsel* in *Nachlass zu Lebzeiten* (Zürich: Humanitas Verlag, 1936).

5. Paul discourages converts from yoking themselves with unbelievers like draught oxen mismatched (2 Corinthians 6:14) but never suggests dissolving a mixed marriage. Sectarian cults that do so are in no way biblical.

6. Roland Allen, *The Spontaneous Expansion of the Church, and the Causes Which Hinder It* (Grand Rapids, MI: World Dominion Press & Eerdmans, 1962), 64–65.

7. Daphne de Marneffe, *The Rough Patch: Marriage and the Art of Living Together* (New York: Scribner, 2018).

telling ourselves stories, many of those cadged from popular illusions. Dissatisfied spouses imagine they formed their identity before this marriage, rather than seeing chances to create their real identity henceforward. Psychotherapy helps people to reform their own stories, fit their life's genuine and changing conditions, and discover fresh satisfactions in living with one another. Thereby some unions apparently doomed to divorce rebound surprisingly into reality. De Marneffe's examples uncover an earthquake fault running beneath much traditional "sacramental" theory and canonical regulation. Western canons assume that beginnings define all, as first love supposedly does. Grace once given should answer every future challenge; so troubled unions are examined to find elements missing from the start that would nullify a marriage, rather than admit its death. Too often in place of pastoral support, church marriage officers resemble court clerks untangling landowner rights.

Such a régime of *ex-post-facto* restatements contradicts the human life that modern people know. More broadly, the same earthquake fault yawns below other conventional ritual theories that stress launching actions. We have seen how Luther (like Theodore) taught Baptism's essence was not the water bath, but the life of growing virtue afterward; and McCauley distinguished the ongoing work of grace as the living heart of Confirmation. Patton found forgiveness a discovery, not an action; beauty speaks already to a working artist before doctrine does; and the storm spirit blows where it will, bringing life and death. All these move into an open future. The world mistrusts rebuilding upon old earthquake faults and conflicted claims. Centering new ritual theory around Matrimony, seen as a path for people to create their Christian identity together, will soundly replace exclusive structures throughout church life—most of those lately shaken.

Public proof that Matrimony naturally reigns over other rituals—including Christian Baptism—is the effort society makes to repair ailing marriages, and Christian support for couples counseling, which has become a secular industry. For despite every fond intention, marriages can sometimes die, and spouses inevitably do. The biblical image that married couples "become one flesh"[8] acknowledges the pain of either death in timeless human experience. Most grown children will have to watch a widowed parent endure that pain.

Commitment superseding other commitments, and changing through life's many changes: these qualities made Matrimony a ready analogy for God's love

---

8. Ephesians 5:31, quoted by Thomas Cranmer, "The Forme of Solemnizacion of Matrimonie," *The Booke of the Common Prayer and Administracion of the Sacraments and Ceremonies of the Churche after the Use of the Churche of England*, 1549.

toward wandering humankind. Isaiah's God rejoices over Jerusalem as a bride-groom rejoices over his bride. Wedding banquets are a happy symbol throughout Hebrew scripture, and in gospel stories about Jesus. Even Hosea's prophetic marriage to promiscuous Gomer becomes a sign of God's love for Israel. Seeing so many bright images and human practice everywhere, we may ask why traditional worship theory has not focused here. Instead, Matrimony was the last added to the Western "sacrament" list. One reason may be that marriages can be happy or painful, fruitful or thwarted, enriched or decayed. Pastors are most often called in to assist troubled couples, while happy ones celebrate anniversaries on their own. From hard experience that too many will recognize, the Bible chronicles the marital faults of David and other heroes. Indeed, the weddings of Samson and Delilah[9] or Ahab and Jezebel[10] led to death for both spouses and for thousands of Hebrews besides.

Weddings figure less in the New Testament. Among Jesus's likely authentic sayings, hearers who dismiss his message are like children refusing to join wedding (or funeral) games that village children play,[11] or arrogating banquet eminence that is quickly discomfited.[12] John's story of a wedding at Cana sets a social context for a miracle: by Jesus's apparent rebuke to his mother, the evangelist actually echoes prophetic speech to preface a symbolic change of water into wine.[13] Alone among epistle-writers, Paul addresses marriage directly, and he barely recommends it, as a state he does not share: only divorce could be more dangerous.[14]

The Heart's Desire

Hellenistic dualism blamed our passions as causes of error and grief, advising us to bridle or root them out. Gregory Nyssen, a resolute monist, held with Genesis 1 that "everything that is, is good, and created amid good."[15] He reasoned that God gives all creatures passions for healthy purposes, only humans misdirect them. Gregory's rehabilitation of anger, for example, anticipates the duple role that aggression fills in modern psychiatry. Gregory devoted his longest commentary

---

9. Judges 16.

10. 1 Kings 16–21, 2 Kings 9.

11. Matthew 11:17 // Luke 7:32. See also Matthew 22:3–12.

12. Luke 12:36, 14:8.

13. 1 Kings 17:18, 2 Kings 3:12. See also chapter 6, notes 26 and 27.

14. 1 Corinthians 7:10–39.

15. Gregory of Nyssa, *The Great Catechism* and *The Making of Humankind*.

to the biblical Song of Songs, a long chain of love poems.[16] The Songs convinced him that humans are moved by desire for the good, the true, the beautiful: that is, for God, as God longs for us too. Indeed, God's desire fuels our desire, and so pulls our progress forever forward. Far from quashing or expunging passion, God saves humanity by working with our desires, reordering those toward healthy life.

Gregory of Nyssa was one of antiquity's last married bishops, and this icon presents his commentary on the Bible's Song of Songs. There he expounds marriage allegorically as a model of human spiritual growth in union with Christ.

Gregory identifies the poem's mother-in-law with God, reasoning that God has no gender, so that a woman can represent God perfectly well. (A novel teaching for the late fourth century! Gregory did have an actual mother-in-law: perhaps she suggested this?) He inspired centuries of mystic authors, though most were monks and nuns. Indeed, one obvious reason why marriage has not become the central model for Christian rituals is that our theories and canons have come chiefly from authors who chose not to marry. Nevertheless, celibate monastics owe their birth to a marriage, and most recall it gratefully. The great Spanish mystics, nearly all celibate, followed Gregory Nyssen's example by evoking marriage with Christ—by the individual soul or

Icon by Mark Dukes, photo by David Sanger

Gregory of Nyssa's last commentary explains the biblical Song of Songs: here in this church Christ marries your soul, while God blesses your union together.

by the worldwide church—using such erotic imagery as Renaissance poets used describing union between lovers. Thus for John of the Cross, a young bride's hymen tear symbolizes every human soul's final union with Christ, who desires her as she desires him.

---

16. Modern historical criticism locates their source in Canaanite fertility rites, a reading nowhere recognized during Gregory's time.

¡O llama de Amor viva
que tiernamente hieres
de mi alma en el más profundo centro!
Pues ya no eres esquiva.
acaba ya si quieres,
rompe la tela de este dulce encuentro. . . .

   O living flame of Love,
   wounding tenderly
   in the deepest core of my soul!
   So you flicker furtive no longer,
   now finish me off if you wish,
   tear the bodily stuff of this sweet meeting. . . .[17]

Partly under monastic influence, Hellenistic dualism flooded Latin pastoral teaching; nevertheless Gregory did influence mystics westward, even where most knew no Greek. German Meister Eckhart and Spaniards Teresa of Ávila and John of the Cross derived their famous ascetical schemes from Gregory's *Life of Moses* and resurgent Renaissance humanism inspired painters in a fashion we now call Spanish Realism. Unlike El Greco with his chiaroscuro canvasses, Spanish Realists painted saints with no iconographic distortion, no clouds, and thunder and lightning.

Bartolomé Murillo's *Death of St. Clare*, now in the Dresden Museum, is a masterwork of the school. His painterly color shift plays powerfully on canvas.

The Death of St. Clare, by Bartolomé Murillo, 1645 CE

17. San Juan de la Cruz (1542–1591), "Llama de Amor Viva," stanza 1.

Murillo depicts the dying Clare and her Franciscan mourners in gray tones. Only Clare herself can see Christ walking toward her deathbed—not majestic or glorified, but in a procession of lively natural colors, like a bridegroom and his company come to claim his longed-for bride, and take her from her sorrowful house to his own joyful one.

As a formal model for ritual acts, marriage may not be quite so ubiquitous as eating and washing. But Matrimony exemplifies the theological maxim *Ex Opere Operato Non Ponentibus Obicem*—grace comes by the very doing it, for those who raise no obstacle. A minister's faults or doubts erect no hurdle, nor does a congregation's imperfect faith. At first the "obstacles" were few: only mockery, malice, or magical intent could block prayer's effect. Later denominational polemic extended the "obstacles" list with dogmatic difference or lack of approval by higher church authority. That extension, however, reversed the maxim's original sense, which had secured grace within God's control alone. Every married couple worldwide knows the power of life committed together—whether in a union orthodox or agnostic, peaceful or stressed, happy or wretched. Even infants can know its blessing day by day.

Eastern and Western marriage theorists differ only slightly. Westerners treat weddings as an exchange of promises that must be made freely and fully, but any bride and groom anywhere in the world can officiate as its ministers. Easterners also view marriage as universal within creation but seeing Christ the divine *logos* as its universal minister, Eastern churches claim an exclusive context for Christians to solemnize it. Under either description, church law bows to marriages already solemnized by whatever ethnic or religious custom. Should families feud, or should one spouse abandon or change faith, their marriage endures. Matrimony's natural created matter suffices for baptismal washing and eucharistic feasting too. Death alone ends the relations that those three rituals set, and the death of a marriage through divorce can scar survivors as deeply as any death. As one Episcopal bishop told a priest whose marriage had died, "Divorce is like pneumonia. You wouldn't wish it on anyone."

Features so widespread make Matrimony the most reasonable model for Christian ritual theory. It is welcome on mission everywhere, and marrying couples and their neighbors are blessed with grace more than they know how to count. Beyond those excellencies, the next chapter will extol how Matrimony brings our heart's desire hallowed living fruit. The human heart's desire has ancient primacy in missionary planning; today it deserves proper honor in ritual planning too.

Elephants mourning their dead

A Farewell to Love

Love knows but one custom more widespread than weddings. When an ele-phant dies in the African veld, her kin gather about her body. For a time they alone will measure, they stand waving their trunks above her. Then as one they turn, and walk their many ways over the savannah. What elephants think or hope for after this life, no woman or man knows.

Yet human beings cannot stop talking about it. Until recently, researchers credited our own *homo sapiens sapiens* with inventing religion, evidenced by the first human burials. Then as sites for Neanderthal, *Homo ergaster*, and *Homo habilis* received more scrutiny, hominids in general seem to have cared for the dead, as very few mammals have done. Peking Man drew a tiger and dragon left and right of graves, although we can only wonder whether meanings a hundred millennia later applied then. Physical anthropologists now rank hominid capa-bility for song older than speaking, and dance older than singing, and funerary custom older than all.[18]

Facing such universality, it is remarkable that no church assigns Christian burial sacramental efficacy. Other faiths, like Tibetan Buddhism, do claim their prayer rites have eternal impact upon one's next incarnation—although nobody returned from the dead has convinced Confucian skeptics that reincarnation

---

18. Gary Tomlinson, *A Million Years of Music*, chaps. ii and iv (New York: Zone Books, 2015). McNeill, chap. 2 in *Keeping Together in Time*.

is anything more than an Indian illusion. And given the estimate that half the humans ever born are alive today, we are mathematically unlikely to collect proof. Notwithstanding, every era, every tribe, every cultic tradition has advanced theories, and most of those have colored Christian believers' hopes. Welcoming at least some, our preachers try to lend the bereaved support and comfort. As Christian mission spreads and ecumenical dialog grows, further ritual accommodation in the service of human hope is a sure and even a healthy outcome.

Deterrence, on the other hand, is a different matter. Francis Bacon mused:

Men fear death as children fear to go into the dark,

and as that natural fear in children is increased with tales,

so is the other.[19]

Hebrew scripture says little about dead people's existence. Early texts picture them lying about weary, powerless, and no wiser than they proved in life.[20] New Testament documents depict the righteous awaiting God's final revelation when wrongs will be put right and hurts healed. Wrongdoers wait meanwhile in a place fiery as an unquenched trash heap,[21] or so cold they wail and chatter their teeth without relief.[22] Synoptic parables paint a brighter vision for the righteous: a posthumous feast chaired by the Patriarchs, with food and drink that evildoers can only envy.[23] This image from contemporary Jewish preaching transfers Isaiah's vision of unbounded company feasting in this life into individual rewards beyond it.[24]

One sole popular belief in life after death lacks biblical support absolutely. That is the medieval vision of Hell with a discrete eternal punishment matching each sin. (As Gilbert and Sullivan's *The Mikado* parodies it, "My object most sublime / I shall achieve in time, / to make the punishment fit the crime, / the punishment fit the crime.") This concept originated where Indian Hindus taught reincarnation: Yama the King of Death and justice prescribes purgation to prepare souls for better *karmic* behavior when re-born on

---

19. Francis Bacon, *Of Death*, 1616.

20. Samuel raised by the Witch of Endor offers no new visionary power, and resents being called up to answer questions. 1 Samuel 28.

21. Mark 9:43, 45.

22. Matthew 13:42, 50; 22:13; 24:51; 25:30; Luke 13:28.

23. Matthew 8:11. Matthew 22:1–14 // Luke 14:16–24. Luke 16:19–31.

24. Isaiah 25:6–8. Perrin, *Rediscovering the Teaching of Jesus*, finds this innovation in both apocalyptic and rabbinical texts (162).

earth. Yama's medicines are painful, like surgery without anesthetic; but they promise advancement toward bliss, which is the Hindu ascetical goal.

When tenth-century Arab armies invaded the Afghan Buddhist heartland and Hindu Kush, they destroyed Buddhist and Christian monasteries. Buddhist monks fleeing slaughter carried that Indian concept west and east across Central Asia, where only fighting Tibetans withstood the Muslim advance. The enlightened world did not end in 1021 as those monks feared; rather within a single century King Yama's hell spread across the walls of Korean and Japanese temples eastward, Khmer monasteries southward, and a church door tympanum at Constantinople. Torcello Island artists planted it gorgeously in Italy, and by 1308 Dante adopted it for his *Comedia*. Buddhist and Christian preachers ever since have made hell's tortures the most popular threat to deter evildoers.

Far from boosting ecumenism, however, this Christian borrowing shocks Indian teachers. Unlike their own short-lived harsh prescriptions, Christian condemnation to eternal suffering disgusts them: here they find our most dangerous theological fault among many. Suffering is the human problem Buddhists chiefly would solve, whereas Christian vision seems to wallow in it. Our reverence for martyrs' pains, with an added hell of eternal retribution, can repel friendly thinkers who acclaim a humane Christian core. Pastor's son Carl Jung once responded to a documentary filmmaker, "My job is not to climb up and join Jesus on his cross; my job is to be true to myself as Jesus was true to himself."

Relish for God's wrath and sinners' torment gained ever-wider European currency after the fourteenth-century Black Death killed half of Europe. Thereupon war and plague images from the Apocalypse invaded funerals and overwhelmed hopeful Bible texts. The new hymn *Dies Irae* inspired Roman Catholic preachers' warnings and romantic composers' operatic arias. Calvinist doomsayers were equally popular: congregations yearly begged Connecticut's Jonathan Edwards to repeat his blistering sermon that began, "Sinners in the hands of an angry God!" and pictured his hearers dangled like spiders over hellfire.

If Christians can now replace such ghastly stuff with alternative scripture, hymns, and prayers, they have the English Reformers to thank. Roman Catholic worship reformer Louis Bouyer called Anglicans the heirs to Renaissance humanism.[25] Seventeenth-century Britain surely knew urban violence, plagues, and civil warfare aplenty—John Donne, the lusty love poet and dean at London's St. Paul's Cathedral, prepared nightly for death in ways that may look morbid to us—but their Book of Common Prayer flushed away the medieval

---

25. L. Bouyer, *Liturgical Piety* (Notre Dame, IN: Notre Dame University Press, 1955).

slurry of hell, and poured in Bible texts beaming with hope, and prayers trusting God's royal grace. Anglican teaching evolved to match, arousing criticism
that for a traditionalist liturgical body Anglicans make weak pulpiteers. San
Francisco's Grace Cathedral dean Alan Jones replied to one protester, "I suppose I can see the logical necessity of hell; only I prefer to believe that no one
is *there.*" American atheist H. L. Mencken gave their liturgical work a rare trib-
ute: "The burial service in the Book of Common Prayer is so beautiful it makes
you wish it was true." True or not: that is one answer believers and atheists alike
are 100 percent certain to learn.

Death and Religion

Mencken returns us to an unsolved query: why care for the dead? Elephants
cannot answer for us. One answer is fear, for which apotropaic rituals and traditions give evidence, driving away ghosts and spirits more primitively thought
sacred. The Navajo reserve a time that a deceased person's ill deeds can spread
to others, so kinsmen must avoid his hovering *chindi* spirit after burial. As a
general rule, taboos reflect earlier religion by banning as ritually impure something more anciently held sacred, like blood. That is why biblical food bans
forbid boiling a kid in its mother's milk, a Canaanite fertility sacrifice,[26] and
why observant Jews today keep meat and milk dishes apart, avoiding accidental
sacrilege. Intentional curses and evil charms might once have summoned the
dead, even using recovered body parts. Yet despite Levitical taboos surrounding corpses, Orthodox Jewish burial customs today are intimate and speedy.
Indeed, the Hebrew Bible editors erased every suggestion that dead bodies or
ghosts have lingering power over the living, for good or evil. The Bible's sole
necromancy ends darkly and is never repeated.[27]

  Since the French Enlightenment, critics have charged that human religion
began with fearing death. It is more likely that religion began from losing someone in death who loved you. That pain draws poetry from the bereaved everywhere, while fear of the dead leaves poets mute. Chinese ancestor worship, a
longstanding target of Christian missionaries, keeps love and thanks at its irre-
ducible core, and converts hope their beloved children will return their self-sac-
rifices with prayers. Reverence for ancestors grounded many ancient human
polities. The Inca carried his forebears' remains with him sewn into leather

---

26. Exodus 23:19, 34:26.

27. 1 Samuel 28.

bags, on administrative visitations up and down history's grandest empire beyond the brief Mongol alliance.

Bishop William Swing tells a moving experience of love surpassing fear in a culture that some might label primitive. At the dedication of a new Episcopal seminary in Papua New Guinea, he was startled to see tattooed tribesmen bring human bones to bury into the foundations. Wondering whether this ritual showed a survival of human sacrifice, he asked the tribesmen why. "This shows we no longer fear the spirits of our ancestors," they replied. For those new Christians, care for the dead outlasted apotropaic fear. Poet Ann Thorp expresses personal modern grief in lyrics that British composer Howard Goodall set to music for a national memorial:

BELIEF

> I have to believe
> that you still exist
> somewhere,
> that you still watch me
> sometimes,
> that you still love me
> somehow.
> I have to believe
> that life has meaning
> somehow,
> that I am useful here
> sometimes,
> that I make small differences
> somewhere.
> I have to believe
> that I need to stay here
> for some time,
> that all this teaches me
> something,
> so that I can meet you again
> somewhere.[28]

---

28. Howard Goodall, composer, *Eternal Light: A Requiem*, for the ninetieth anniversary of the peace ending World War I, 2008.

Care for the dead proves more universal than all rituals churches class as sacraments or mysteries, because humane duty here respects no restrictions. Sophocles's play *Antigone* upholds it against every other argument, and his tragedy won Athens's first prize. Soldiers often return to battlefields to bury fallen comrades at their own risk without strategic gain. Knowing that worms will devour those bodies, whether buried or unburied, does not deter them. Indeed, sailors "bury" bodies dead at sea hoping that watery creatures *will* consume them before they float again to the surface. No rubric or canon disqualifies any minister of burial; and afterward society defends human remains from interference unless authorized, as by court order. Church synods and councils may regulate the times and places of burials, enjoin or forbid cremation, and dictate what rites are followed; but none dare demand ignoring a human corpse. At the funeral of a celebrated Jewish newspaperman whose son was a student at the Cathedral school, an angry visitor demanded: "Why is Grace Cathedral burying a Jew?" Dean Alan Jones answered: "Because he's dead." No ritual action obeys more blunt logic.

For all our rich concepts and history, then, do we human beings differ so far from elephants?

Zilu asked how to serve the spirits and the gods.

The Master [Confucius] replied, "Not yet being able to serve other people,

how would you be able to serve the spirits?"

Zilu said, "May I ask about death?"

The Master replied, "Not yet understanding life,

how could you understand death?"[29]

---

29. Confucius, *Analects* 11:13, fifth century BCE, Roger Ames and Henry Rosemont, *The Analects of Confucius: A Philosophical Translation* (New York: Ballantine, 1998) 144.

CHAPTER SIX

THE SIGN OF DESIRE: DAUGHTERS AND SONS

Cradling my nursing baby in one arm and the phone in my ear, con-
ducting an interview with some serious personage, I could hardly
contain my happiness. I don't really advocate trying to interview with
a baby on one arm. But that one moment, ridiculous as it sounds,
stands out because it was the first time I felt both my selves fit
together with an audible click.[1]

—SUSAN CHIRA, JOURNALIST

A mong other advantages, taking marriage for our model Christian ritual
will welcome natural desire at the core of them all. Some Christian teachers have warned against desire, almost as a habitual ethical assumption,
but their horror is not scriptural. The Hebrew Bible did not divide our nature
into good and evil; instead, rabbis found two healthy human impulses: *yetzer
ha-tov* and *yetzer ha-ra'*,[2] sometimes in tension. The first term translates clearest
as "productive urge." The second appears in Paul's Greek as *sarks*, misleadingly if
accurately translated as "the flesh." But neither urge is morally simple.

> The rabbis declare that God created both the *yetser tov* and the *yetser ra'*
> (Berakoth 61a). The command to love God "with *all* your heart" they inter-
> pret to mean "with both your impulses" (Berakoth 54a), since both human
> elements can be employed in the service of God. "Were it not for the *yetser
> ha-ra'*, no man would build a home or get married or follow an occupation
> (Genesis Rabbah 9:9).[3]

---

1. Susan Chira, *A Mother's Place: Taking the Debate about Working Mothers beyond Guilt and Blame*
(New York: HarperCollins, 1998), cited in Daphne de Marneffe, *Maternal Desire: On Children, Love, and
the Inner Life* (New York: Little, Brown, 2004), 181.

2. Joyce Eisenberg and Ellen Scolnic, *The JPS Dictionary of Jewish Words* (Philadelphia: Jewish Publication Society, 2001/5761), 177.

3. Philip Birnbaum, *A Book of Jewish Concepts* (New York: Hebrew Publishing, 1964 rev. 1975), 271–272.

119

Sin spoils human life, of course: the flesh can fuel infidelity or rape as well as marriage. Declaring that "we have crucified the flesh," Paul means that Christ's spirit directs Christians wholly for God's service, just as Christ directed his own undivided human nature.[4] But in Hellenistic dualist soil, Paul's subtle language sprouted a rigorist strain that never withered away afterward.[5] Some moderns express surprise that the very Greeks whose early poets and artists cultivated bodily beauty in athletics and in sculpture, later shifted toward disapproval. For Platonist philosophers, however, humankind's chief problem is our bodies, which effectively entrap our souls. Our physical desires are easily corrupted, and hence corrupting: an ethical cause for restraint, or even abstinence. Christian moral instruction bore that dour attitude forward for centuries, giving natural desires a nod but rarely encouraging them.

On the other hand, desire has had a line of classical champions too, whose thought preserved humanism inside the Christian margins, and whose writings draw fresh attention today. The fourth century's Gregory of Nyssa was the most systematic of these. Modern students admire his monist reading of biblical creation, his emphasis upon moral progress, and his apophatic principle that God lives in darkness, so we know only what God *does*. All these distinguished Gregory Nyssen among orthodox theologians for centuries afterward. His most singular teaching agreed with Jewish rabbis that all passions—including sexual passion—are wholly a gift from God, who has installed them for all creatures' well-being.

Evil arises as humans misdirect our passions away from goodness toward lesser goals, Gregory reckons, which soil our souls so we cannot see God reflected naturally within us, to guide us. So God has sent us his Son for a model. Imitating Christ, guided by his Spirit, we can learn to recognize God's image planted in the whole of humankind, and redirect our lives toward the Good, True, and Beautiful which we naturally desire. Sexual passion, for example, is how God outmaneuvers death. Sinners inevitably die; but knowing that they must die, God has created sexual generation to extend our race through time, until Christ's appearance could teach benighted sinners how God designs us to live, and Christ's Spirit could quicken us to live so.[6]

---

4. Galatians 5:24; Romans 7:5, 8:8.

5. Kenneth Kirk, Lecture IV "Rigorism" in *The Vision of God: The Christian Doctrine of the Summum Bonum* (New York: Harper & Row, 1931; New York: Harper Torchbooks, 1966), 174–234.

6. This short précis outlines Gregory's anthropology in his treatises *On the Making of Humankind, The Great Catechism*, and *The Soul and the Resurrection*. All three draw constantly upon the Bible, at a length too great to detail here. See W. Moore and H. A. Wilson trans., Schaaf, *Nicene and Post-Nicene Fathers*, Second Series, vol. 5 (Grand Rapids, MI: Eerdmans, 1892).

Theologians today find contemporary parallels outside religious discourse. For example, Freudian depth psychology, if vulgarly thought sex-centered, actually focuses upon desires in conflict, and sex is one outstanding locus (among others) for conflicting desires concealed even from their conscious human subjects. Freud's writings created a new popular awareness of childhood experience recurring disguised within adult experience. A psychoanalyst uncovers those connections that spark our behavior unseen—always with the therapeutic aim of freeing our active lives from chains we forged in our past, like Dickens's Jacob Marley. Relief of suffering and effective living mark the true Freudian goal; as his followers quip, "Understanding is the booby-prize."

Freud's skepticism of all religion is well known, and to some degree enrolls many psychiatrists today, but he made an equally harsh attack upon scientific positivism and its faith in educated social progress. Following Emil Durkheim, mid-nineteenth-century anthropology had identified "alienation" as a logical fault, whereby primitive groups mistake their own human imaginings for external reality, and project those "alienated" values upon their gods as cosmic laws inspiring wars and other tragedies. Scientific positivists proposed to replace such errors with truths tested and proved by evidence, as physics is. But Freud found disappointed desires ruling human life from infancy onward—and worse yet, hiding in the human unconscious, which knows neither time nor death. As psychoanalyst Stanley Leavy summarizes, "Concealment is not just episodic, like lying or other forms of conscious dissimulation. It is habitual, literally characteristic . . . Because we cannot always have what we want, we pretend to ourselves that we want something else."[7] Thus, rational happiness will always elude society. Freud wryly commented that even psychoanalysis at best merely changes neurotic suffering into "ordinary misery."

Not all Freud's followers have shared his pessimism. One example of new psychological reflection is Daphne de Marneffe's book *Maternal Desire*. De Marneffe observes that despite centuries of writing about women, and more recently even by women, the female desire for children has received little or no examination. Modern feminist writers have adjudicated motherhood-versus-career as an economic and social contest, not hearing women's common desire to give birth and—especially—to care for the young. Such deafness is remarkable, given this powerful longing's economic and social effect.

---

7. Stanley A. Leavy, *In the Image of God: A Psychoanalyst's View* (New Haven, CT: Yale University Press, 1988), 54 and 65.

If adolescents did not want babies, they would not have them. But they do want them. Indeed, many seem to fear infertility, craving pregnancy and motherhood . . . The desire to be pregnant and to have a child makes the prevention of adolescent childbearing a formidable task.[8]

De Marneffe comments: "The unthinking intensity of the desire for a child is not only the province of impulsive, confused teenagers." Karen Horney in 1926 rebutted Freud's presumption that women want children to compensate for lacking a penis:

At this point I as a woman, ask in amazement, and what about motherhood? And the blissful consciousness of bearing new life within oneself? And the ineffable happiness of the increasing expectation of the appearance of this new being? And the joy when it finally makes its appearance and one holds it for the first time in one's arms? And the deep pleasurable feeling of satisfaction in suckling it and her happiness of the whole period when the infant needs her care?[9]

Desire Is Everywhere

Making such a shift in awareness, we can better appreciate Jesus's singular teaching habit. The parable exemplars Jesus chooses controvert common ethics: law-breakers, pre-moral children, selfish opportunists, and pushy women predominate.[10] Far from providing a gratuitous shock, these protagonists exemplify human desire and risky action taken in the face of known social restraints. *Midrash* explanations appended within the gospels underscore that challenge: ". . . for the children of this age are more astute in dealing with their own kind than the children of light."[11] "If you then, bad as you are, know how to give your children good things, how much more will your heavenly father give good things to those who ask him!"[12] Jesus's parables rank desire for God's reign as the highest motivation, superseding other sacred duty. Thus scholar Norman Perrin chose as Jesus's most radical saying, "Leave the dead to bury their own dead," where Luke adds, "but for you, go proclaim the Kingdom."[13]

8. Judith Musick, cited in de Marneffe, *Maternal Desire*, 202.

9. Karen Horney, "Flight from Womanhood" (1926), cited in de Marneffe, *Maternal Desire*, 62–63.

10. See chapter 7 "The Seer's Sign: Rivers in the Desert."

11. Luke 16:8.

12. Matthew 7:11.

13. Matthew 8:22 // Luke 9:60. Perrin, *Rediscovering the Teaching of Jesus*, 144.

Renaissance Protestants knew well the passion for God's truth and its risks. Cranmer's first Book of Common Prayer climaxed the baptismal profession of faith with this dialog from the medieval Sarum rite: "What doest thou desire?" "Baptism." "Wilt thou be baptized?" "I wyll." And yet no other rites vocalize the desire that moves candidates to undertake them. In post-Christian society, our refusal to talk of desire earns neither attraction nor support. Loving friends attending a Christian service today want to know that we *want* what they see done: that is what they care about most. Indeed, God is such a friend.

> No one I've ever met has asked, "What is virtue?" Instead, they fall in love with a person, or they fall in love with a god, or with a way of being in the world, or with some hero that they try to imitate. It's our desires that come first, and our desires are aroused not by an abstraction but by a specific story, a specific person, a specific concept of the good.[14]

Parenting

Naming our desire for God and God's desire for us in pastoral liturgies will be easier if we listen to the Bible. For example, some critics of religion argue that Christians project upon God our struggles with relating to our own parents—the very experience that fills psychoanalysis. Because no family is perfect, calling God Father can recall uncomfortable memories, which Mother images soften only slightly. Worse yet, an unsavory fungus of patriarchy embitters much so-called "biblical" preaching. Hence modern worship books prefer task-based "Teacher," "Advocate," "Creator," or "Forerunner" in place of the emotional relationships "Father," "Lord," "Master," or "Redeemer."

By strong contrast, however, the Bible's talk of God rarely invokes the human experience of *having* parents, and far more the widespread experience of *being* a parent, with its joys and (especially) its frustrations.

> When Israel was a youth, I loved him,
>
> and out of Egypt I called my son.
>
> But the more I called, the farther they went from me . . .
>
> Yet it was I who taught Ephraim to walk,
>
> It was I who took them in my arms.

---

14. *New York Times* columnist David Brooks, in Matt Fitzgerald, "Chasing Beauty, Finding Grace," *The Christian Century*, February 1, 2017, 28.

I drew them with human cords, with bands of love;
I fostered them like one who raises an infant to his cheeks.
Yet though I stooped to feed my child,
They did not recognize I was their healer . . .
My people are bent on rebellion,
But though they call in unison to Baal
He will not lift them up.
How can I hand you over, Ephraim,
Or deliver you up, Israel?
My heart recoils within me,
my compassion grows warm and tender.
I am not going to let loose my fury,
I will not turn and destroy Ephraim,
For I am God, and not a man,
The Holy One present among you;
And I will not come with threats. [15]

Can a woman forget her baby nursing at her breast?
Or feel no pity for the child she has borne?
Even if these were to forget,
I will not forget you.[16]

Jerusalem, Jerusalem, you who kill the prophets
and stone those who are sent to you!
How long have I yearned to gather your children together
as a hen gathers her brood under her wings;
but you would not let me.[17]

Here the stresses of mothering and fathering speak up, evoking the passionate care that parents have for their children despite misbehavior or mischance. All primates exhibit it, as do most mammals for at least some time. Indeed, the

---

15. Hosea 11:1–9, NAB.

16. Isaiah 49:15, NJB.

17. Matthew 23:37 // Luke 13:34, NEB and NJB.

experience of parenting transforms lives, whatever triumph or sorrow may follow. King David's lament over the death of his rebel son Absalom sounds tragically familiar in some parents' ears and has inspired great composers.[18] A recent generation of gay Americans married heterosexual spouses to conform with convention, and later divorced after pain on all sides. Yet divorcés report that their children are the one thing neither side regrets. European polities increasingly stipulate paternal as well as maternal leave from work. Here is the context in which biblical talk enables church planners to shape worship that truly fits our times.

On biographical points, scripture is often silent: Jesus's personal connection with children, for example. No Bible text says Jesus or any New Testament writer sired children. To a historian this omission by itself does not prove all were unmarried and childless, however. Progeny often go unnamed in ancient documents, when child mortality claimed half of births.[19] Moreover, the eras that canonized those texts revered the celibate life. In Jesus's case, Jewish commentators argue that a rabbi had to marry, so the gospels' silence may mean Jesus had married as a matter of course. For that same reason, Paul felt constrained to explain his abstinence.[20] At least on this point, Paul's defense speaks for itself: he had no children. We may infer that Jesus lacked children, too, since the gospels mention his mother and siblings without them.[21] When the Romans executed his brother James, churches had no recourse to a hereditary teacher line, the way Muslims installed a caliphate from Muhammad's descendants.[22] Matthew's gospel employs children to symbolize believers generally,[23] and most child images in the gospels actually point toward the church. Yet two synoptic sayings suggest Jesus enjoyed childlike behavior. One passage likens those opposing his preaching to village children who refuse to join in games.[24] The second

---

18. 2 Samuel 18:33. William Billings's straightforward eighteenth-century choral setting is widely sung, as are more elaborate Renaissance works by Weelkes and Tomkins.

19. See further discussion of this unhappy issue below.

20. 1 Corinthians 7.

21. Mark 3:31–35 // Matthew 12:46–50 // Luke 8:19–21. Matthew 13:55, John 2, 19:25–27.

22. Hans von Campenhausen, "The Authority of Jesus's Relatives in the Early Church," in von Campenhausen and Henry Chadwick, *Jerusalem and Rome: The Problem of Authority in the Early Church*, Facet Books Historical Series 4 (Philadelphia: Fortress Press, 1966). For a parallel example of vague heredity, the *Great Paranibbana Sûtra* (Sanskrit text) says the Buddha converted his family first, and then founded many monasteries, but the Sûtra does not specify which generation those first converts belonged to.

23. Green, CR, *The Gospel According to Matthew.*

24. Matthew 11:16–19 // Luke 7:31–35.

admires children's simple aggression toward proffered gifts: "No one who will not receive my message the way a child receives will get God's reign."[25]

Jesus's attitude toward his own parents is likewise obscure. His few family dialogs in the gospel texts too obviously conjure scriptural predecessors. For example, his apparent rebuke to his mother before changing water into wine at John 2:4 quotes the Hebrew formula *"Ma li walach/w'lachem?"* spoken just before prophets Elijah and Elisha perform saving miracles, or King David rescues criminals from death.[26] It is heard again (in Greek *"ti emoi/hêmin?"*) before the synoptic gospels show Jesus casting out demons.[27] These editorial echoes assert Jesus's prophetic heritage, not his inner feelings. More intriguingly, Jesus's choice to call God by the Aramaic *Abba*, "Papa," touched the modern critic Joachim Jeremias as singularly intimate; but other scholars demur.[28] Our modern experience of *having* parents can tint our own childhood memories either light or dark, but it cannot dictate either coloring for Jesus's family life.

Family Feelings

Among signs of human desire, children are the widest understood. Gregory Nyssen's siblings Basil and Macrina embraced the rising celibate standard for Christian leaders, while Gregory lamented that children are "born only to feed Death." Raymond Van Dam infers here that Gregory pessimistically refrained from fatherhood, and that his treatise *Peri tês Parthenias* shows his intellectual preference for celibacy, which he disobeyed briefly when he "followed his heart" by marrying the lady Eusebeia.[29] But alas, a different and sadder inference is far likelier. Because Gregory Nyssen bore the Christian name of his father and grandfather, Van Dam observes also that he was responsible—as his siblings Basil and Macrina were not—for carrying on their family line. Modern readers dare not overlook infant mortality and women's childbed deaths. Before Louis Pasteur discovered germs, their reign was terrible: the eighteenth-century composer J. S. Bach lost one wife and ten of his twenty children, for example, and

---

25. Mark 10:15 // Matthew 18:3 // Luke 18:17.

26. 2 Samuel 19:22, 16:10; 1 Kings 17:18. 2 Kings 3:13.

27. Mark 1:24, 34 // Luke 4:34. Mark 5:7 // Matthew 8:29 // Luke 8:28.

28. Joachim Jeremias, *The Central Message of the New Testament* (New York: Charles Scribner's Sons, 1965; reprinted Philadelphia: Fortress Press, 1981). Geza Vermès reviews this discussion in *Jesus the Jew: A Historian's Reading of the Gospels* (New York: Macmillan, 1973), 210–213.

29. Raymond Van Dam, chap. 7 in *Families and Friends in Late Roman Cappadocia* (Philadelphia: University of Pennsylvania Press, 2003).

David Sanger

Martyrs Anne Frank & Iqbal Masih, icons by Mark Dukes

Mozart five of his seven siblings. The infant mortality rate (IMR) has broad causes and impacts such as agricultural failure and warfare, and today it provides the leading index of economic development. Nations that reduce their IMR to 10 percent have never seen it rise again above that threshold. Barely a century and a half after Pasteur, statisticians reckon that already half the humans ever born in our race's history are alive now.[30]

In their more mournful world, ancient documents do not name stillborn babies or short-lived infants, out of regard for ancestors whose names they might have carried. For the same reason, some Middle Eastern peoples still do not formally name offspring before a seventh birthday proves their viability. We can presume that in Gregory Nyssen's time, like Bach's, half the infants born died soon. Gregory's compassionate lament for dead newborns, an emotional cry rare in patristic literature and echoed by Augustine, most likely expresses his own personal loss. No record says progeny survived Gregory; and we do

---

30. "The Delhi Declaration on Ending Preventable Maternal and Child Deaths," 2015, from *The Call to Action Summit* co-hosted by the Ministry of Health and Family Welfare, Government of India and the Health Ministry of Ethiopia, in partnership with the Bill & Melinda Gates Foundation, the Tata Trusts, UNICEF, USAID, and WHO.

not know whether his beloved Eusebeia did. His treatise extols *Parthenia* in spiritual and moral terms, as a quality attained, rather than lost, through life experience. The treatise would best be titled—not so crudely *On Virginity*—but echoing Buddhist ideals that Christians know well enough, *On Overcoming Attachment.* Most importantly, above all those passions Gregory calls our Creator's gifts, parental desire for children is salvific and necessary. How else could sexual generation ensure our race's survival until Christ appeared, as Gregory taught was God's foreknowing plan?[31] Gregory's crucial reliance upon sexual generation to overcome evil contradicts any imputed pessimism about children or an ethical preference for celibacy. But alas, such arguments would soon be heard from many other Christian teachers.

Augustine became a truer pessimist. At first a joyful father, Augustine painfully but obediently banished his Punic wife of thirteen years, and later their cherished but doomed son Itanbaal (Latin *Adeodatus*, Gift from God), in order to fulfill his aristocratic mother's scheme that he become a catholic bishop. His argument that babies' facial expressions prove original sin projects his own grief and envy upon the innocent.[32] Only a church dominated for sixteen centuries by celibates could derive ethics from such a repressed—if brilliant—exemplar, and sidestep Gregory Nyssen's courageous universal humanism. (On the other hand, Augustine did have one excuse medieval schoolmen lacked: he knew neither Gregory nor Greek.) As a single gay man myself, I was unlikely to know parenthood's joys or sorrows until St. Gregory's co-founders Donald and Ellen Schell and I moved into a duplex house. There for eight years their four hilarious offspring brightened my daily life. (No sorrows!) Later I met my husband through an internet matchmaking service where I had simply written: "Must love children." That was then a tight filter, but our marriage by an Episcopal bishop has brought me two children and even three grandchildren so far. . . .

Cappadocian theologians supremely stressed warm family feeling. Probably no other ancient Christian writer extolled a sister the way Gregory Nyssen extolled Macrina, crediting her with his own boldest ideas, even if he did so as a literary device.[33] Their celibate brother Basil's sermon on the foolish rich farmer[34]

---

31. *On the Making of Humankind.*

32. Augustine, *Confessions*, Book 1, Chapters 6 and 9.

33. Gregory Nyssen, *On the Soul and the Resurrection*, keeps this fond convention throughout, but other treatises (*The Great Catechism, The Making of Humankind, The Life of Moses*) just as thoroughly omit it. See note 6, above.

34. PG 31, Basil's Homily 6 on Luke 12:18: "I will pull down my barns." F. Toal, *Sunday Sermons of the Great Fathers* (Chicago: Regnery and London: Longmans, Green, and Co., 1959), 3:325–332.

climaxed famously by describing the anguish of a starving father selling one favorite child into slavery in order to feed the rest. Preached during a famine, Basil's dynamite sermon burst open a flood of civic charity at Constantinople, setting a high-water mark for social activists ever since. As a monastic reformer, Basil argued that ascetics must no longer live alone with no one to show charity to. Under his influence, the "cenobite" (shared living) monastic pattern from upper Egypt overtook the lower Egyptian solitary anchorite athletes who had first inspired imitators abroad.[35] Such examples show how our natural human desire for the good and for natural familial affection can transform both our faith institutions and our corrupt public life. And like a woman planning one child, then desiring another, and another, our hunger for the good grows with every taste.

"Rites of passage" found in many cultures can inspire church planners when their true rewards are understood. Even more directly than they shape children's growth, Jewish bar mitzvah and Hispanic quinceañera ceremonies encourage parental rejoicing in the first place. Precocious children still have toy-like notions of adulthood: hence the Jewish joke about a rapturous bar mitzvah boy declaring, "Today I am a fountain pen!" rather than the proper ending "a man." Rites of passage are valued long afterward: youngsters will get full gratification when in turn they become parents. That is why many Jewish families continue circumcision, and why some Episcopalians press for "restoring Confirmation" after the prayer book has reunited that act with Baptism. Their nostalgia for a "lost" sacrament expresses a parent's enduring desire to rejoice in their children, which worship planners might better satisfy otherwise.

Most recollections of Christian Confirmation center on bodily touch. After restoring infant Communion, and after learning that Confirmation by bishops is an odd Anglican quirk with an odder history—the American Episcopal House of Bishops refused nevertheless to drop episcopal Confirmation, cherishing their sole corporal contact with each church member. In fact, Egeria's fourth-century pilgrimage memoir records how that very contact concluded every Jerusalem service, even summoning the bishop briefly into church so that people could "come to his hand" for a blessing.[36] St. Gregory's congregation always do so (very speedily, while singing to the bishop "God grant her

---

35. Kirk, *The Vision of God*, 264–268.

36. George Gingras, *Egeria: Diary of a Pilgrimage*, Ancient Christian Writers Series (New York: Newman Press, 1970).). This ritual, called the Missa, is announced but not enacted ending every Latin eucharist—hence the Latin name Mass.

many years!"). Modern renewal has so far proposed no palpable substitute, nor
any gesture anchoring a teenager's loyalty so well. Friendly hugging and kissing
during the liturgical Peace, or laying hands on shoulders surrounding a birthday blessing, or joining hands at the Lord's Prayer: these informal parish developments recall physical affection we knew in our youth, as traditional rites of
passage are meant to do. Today's official worship commissions have ever more
opportunities to design by highlighting biblical wonders:

> O praise the Lord, ye servants all,
> Praise ye his name for ever!
> From rise of sun till evenfall
> Praise him by thy endeavor!
> For who is like unto the Lord
> That doth uphold us by his word,
> And who forsaketh us never.
>> Though he is high above the earth,
>> He seeth all things duly.
>> Of simple hearts he knows the worth,
>> And those that seek him truly.
>> The humble man he setteth high
>> From out the mire of misery,
>> His feet he stablisheth newly.
> The barren woman sings his praise,
> Her joyful heart upraising.
> Her children serve him all their days
> In happiness and praising.
> Above the heavens his glory is,
> And they that seek to know his ways
> Find his great mercy amazing.[37]

---

37. Psalm 113 in metrical verse by John Calvin, *Strasbourg Psalter*, 1539, trans. K. W. Simpson, 1932, in
E. H. Geer, ed., *Hymnal for Colleges and Schools* (New Haven: Yale University Press, 1956).

CHAPTER SEVEN

THE SEER'S SIGN: RIVERS IN THE DESERT

Look, I am doing something new. Now it springs forth: can you not see it? I make a way in the wilderness, and rivers in the desert, for my chosen people to drink.

—ISAIAH 43:19–20

The prophet Isaiah evokes a reality most people can imagine. South Africa's Kalahari Desert is dry and empty over half the year, except for a few roaming beasts, much the way biblical writers describe Middle Eastern deserts. Then each January, summer storm clouds form over Angola's mountains hundreds of miles north. Southward their thunder cannot be heard; in fact, their rainwater never achieves the sea, because the seasonal Okavango River floods the Kalahari plain, spreading broad beyond any channel. Wherever the delta runs, life forms spring up that were invisible. Those thrive and interact until the flood ebbs, and they return into the earth to await next summer's storms. Rivers in the desert raise surprising life.

On the other hand, rivers in the desert bring death. Each summer, Utah's Zion National Park fills with hikers and campers who have voted Zion the most beautiful United States park. When afternoon thunder is heard far off, rangers call visitors quickly from the riverbeds, because flash floods come suddenly. Each season dozens of people drown who camped or hiked by pretty mountain streams, or whose cars did not cross a dry canyon in time.

I shall never forget my own first visit to Zion National Park, America's most dramatic wonders within an intimate landscape. Such awesome beauty attracts humans to hike and climb, and our race is prone to risk-taking. Psychologist Craig Anderson leads teenage groups to wonder at nature's power, and he records their response of self-abandonment. One wrote, "Today was the first time I ever went water rafting. I was totally scared about the rapids but I conquered my fears. I also jumped into the water even though I couldn't swim."[1] Rudolph Otto famously summarized such duple power as *mysterium fascinans et tremendum*, a mysterious energy that at once draws us and shakes us up.[2]

Water brings both life and death everywhere. Insects are nature's hardiest life forms, surviving nuclear radiation and all efforts to eradicate them. Throughout 250,000 years of hominid history we have extinguished only one insect, and that by accident. The Rocky Mountain locust was more terrible than biblical scourges, and decade after decade darkened skies across the prairie. "[O]ne famous sighting in 1875, estimated at 198,000 square miles (greater than the area of California), weighing 27.5 million tons, consisted of some 12.5 trillion insects—the greatest concentration of animals ever speculatively guessed, according to the *Guinness World Records*."[3] When farmers tried to beat them away, locusts ate their broom handles first, then the farmers' clothes, then every standing tree and plant, before disappearing for another deceptive decade's rest. But the dread Rocky Mountain locust had an unknown fatal flaw. The insects laid their eggs in dry creek beds along the prairie edges, just above spring runoff. Humans extending farmland by irrigation soaked those immemorial dry banks, until after two drowned hatching cycles the unconquerable Rocky Mountain locust became extinct.

The prophet Isaiah never knew the great prairie, but had surely heard of Egypt's double river. Blending Blue and White branches, the Nile crosses a burning desert where my plane could see it for a hundred miles. Each year the Nile overflows its banks, spreading a broad green ribbon through the yellow sand, and watering crops that fed ancient Egypt's whole populace and their trading partners beyond. Isaiah may have drawn his image from that famous natural wonder. Yet the Nile's bounty is double-faced: it also hides dread parasites. Humans are the sole hosts for blinding bilharzia worms, whose breeding cycle completes within twenty-four short hours. Such species have never been extinguished, because people cannot stay out of the Nile for a single day. Other streams further south give Africa's painful Guinea worm a similar longevity. Despite drugs that can eradicate it from humankind, it lives on in rivers to reinfect us, because it has found another host: dogs. The prophetic promise "I will do a new thing, I will make rivers to spring up in the desert" evokes both salvation and peril at once.

1. Reported by psychologist Craig L. Anderson, PhD, following a group study of awe in nature, 2016.

2. Rudolf Otto, *Das Heilige: Über das Irrationale in der Idee des Göttlichen und sein Verhältnis zum Rationalen* (Breslau: Trewendt & Granier, 1917).

3. *Wikipedia*, s.v. "Rocky Mountain locust," last modified December 30, 2018, *https://en.wikipedia.org/wiki/Rocky_Mountain_locust*.

The Blue Nile flows from Lake Tana, Ethiopia

Promises of God's Spirit have a like duple force. Hebrew scripture portrays prophecy as God's Spirit at work, and Christians pray for God's Spirit to bless and sanctify worshippers, bread, wine, water, oils, and every human labor, yet even at ordinations where the Spirit comes as promised, the church wins no control.[4] Presumptions to channel grace have brought disaster to churches, much as flash floods do. Schisms, inquisitions, and bloodshed ought by now to have warned us off such folly.

Moreover, God's Spirit is not nice. Unlike the bland Latin rendering "Spiritus," or a recent Trinitarian fashion feminizing it (the Hebrew gender is ambiguous), the Hebrew *ruach* is ever a violent wind. The opening Genesis creation story begins with earth as a lifeless mass awash in a dark sea, as a storm wind— *ruach elohim*, "God! what a wind it was!"—whips up the waters every which way. And then God said. . . .[5]

Eons afterward, Ezekiel summons the wild *ruach* (no mere "breath") blasting upright the scattered bones of Israel's fallen warriors.[6] Renewed conflict must follow, with more life and death yet ahead for those former slain, as they later lay ahead for prophet Jesus.

---

4. See chapter 4 on mystery.

5. Genesis 1:1–2:4. See chapter 4 on mystery, above.

6. Ezekiel 37:9–10.

The Inner Cause for Rage

Jesus's contemporary reputation for healing, and his reputation for offense, polarize gospel accounts of his ministry, where crowds echo opposing beliefs, sometimes both at once. Seventeenth-century English hymn writer Samuel Crossman framed a tantalizing question:

> Why? What hath my Lord done?
>
> What brings this rage and spite?
>
> He made the lame to run,
>
> He gave the blind their sight.
>
> Sweet injuries!
>
> Yet they at these
>
> Themselves displease
>
> And 'gainst him rise.[7]

Public opposition to Jesus, and his renegade's punishment imported from Rome's rival Persia, have drawn different explanations. Most tell us more about today's popular interpreters than about Jesus's life, for which we have scarce information outside the Bible. Anachronistic writers today conjure nineteenth-century nationalism, colonial oppression, collaboration and resistance, such as our newspapers teach us to recognize. Although Jesus actually pursued his short Galilee career under a native Jewish government outside direct Roman military rule, these writers speculate that he was a political agitator, or that occupied Jerusalem feared him as one. That reading dismisses gospel hints otherwise, as though the editors had scrubbed Jesus clean for a Roman Empire readership. But in face of so little evidence we must hear what the gospels tell.

Evangelists' apologies that God wanted a backsliding multitude to die, while a few hearers converted and lived, show the painful earmarks of later church struggles. Some apologies even overturn the very parables about God's creative power that they pretend to explain.[8] But the passions, our earliest stories, offer one very different explanation: Pilate knew that Jerusalem's religious leaders had delivered Jesus to him out of envy.[9] The Hebrew Bible assigns envy primacy among sinful motives (above pride, which medieval schoolmen

---

7. Samuel Crossman (1624–1683), "My song is love unknown."

8. For example, Matthew 13:10–15.

9. Mark 15:10 // Matthew 27:18.

preferred), and Mediterranean folk superstition still sells charms for warding off envy. Sociologist Joseph Campbell attributes American middle class conformity to a protective strategy: teaching children to attack themselves, and so forestall envious attacks by others.

Adrian van Kaam spies lethal envy behind the Genesis myth of humanity's first murder. Cain kills Abel because God welcomed Abel's sacrifice of meat animals, and not Cain's sacrifice of agricultural crops.[10] Jealous tension between herding and planting economies, repeated throughout world history, underlies that story. But Envy differs from jealousy. Jealousy wishes we had something that others enjoy; envy only wishes they did not enjoy it. The Cain and Abel myth epitomizes envious logic: since there is not enough reward for everyone to receive a fair share, we attack and destroy competitors, whether or not violence can augment our own share as a result. Among the many competitive advantages provoking envy—beauty, intelligence, birth, skill, wealth, power—van Kaam names as chief: originality. Originality creates an asset that does not exist otherwise, so no rival can compete with it. Only destruction can silence an original person's claim upon approval. The envious destroyer may not win assets, but can at least remove competitors.[11]

Jesus's popular reputation as a healer, and his regal *praüs* forbearance in the face of calumny,[12] might have made cause enough for envious attack, but his ministry was original as well. His contemporaries boasted prophets like John the Baptizer: most preached an eschatological future to prepare for; whereas Jesus's parables focused uniquely on God's reign already come upon the ready and unready alike, demanding our urgent response.[13] The Baptizer's fellow futurists included rebels armed against Roman dominance, whereas Jesus's most radical sayings advise accepting insults and serving *corvée* labor longer than forced to.[14] The Baptizer advocated reforms to lift the national ethic high, and upheld heroes all could respect, whereas Jesus made criminals and ornery women his favorite exemplars. The parables' rule-breaking heroes may explain what disquiet Jesus aroused. Over a dozen portray alert opportunists seizing quick chances like those God brings us, while respectable purists miss theirs.

---

10. Genesis 4:1–16.

11. Adrian van Kaam, *Envy and Originality* (Garden City: Doubleday, 1972), 21–23.

12. See chapter 3, "The Church's Sign: Baptizing the World."

13. See chapter 1, "Jesus's Sign: The Welcoming Table."

14. Matthew 5:39–42, Luke 6:29–30.

(a)	Mt 13:44	Hidden Treasure (the finder steals it, against law)
	Lk 16:1	Cheating Bailiff (defrauds his boss)
	Mt 25:14, Lk19:12	Entrusted Money (boss is the local crop thief)
	Mk 12:1, Mt 21:33, Lk 20:9	Peasant Rebellion (murderous mob)
	Lk 18:1	Unjust Judge (demands bribes from all)
	Mt 11:12, Lk 16:16	Violent People (aggressive opportunists)
	Mk 10:15, Mt18:3, Lk18:17	Grabby Child (not politely waiting his turn)
	Lk 15:11	Man with Two Sons (admits he wrongs the elder)
	Mt 13:33	Leaven (woman hoards it despite Passover)
	Mt 8:22, Lk 9:60	Not Burying the Dead (sacrilege)
	Mt 20:1	Generous Employer (defies public envy in order to get in his harvest on time)
	Mk 7:15	No External Action Defiles (breaks taboos)
	Lk 10:29	Good Samaritan (Samaritans deliberately defiled the Jerusalem temple at Passover)
	Luke 18:10–14	Tax Collector (admits his greedy wrongdoing)
(b)	Lk 19:1	Zacchaeus (tax gouger)
	Mk 7:24, Mt 15:28	Pagan Woman (classical enemy: a Philistine)
	Mk 5:34, Mt 9:22, Lk 8:48	Unclean Woman (defiles a Jewish teacher)

More stories show cunning responders as lawful winners, and fools as losing while bringing disaster upon those around them. Two protagonists were so upsetting that Christian preachers have shouted down the storyteller ever since. In both these parables, blunt repetition makes their moral flaws plain. Yet conventional homiletic has identified both men with God—contrary to Hebrew and Greek scriptures, which insist that God needs take nothing from humans, and plays no favorites (apart from his friend Moses).

In one, a leader going on a long trip summoned his underlings, and entrusted money to each according to his abilities. Most put their money to work earning more, but the one who received the least only buried his. When the boss returned, he rewarded each profit-maker with increased authority. But the last man defended his action: "I knew you are a hard man, reaping and gathering where you did not sow, and I was afraid and hid your money: here you have back what is yours." The boss answered, "You lazy bad servant! You knew that I reap and gather where I did not sow. At least you should have farmed my cash out with the usurers making Mafia loans, so I'd get it back with interest. Take his money away and give it to my most profitable agent!"

Undercutting pious later allegories, the boss entrusting his money to both wise and foolish underlings confirms twice that he is the local crop thief—the most pernicious and hated figure in any farming village.[15] He rewards astuteness, not ethics. Indeed, the usurers he approves are the farmers' second worst scourge, repeatedly driving their village and their nation into bankruptcy.

Again, preachers have smothered the most insidious of Jesus's stories under devotional pillows for millennia: the Man with Two Sons, commonly called "The Prodigal Son."[16]

A man had two sons. The younger asked his father, "Give me my inheritance." So he divided the property between them. Days later, the younger son took it all abroad, where he squandered it in loose living. When he'd spent it, a famine came and he was needy. So he took a local job feeding pigs—whose food he would gladly have eaten, but nobody gave him anything. Coming to himself, he said: My father's many hired servants have more than enough food, while I die of hunger. I will go tell my father, "I have sinned against heaven and before you, and can no longer be called your son. Treat me as one of your hired servants." But as he went, his father saw him a long way off, had compassion, ran and hugged and kissed him. The son began, "Father, I have sinned against heaven and before you, and can no longer be called your son." But the father interrupted: "Quick! Put our best robe on him, and shoes and a ring; and kill the fatted calf for a public feast, for this son of mine was dead and is alive again; he was lost and is found." And they began to celebrate.

When the older son came home from farm work and heard music and dancing, a servant explained: "Your brother has come, and your father has killed the fatted calf, for receiving him safe and sound." He angrily refused to go in, and when his father urged him he said: "For these many years I served you, never disobeying, while you never let me share even a baby goat with my friends. But this son of yours, who has devoured your living with whores—for him you killed our one fatted calf." The father answered, "My dear child,[17] you have indeed faithfully stood by me, and everything I still own is yours by law. But feasting suits us because your brother, who was as good as dead on his return, can now live, no longer lost to us."

Here conventional preachers take the wrong lesson. As Jeremias's and Perrin's careful commentaries prove, this parable offers no model of divine forgiveness: the father does not stand in allegorically for God, nor the elder son for Pharisees.[18]

---

15. Matthew 25:14–30 // Luke 19:12–27. Conventional title: "Parable of the Talents."

16. Luke 15:11–32.

17. Jeremias distinguishes the affectionate term *teknon*.

18. Joachim Jeremias, *The Parables of Jesus*, trans. Samuel Henry Hooke (London: SCM Press, 1958). Norman Perrin, *Rediscovering the Teaching of Jesus* (London: SCM Press, 1967), 94–98, author's translation.

Possibly carved out of a local scandal, every blow breaks hallowed custom. For reasons we do not know (besotted favoritism?), the father forsakes his duty to teach his sons wisdom, and allows his younger son to cash out early. Thereafter the whole remaining estate (family, hirelings, sharecroppers) must live on near half rations until the father dies. ("This son of yours who has devoured *your living* with whores. . . .") Jeremias writes that if a Middle Eastern youth today gamed inheritance law, impoverishing his household ("I have sinned against heaven and in your sight"), then returned empty-handed to shame them after tending unclean pigs, outraged villagers would kill him. But the father spies him coming from afar off and in a flash thinks how to avoid his likely murder. The father runs to meet him safely outside the village, interrupts his prepared speech about lethal wastefulness, vests him quickly with misleading tokens of wealthy homecoming (best robe, shoes, rings) and summons the village loudly to the biggest feast he can still afford ("the fatted calf") where well-fed diners will forfeit their claim on his life.

The elder son has lived loyally on bare rations and refuses to join his father's assault on customary morals. In a much-misunderstood reply, the father concedes that his elder son is right! "My dear child,[19] you have indeed faithfully stood by me, and everything I still own is yours by law. But feasting suits us because your brother, who was as good as dead on his return, can now live, no longer lost to us." We do not know how the younger son will live afterward; he may hope to hire himself out, but the older brother will hardly accept. Yet the father has got what he wants. By cheating his faithful son and hoodwinking the neighbors—just in time—he manipulates the local net of duty, revenge, and "protection" like a Sicilian Mafia capo. Far from symbolizing God's forgiveness, here a besotted bungler responds astutely to opportunity: Act quick, and justice and custom be damned! We can only imagine which among Jesus's hearers liked this story of so many customs broken—by all save the robbed faithful son, whom Christian preachers may pillory, but his father and Jesus do not.

Ambivalence and Freedom

Even worse than his seditious parables, Jesus himself crossed rising purity barriers to consort and dine with the unqualified. Here is the sole accusation that the synoptic gospels report as true, and not a false charge against him.[20] Jesus's hearers were either attracted or repelled; the mob was both, and could cry, "Crucify him!" Freud coined the word "ambivalence" to mean simultaneous positive and

---

19. Jeremias distinguishes the affectionate term *teknon*.

20. Mark 2:16, Matthew 9:11, Luke 5:30. See chapter 1.

negative feelings toward the same object. Ambivalence springs up at every human encounter with power. History offers provocative examples of power raising life and death at once, like a desert river. For example, modern hopes that religions can live in harmony are our loftiest inheritance from the Mongol marauders— well above the violin bow, stirrup, eyeglasses, dinner fork, and compound archery bow. Mongol tribes of three religions followed Genghis Khan's mystic vision. One third (the Keraits) were Syrian Christians, including Kublai Khan's mother Sorghaghtani. Their united armies would massacre cities that resisted them; but any that accepted Mongol rule and taxes might practice their own religion freely thereafter.[21]

By contrast, Arab invaders converted defeated peoples at sword-point, as Mongol looters had not done. Persia's horrified Il-Khan Hulegu, a traditional Mongol animist with a Christian wife, sent her bishop Rabban Bar Saúma from Baghdad seeking Western allies to defend his religious plurality against Arab armies. The pope and European kings welcomed Bar Saúma graciously, but sent no troops. (Would our news today read differently if they had?) Sure enough, a century later the Turk Tamerlane—a fake Mongol, so never titled Khan—converted to Islam and piled mountains of skulls outside central Asia's Buddhist, Christian, and Manichee monasteries. Genghis Khan's universal vision did endure in Kublai's China[22] and in India, where Mughal (Mongol) emperors like Jahangir hosted religious rivals for theological discussions, some heated, all safe.

The Mongol Khans' neutral religious state—the world's first—arose just when Europe's rulers began crusades, inquisitions, pogroms, and exclusions lasting nearly a millennium. Outside India and China, the Mongol religious peace disappeared like watery Kalahari denizens vanishing into the desert when the life-giving streams dried up. As in the Kalahari heat, it long seemed no Mongol progeny had survived.

Yet just like the Kalahari, a diverse Europe welled up in a desert flash flood three centuries later, and from a new windstorm gathered in Italian mountains. This book's first chapter retold how our modern concept of history began with art historians distinguishing the Italian "Renaissance" era.[23] Fifteenth-century artists recognized a gap between past peoples and

21. John Man, *Genghis Khan: Life, Death and Resurrection* (London: Bantam, 2004). Jack Weatherford, *Genghis Khan and the Making of the Modern World* (New York: Three Rivers Press, 2004).

22. John Man, *Kublai Khan: From Xanadu to Superpower* (London: Bantam, 2006).

23. Jacob Burckhardt, *The Civilization of the Renaissance in Italy*, trans. S. G. C. Middlemore (London: Kegan Paul & Co., 1878), and Johan Huizinga, *The Waning of the Middle Ages*, trans. F. Hopman (Harmondsworth, Middlesex, England: Penguin Books, 1922).

themselves, and painted antiquity as a world unlike medieval conventions. Northern humanists like Erasmus soon followed, setting aside medieval Latin to translate scripture direct from ancient texts. Their mistrust of hallowed authorities changed the world for us. A bare century beforehand, Jan Hus had gone to the stake; whereas Luther with like ideas did not. And though Emperor Charles V died fearing God would punish him for failing to burn Luther at the 1495 Diet of Worms, that Diet showed the new mentality ascendant, popular, and irreversible. For two more bloody centuries, Catholics and Protestants did battle over opposing concepts of inspiration; yet both sides addressed questions we recognize today.

Prophetic Responsibility

Now a flash flood from another more recent storm may yet drown both aging rivals. The twentieth-century downpour of Marxist idealism flooded public awareness with secular critique—and then suddenly ebbed, stranding social justice for churches to preach about. Churches responded like life forms vying for Kalahari savannah territory. America's Civil Rights Movement transformed a few conservative backwaters into liberal currents: Episcopalians, for example. But their opponents channeled grudges into a torrent of political reaction. *Ruach* blows throughout our world, disruptive as well as creative. All who hope for justice and peace must league together. Here is today's most urgent reason for building broad worship participation: like Jesus and other biblical prophets, our congregational activists and leaders will be layfolk.

Televangelists claim wrongly that God's mysterious plan promises the faithful personal salvation or profit. Chapter 4 shows how since the seventh century BCE, Jewish and Christian preachers have bound worship up with justice and generosity toward the poor. Amos, the earliest literary prophet, welds those causes together by the hottest rhetorical argument in the whole Bible.[24] His contemporary Levitical "holiness code" commands much the same ethic within its recital of cultic rubrics.[25]

Christian, Jewish, and Muslim writers have tightened that moral union ever since. Gregory Nyssen's brother Basil of Caesarea quipped, "Those extra shoes in your closet—they belong to the poor," and he coined the patristic era's most radical motto, "Property is theft!" (Karl Marx, unaware, mocked Prudhomme for saying so, but the Catholic Prudhomme had quoted St. Basil on purpose.)

---

24. Amos 1–2.

25. Leviticus 19–22.

Christian lay voices chimed in with mixed success. Ukraine's Nikolai Gogol' was one lay author of early nineteenth-century Slavic religious renewal. His worship commentary painted devotional colors. Yet like Lermontov and Dostoyevsky, Gogol's novels and plays highlighted urgent social crises. *Dead Souls* pilloried Russian slavery (called serfdom), and helped bring emancipation in 1861. Sadly enough, the glories that Gogol' extolled in Orthodox worship could not suffice for the author's countrymen, or even for himself. He emigrated to Italy. And after eight decades of anemic reform, an atheist revolution castigated Russia's church for the piquant failure so prophetic in Gogol's parody—

And what a devout man Ivan Ivanovich is! Every Sunday he puts on his coat and goes to church. When he goes in Ivan Ivanovich bows in all directions and then usually installs himself in the choir and sings a very good bass. When the service is over, Ivan Ivanovich cannot bear to go away without making the round of the beggars. He would, perhaps, not care to go through this tedious task, if he were not impelled to it by his innate kindliness. "Hello, poor woman!" he commonly says, seeking out the most crippled beggar woman in a tattered gown made up of patches. "Where do you come from, poor thing?"

"I've come from the hamlet, kind sir; I've not had a drop to drink nor a morsel to eat for three days; my own children turned me down."

"Poor creature! What made you come here?"

"Well, kind sir, I came to ask alms, in case anyone would give me a copper for bread."

"Hm! Then I suppose you want bread?" Ivan Ivanovich usually inquires.

"Yes I do! I am as hungry as a dog."

"Hm!" Ivan Ivanovich usually replies, "so perhaps you would like meat too?"

"Yes, and I'll be glad of anything your honor may be giving me."

"Hm! Is meat better than bread?"

"Is it for a hungry beggar to be choosy? Whatever you kindly give will be greatly appreciated." With this the old woman usually holds out her hand.

"Well, go along and God be with you," says Ivan Ivanovich. "What are you staying for? I am not beating you, am I?"

And after addressing similar inquiries to a second and a third, he at last returns home or goes to drink a glass of vodka with his neighbor, Ivan Nikiforovich, or to see the judge or the police captain.[26]

---

26. "Tale of How Ivan Ivanovich Quarreled with Ivan Nikiforovich" (1835), *The Collected Tales and Plays of Nikolai Gogol* (1809–1852), Leonard J. Kent ed. (New York: Random House, 1964), 375ff.

CHAPTER EIGHT

THE PEACEMAKER'S SIGN: RECONCILIATION

We cry peace and cry peace, and there is no peace. There is no peace because there are no peacemakers. There are no makers of peace because the making of peace is at least as costly as the making of war—at least as exigent, at least as disruptive, at least as liable to bring disgrace and prison and death in its wake.

—DANIEL BERRIGAN, SJ[1]

The critics are quite right in supposing that a fully satisfied human, with no failures, no sense of wrongdoing, no griefs, no fears, no longing for the eternal, would have no occasion to look to God. But it is they who are indulging in fantasy when they imagine such a creature and suppose it to be human.[2]

—PSYCHOANALYST STANLEY LEAVY[2]

The Beatitudes' *praüs* (purposeful forbearance)[3] overcomes an opposite behavior, with examples easy to find: revenge. In some Mediterranean cultures as in American gang life, revenge carries the extra freight of sacred duty; but in fact among many animals alongside hominids, it is commonplace. Neuroscientists locate the desire for revenge in one of the oldest human brain areas, the dorsal striatum, and "researchers estimate that 20 percent of all homicides worldwide are motivated by revenge." Among social-bonded species (chimpanzees, crows, wolves, dolphins) "revenge serves the group by protecting individuals from victimization."[4] European Renaissance culture enshrined

---

1. Quoted by Jim Wallis in *Sojourners*, August 2016, 18.

2. Leavy, *In the Image of God*, 68.

3. See chapter 3 on Baptism.

4. Michael McCullough, *Beyond Revenge: The Evolution of the Forgiveness Instinct* (San Francisco: Jossey-Bass, 2008), chap. 2. James Thornton, "Revenge," *Men's Health*, September 2015, pp.110–118, summarizes other recent scientific publications.

revenge. Shakespeare made vengeance his dramatic engine throughout *Hamlet*, *Romeo and Juliet*, and *Richard III*, where it replaces the Greek tragic motive of *areté*, heroic pride. In a triumphant musical chorus that disquiets audiences today, the darker of two endings to Mozart's opera *Don Giovanni* celebrates damnation as a "poetic justice" inherited from Tirso de Molina's play 150 years before.[5]

By contrast, the mental work of assessing costs and benefits belongs to a later-developed brain area, the medial prefrontal cortex, and this area reckons that revenge pays off poorly. "People who are given the chance for payback think it will make them feel good, but most actually feel bad afterward."[6] Among beasts, an instinct for forgiveness boasts biological evidence, and so may be a widespread evolutionary adaptation.[7] But while Homer's *Iliad* shows Priam successfully persuading Achilles to release fallen Hector's body, the tragedies upheld Greek religious thought by affording forgiveness no place. Exploring that gentler path was an innovation of Renaissance literature. Shakespeare's *Winter's Tale* and *Pericles* exalted it for their dramatic solution, a pattern that baroque dramatists would echo. The reconciliation ending Beaumarchais's *Marriage of Figaro* provided Mozart one of his most popular opera plots. The greatest drama of Spain's Golden Age, Calderón's *La Vida es Sueño* (*Life Is a Dream*), turns centrally on forgiveness, and even today rivals *Hamlet* for Spanish productions.[8]

On a world scale, perhaps, peacemaking takes tougher calculations, and responds slower to ethical argument. Harvard/Radcliffe researcher Helena Meyer-Knapp finds that nations typically turn toward peace after suffering military losses and political upset. Forgiveness can wait a generation or more afterward, as Americans found in the Vietnam War.

> Ending a war is always a choice, and no particular timing makes it inevitable. The choice rests in the hands of the weaker, most likely to "lose." The stronger ones must keep fighting, until the weaker ones conclude the time has come to stop. And the choice rests in the hands of a very small group of political leaders, often a new generation of leaders who have ousted the ones most heavily invested in combat.[9]

5. Tirso de Molina, *El Burlador de Sevilla y convidado de Piedra*, 1616, pub. 1630, re-written by José Zorrilla as *Don Juan Tenorio: Drama religioso-fantástico en dos partes*, 1844.

6. Timothy Wilson, quoted in Thornton, "Revenge."

7. McCullough, chap. 6 in *Beyond Revenge*.

8. Pedro Calderón de la Barca, *La Vida es Sueño*, 1635.

9. Helena Meyer-Knapp, *Dangerous Peace-Making* (Olympia, WA: Peacemaker Press, 2003).

God's Wrath and Friendship

The Hebrew Bible projects both human revenge and forgiveness upon God. Far from reconciling those instincts, the editors may mount them side by side. When direct contradiction results, their later theology of divine mercy literally over-writes more ancient deterrent threats.[10] Yet some prophetic warnings of divine wrath still appear unedited, reserving compensating promises for other passages. Revenge predominates in the Canaan conquest stories. God's ban on Amale-kites condemns every living being to destruction: an explicit vengeance—not for their violence, but for the contrary: their defensive dodge of confrontation.[11] Saul's initial failure to destroy them cancels his divine mandate to rule Israel, so the prophet Samuel brutally finishes his job. For at least this early biblical writer, blocking God's mysterious plan offers cause enough for genocide.

More ingeniously, however, Hebrew scripture's editors build a narrative convention to downplay earlier legends of God's revenge. Later called *halakah* (walking about), this form typically tells how a human teacher acquired his most distinctive teaching, often by divine correction of some lower understanding. Within the Bible story, *halakah* appears first at Genesis 19, where Lot bargains with God to rescue the sinners of Sodom. Granting pardon for smaller and smaller numbers, God finally allows that should Lot find one single righteous person at Sodom, all will be spared. Lot cannot find one, and the city is destroyed. Again, at Exodus 32 and Deuteronomy 9, Moses bargains likewise with God, only this time he successfully rescues the Israelites who worshipped the Golden Calf.

This second *halakah* was inserted during the same era as Joel's novel prophecy of divine mercy,[12] and it reflects recent scandal when King Jeroboam set up a bull image outside the Jerusalem temple.[13] Some modern readers have misread both stories as evidence for God's change of mind. On the contrary, both bargaining rituals employ a common storyteller's technique to emphasize how inexhaustibly generous God's patience always proves. Daily bargaining is ubiquitous in the Middle East even today. The Hebrew editors likely chose a familiar *halakah* form because their new doctrine was controversial; pagan cults knew nothing like it. So they portrayed God apparently learning through

---

10. Exodus 34:6–8, cf Deuteronomy 7:9–10.

11. 1 Samuel 15.

12. Joel 2:13–14, a text that editors reinserted ten more times around the Pentateuch. "God is gracious and compassionate, slow to anger and rich in steadfast love *(chesed)*, and relents from inflicting disaster" (NJB). See chapter 1, on Jesus's claim to orthodoxy.

13. 1 Kings 12:28.

argument. Both these stories actually emphasize God's royal *praüs* virtue, holding to long-term purpose and never distracted by anger.[14]

Ancient readers wondered how Moses's bargaining succeeded where Lot and Abraham, though entrusted with God's promises, failed. Rabbinical commentators pointed to the patriarchs' misdeeds, saying those may have compromised their spiritual power, but Gregory of Nyssa's final book, *The Life of Moses*, names a different ideal to guide humankind:[15]

> These things concerning the perfect virtuous life . . . we have written briefly for you, tracing the life of the great Moses in outline like a pattern of beauty, so that each one of us might copy the beautiful image shown to us by imitating his way of life. What more trustworthy witness that Moses did attain the perfection which was possible would be found than the divine voice which said to him: I have known you more than all others? It is also shown in the fact that he is named the "friend of God" by God himself,[16] and that [Moses,] by preferring to perish with all the rest if the Divine One did not through his good will forgive their errors, stayed God's wrath against the Israelites [worshipping the Golden Calf]. God averted his judgment so as not to grieve his friend. All such things are a clear testimony and demonstration of the fact that the life of Moses did ascend the highest mount of perfection.
>
> . . . It is time for you to look to that example, and transferring [it] to your own life, be known by God and become God's friend. This is true perfection: not to avoid a wicked life because like slaves we servilely fear punishment, nor to do good because we hope for rewards, as if cashing in on the virtuous life by some business-like deal. On the contrary, disregarding all those things we do hope for, and have been promised us, we regard falling from God's friendship as the only thing dreadful and we consider becoming God's friend the only thing worthy of honor and desire. This as I have said, is the perfection of life.[17]

---

14. See chapter 3, on the Matthean Beatitudes.

15. Gregory quotes the Septuagint at Exodus 33:12, 17.

16. "YHWH would speak to Moses face to face, as a man talks with his friend. . . . Moses said to YHWH, 'How can it be known that you, your people and I, have found favor with you, except by your going with us?' YHWH said to Moses, 'This request too, which you have just made, I will carry out, because you have found favor with me and you are my intimate friend." Exodus 33:11, 17.

17. *The Life of Moses*, AD 395, trans. Abraham Malherbe and Everett Ferguson (New York: Paulist Press, 1978). Paul's Galatian and Roman letters argue differently: that by breaking and thereby superseding Moses's Law, Jesus returns to Abraham's primal style of faith. Yet Paul insists that the Law's commandments remain "holy and just and good" (Romans 7:12).

Christian preaching puts pardon at the gospel's heart, and the passion texts assign explicit forgiveness to Jesus. Since the passions carry our earliest narrative material about him, it is tempting to trust their details, including Jesus's words quoted there. But we receive these words already highly edited, as when Mark and Matthew elaborate Luke's plain report that Jesus died with an inarticulate cry.[18] The elaborators replace that cry with the opening verse of Psalm 22: "My God, my God, why have you forsaken me?"—a psalm that ends in triumph, as readers and singers knew. Indeed, all Jesus's reported words from the cross echo sermons, not least "Father forgive them, for they know not what they do."[19] We must sift verbatim pardons here and in the healing stories with caution.

On the other hand, Jesus's most socially radical words in the gospel texts swear off retribution, and imply something like pardon toward those in power who wrong us. "When slapped, turn the other cheek," and "Give away twice the clothing that justice claims," and "Walk an extra mile beyond what authorities force you to."[20] Their authenticity rating is high because these sayings contradict commonplace advice, and no known contemporary teacher taught so. They exhort us to *praüs* behavior in face of foes; and they fit Jesus's repeated demurrals of kingly power throughout his ministry and capital trial.[21] Thus, these sayings confirm Matthew's third Beatitude as an accurate color for Jesus's portrait, possibly the most faithful tint of all.

Forgiving and Forgiveness

> God will forgive me: it's His trade.
>
> —DYING WORDS OF POET HEINRICH HEINE, 1856

After two millennia of preaching, we can only regret how rigorists have overturned those texts, and focused people's prayers on receiving forgiveness instead. George McCauley, SJ, reports a consistent classroom experience. Under the chalkboard title "Sacrament of Reconciliation," he sketches two men, one kneeling before the other who wears a priest's stole. Asked what is happening there, the students invariably reply: "The kneeling man is confessing

---

18. Mark 15:34, Matthew 27:46, Luke 23:46.

19. Luke 23:34. This verse does not appear in all manuscripts, possibly omitted through anti-Semitism. But the parallel of Stephen's death at Acts 7:60 suggests this was in Luke's original.

20. Matthew 5:38–42.

21. See chapter 2 on authority.

his sins and receiving pardon." They never say: "The church is forgiving that man's sins." Yet the New Testament contains countless exhortations to forgive, while only two bid us seek one another's pardon. Even the Lord's Prayer gives forgiveness first, an implied condition for receiving it.[22]

Oxford Bishop Kenneth Kirk's classic work *The Vision of God*[23] chronicles the long history of Penitential customs East and West, which replaced ready forgiving and re-cast the Church as a rigorous judge dealing out pardons in exchange for reparations from sinners—that is, from all human beings. Here rises the final barrier to communion that most Christians know. Borrowing a single gospel verse—"Whose sins you forgive, God forgives, and whose sins you retain, God retains"[24]—churches have erected a turnpike blocking the baptized from Communion, which swings open only upon repeated absolutions. This barrier opens in response to sinners' remorse, professed individually or corporately.

Although Martin Luther insisted that Jesus's cross had won universal pardon, and that clergy only "declared" it before Communion, nevertheless Lutheran and Anglican layfolk perceive an official visa stamped at this boundary, much as "conservative" Roman Catholics have done since medieval times. Kirk fingers monastic discipline as the maquette that shaped centuries of Communion practice, replacing the more ancient episcopal absolution for heinous crimes. The twentieth century's steep decline in monastic vocations has left a gap that ritual engineers may bridge otherwise. The hoary "Sacrament of Penance," misunderstood just as McCauley sketches it, has not withstood cultural change. More Christians come forward to receive Christ's Body and Blood today, but fewer seek individual absolution and advice from a confessor. Thereby Christians lose a regular opening for spiritual counsel, and turn perforce to paid counselors instead. Some Eastern bodies still uphold monastic discipline by exhorting people to confession and then to communion at every Eucharist; but that full régime has shown only modest success in scattered places. Spiritual counsel comes by other paths today, not necessarily in church.

---

22. In Matthew's Greek, our forgiving appears in the perfect tense for completed prior action. Matthew 6:12 // Luke 11:2. (A vote from Q would be hypothetical, like that document itself. See chapter 1, note 20.)

23. Kenneth Kirk, *The Vision of God: The Christian Doctrine of the Summum Bonum* (New York: Harper & Row, 1931; New York: Harper Torchbooks, 1966).

24. John 20:23. The passive voice is a conventional Semitic periphrasis for God's action.

Furthermore, active forgiving makes a poor disciplinary requirement. Methodist pastoral counselor John Patton argues that forgiveness comes by an inward personal process that church authority can encourage but cannot command.[25] So churches err by telling people they ought to forgive their injurers, thereby adding a weight of obligation to their sense of hurt. From years of interviews, Patton finds that actual forgiveness happens when people discover that they *have forgiven* their foes, and have abandoned their desire to keep apart from them. We may note that the Lord's Prayer implies just this, when we ask God to forgive *as we have forgiven*.[26] Tallying up wrongs from either side is hopeless, and will never prove who owes whom reparation. Instead, forgiveness creates a new world of relations and actions. Perhaps that is why Matthew's nine Beatitudes do not make forgiving a duty for suffering churches: instead, Matthew's expanded blessing on the persecuted promises surprising rejoicing, through all the virtues that Jesus's life and death exemplified.

David Sanger

Archbishop Desmond Tutu, icon by Mark Dukes

The twentieth century closed with people of varied faiths wanting reconciliation on a worldwide scale. In Argentina, Bosnia, and Cambodia today, survivors live in daily contact with their former torturers and the murderers of their families and friends.[27] Following the fall of South African apartheid, President Nelson Mandela and Anglican Bishop Desmond Tutu developed a "Truth and Reconciliation Committee" to forestall a bloodbath of revenge. Local

---

25. John Patton, *Is Human Forgiveness Possible? A Pastoral Care Perspective* (Nashville: Abingdon, 1985).

26. For Greek grammar, see note 22, above, and chapter 1 note 20.

27. Robert M. Sapolsky, "War and Peace," in *Behave: The Biology of Humans at Our Best and Worst* (New York: Penguin Press, 2017), chap. 17, 638–642. Truth and reconciliation processes have made peace, but often without mutual satisfaction.

persecutors, imprisoners, torturers, and murderers who came forward to admit publicly what they had done were released from punishment to reenter the new South African society. Thereby they released their countrymen in turn. Many victims' families have embraced their former foes, sometimes but not always with tears on both sides. Other nations have been less daring, and their people carry yet the weight of personal resentment and stealthy retribution. It may be still too soon to assess the Truth and Reconciliation Commission's political success; but twenty-five years of public peace have given that nation hope.

The emotions attending reconciliation have theological value. Thomas Aquinas wrote that "religion begins in awe, and ends in affection." Only affection triumphs truly over superstition—the Protestant Reformers' goal— enabling worshippers to feel awe without dreading God's punishment, or their own failings and low self-worth. Better yet: affection leads naturally to peace-making, and thereafter to conversion of life.

> If we think only of ourselves, forget about other people, then our minds occupy very small area. Inside that small area, even tiny problem appears very big. But the moment you develop a sense of concern for others, you realize that, just like ourselves, they also want happiness; they also want satisfaction. When you have this sense of concern, your mind automatically widens. At this point, your own problems, even big problems, will not be so significant. The result? Big increase in peace of mind. So, if you think only of yourself, only your own happiness, the result is actually less happiness. You get more anxiety, more fear.[28]

Entering a Byzantine, Syrian, or Russian church today, we see layfolk greeting the saints painted on walls like beloved forebears, many people prostrating themselves with emotion and kissing the icons, while the clergy and choir carry out ritual actions and sing proper texts. Most famous perhaps, the icon of *Christos Pantokratôr* centers ceilings: a bearded Jesus, holding a book, looks down at worshippers. That image derives in fact from classical portraits of Zeus. Medieval Russians mistakenly rendered the Greek title *Vsyederzhytel'*, or Almighty. So Western art historians describe an imperial commander who reproves awed believers cowering below. Reading Byzantine letters and documents directly, however, Thomas Mathews discovers instead a warm sense of

---

28. The XIV Dalai Lama. See also the Dalai Lama, Desmond Tutu, and Douglas Abrams, *The Book of Joy* (New York: Penguin Avery Random House, 2016), passim.

reassurance, inspired from the second common meaning of the verb *kratein*: not to rule, but to hold,[29] so *Pantokrator* means all-holding. Byzantines entering a church saw Christ's image overhead and felt as moderns might sing with feeling: "He's got the whole world / in his hands. . . ." Icons of Mary and Jesus painted in restrained Hellenistic style likewise carry warm titles evoking a mother's inexhaustible love for believers, who return their own love in prayer. Eastern Easter liturgies typically erupt in threefold kisses among the congregation and clergy. (Western Christians exchange the same joy informally when leaving their Christmas and Easter celebrations.)

The Kiss of Peace

Christian worship renewal has revived one powerful scriptural gesture—even more powerful, some say, than renewing the Western vernaculars was. That gesture is the liturgical Kiss of Peace. Whether enacted with a Greek threefold buss, a Yankee handshake, or a California bear hug, the Kiss actualizes here and now the very world that Christians pray for. So it is Jesus's teaching enacted in palpable common touch.

That is hardly a modern innovation. Four of Paul's letters mention a worshipful Kiss, which shortly appears in baptismal documents.[30] In second-century churches, neophytes baptized naked were clothed afresh and brought to a minister (typically a bishop) who blew into their mouths the way Genesis 2 shows God blowing wild *ruach* wind into Adam, giving him life. Predictably enough, those newly baptized can become troublemakers as Adam did. The editors describe God disappointed often enough in Adam's behavior—and soon Israel's behavior—but never surprised.

At the liturgical Kiss, three spiritual changes happen at once. First, isolated worshippers turn to embrace others around them, and become a creative body—a potentially disruptive body, like the fallen Israelite soldiers in Ezekiel's vision.[31] Second, the Kiss actively realizes forgiveness. The New Testament often summons our forgiveness, rarely if ever exhorting us to receive it. Conscientious worshippers know we must kiss people we otherwise avoid, and so

---

29. Thomas F. Mathews, chap. 2 in *Byzantium: From Antiquity to the Renaissance* (New York: Abrams, 1998, 2010).

30. Edward L. Phillips, chap.2 in *The Ritual Kiss in Early Christian Worship* (Cambridge: Grove, 1996).

31. Ezekiel 37:10.

weaken our desire to remain apart from them. Counselor John Patton finds that shift is pardon's essential core.[32]

Third and deepest in biblical terms, this concrete ritual gesture dissolves the poison of envy. Envy, not pride, is the Bible's original sin, whereby Cain kills Abel.[33] Envious thoughts spring up constantly during church services as everywhere else—even Pilate recognized them[34]—and cannot be stifled by thought control. But the act of hugging or kissing people whom we envy can convert resentment into fellow feeling, and into pleasure at embracing our fellows' virtues—including their originality and other excellencies we admire. McCullough chronicles the changes that willing collaboration achieves between rival gangs long practiced at verbal insult, physical violence, and revenge.[35]

Over millennia, the Kiss of Peace has fit into Christian services at many points. Among those, Alexander Schmemann argued for a liturgical order differing only slightly from standard Western renewal: the People's Prayers; then the procession bringing bread and wine to the table; followed by the Peace; and immediately the Preface, "Lift up your hearts." In consultation, Schmemann admitted he had found no ancient ritual written exactly this way, nevertheless he was convinced it showed the natural ritual sequence.[36] Indeed, from Robert Taft's study published shortly afterward, we conclude that it developed just so for congregations at Constantinople.[37]

Matthew's biblical text also presages Schmemann's intuited order. "If you bring your gift to the altar, and there recall that your brother has anything against you, leave your gift there at the altar, go first and be reconciled with your brother, and then come and offer your gift." Remarkably, this is the sole ritual action series the New Testament enjoins, and may reflect worship at Matthew's church.[38] By contrast, reports of Jesus's Last Supper, which the synoptic

---

32. Patton, *Is Human Forgiveness Possible?* See note 25, above.

33. Genesis 4:1–16. See chapter 7, "The Seer's Sign: Rivers in the Desert."

34. Mark 15:10 // Matthew 27:18 "Pilate knew that it was out of envy that they had handed Jesus over." NAB translation.

35. *Beyond Revenge*, chapter 9 on the "Robbers Cave Study."

36. Consultation with the author at St. Vladimir's Seminary, Tuckahoe, NY, 1973.

37. Robert Taft, *The Great Entrance* (Rome: Pontifical Oriental Institute, 1975). In Byzantine use the minister prays simultaneously with hymns and litanies sung by the congregation or choir. Hence "offertory prayers" did not actually interrupt Byzantine laypeople's course, which followed Schmemann's intuition.

38. Matthew 5:23–24. Some translations preserve the verb *prosférēis*, a discrete action of bringing. Armenian and Byzantine ritual feature a dramatic procession with gifts to the altar table, a ceremony lately becoming more common in Western renewal. Chapter 2, above, proposes this ritual creates a natural liturgical symbol for justice.

editors copied from 1 Corinthians 11, presume the commonplace phases of a Hellenistic symposium. Being commonplace, they cannot prove Jesus's behavior sequence that night in the way Renaissance reformers supposed.[39]

Therefore St. Gregory's Church adopted Schmemann's order of events—a mild change in rubrics, but a strong change in congregational feeling. The Kiss of Peace and an immediate Preface dissolve visitors' shyness, and move the whole congregation emotionally upward to the Great Thanksgiving Prayer and climactic Communion. Moreover, our tactile human intercourse at the Peace enlivens our physical experience of communion with Christ in his Body and Blood. Like Genesis's *ruach*, grace will spread uncontrollably thereafter. As Annie Dillard writes:

> On the whole, I do not find Christians, outside of the catacombs, sufficiently sensible of conditions. Does anyone have the foggiest idea what sort of power we so blithely invoke? Or, as I suspect, does no one believe a word of it? The churches are children playing on the floor with their chemistry sets, mixing up a batch of TNT to kill a Sunday morning. It is madness to wear ladies' straw hats and velvet hats to church; we should all be wearing crash helmets. Ushers should issue life preservers and signal flares; they should lash us to our pews. For the sleeping god may wake someday and take offense, or the waking god may draw us out to where we can never return.[40]

---

39. (See chapter 1.) In John's Last Supper story (13:14) Jesus does command imitative washing of one another's feet, but without specific ritual placement.

40. Annie Dillard, *Teaching a Stone to Talk* (New York: Harper & Row, 1982), 52–53.

CHAPTER NINE

THE HEARER'S SIGN: THE WORSHIP YEAR

Parable of the Old Man and the Young

So Abram rose, and clave the wood, and went,
And took the fire with him, and a knife.
And as they sojourned both of them together,
Isaac the first-born spake and said, My Father,
Behold the preparations, fire and iron,
But where the lamb for this burnt-offering?
Then Abram bound the youth with belts and straps,
and builded parapets and trenches there,
And stretchèd forth the knife to slay his son.
When lo! an angel called him out of heaven,
Saying, Lay not thy hand upon the lad,
Neither do anything to him. Behold,
A ram, caught in a thicket by its horns;
Offer the Ram of Pride instead of him.
But the old man would not so, but slew his son,
And half the seed of Europe, one by one.

—WILFRED OWEN, 25, KILLED IN ACTION SEVEN DAYS
BEFORE THE ARMISTICE, 1918

Origen in the third century set the Bible at the heart of Christian teaching, where it stays. Other faiths' theological methods, equally sophisticated, may comment upon tradition or metaphysic first. Reading scripture first determines both our conservation and reform—sometimes even revolution.

Historical research today focuses upon the Christian calendar: what it is for, how it began, what it means to churches who disagree about so many other

things. Some Renaissance Reformers tried to dispense with festivals and seasons altogether, noting that the Old Testament prophets and New Testament
writers discount those anyhow.[1] Many of their modern Evangelical heirs shun
official reading plans, preferring fresh inspiration each week: what the preacher
should say, and what Bible passages will lend support. They can hardly feel surprise when favorite Bible selections recur Sunday after Sunday. But can they
think that gives scripture a full voice?

Religious calendars have typically sprung up from two independent root
systems. Hebrew Bible feasts traced the cyclical events of agricultural life: when
the crops were best planted, when the lambs were born, when the harvest was
in. Each festival called up thanksgiving prayer and future hope. But the Christian calendar most churches now use tracks a different course. Lutheran historian Max Johnson pictures the start of our familiar Christian year, "Out of
the original kerygmatic sea, the events of Jesus's life first washed ashore on the
Jewish feast of Pentecost," and churches then distributed those around periodic
beachheads of readings—not agricultural tasks—by processes that historians
trace today.[2] Thus Pentecost, before Easter, is the Christian source festival.
Even Good Friday came later, reflecting how the gospels tie Jesus's execution
somehow to Jewish Passover, which conflates agricultural and pastoral festivals.
No one knows which months (or years!) Jesus was actually born or taught or
healed the sick. Our readings cycle originated otherwise. Its growth was unsys-
tematic, and saw conflicts among congregations.

Recent efforts to explain our complex worship year as naturally based, like
the Hebrew calendar, are anachronistic. For example, Victorians speculated
that the Roman Christmas date near the December solstice mirrored the pagan
Feast of the Unconquered Sun, but that feast was actually invented by "Apos-
tate" Emperor Julian to override already popular Italian Christian celebrations.
And nothing significant happens on either summer or winter solstice day that
a Christmas feast might baptize. Weather shifts float by weeks afterward upon
ocean currents that neither biblical nor pagan peoples knew about. Life in
opposite hemispheres counters every shift. In all cultures the real "dying" or
"birth" of the natural year obeys agricultural urgencies: new planting (China,
Greece) or the harvest (Palestine, Ethiopia). Through the eighteenth century,
European civil calendars turned not in January but with the spring rains—a

---

1. For example Amos 8:5, Isaiah 1:11–17, 1 Thessalonians 5:1.

2. Max Johnson, in a discussion paper for the Early History of Liturgy Seminar, North Academy of Liturgy, 2002.

natural event near the Christian Annunciation festival—which is why North Americans still pay taxes in April. Our worship year is simply (or not very simply!) a lectionary, a way of reading the Bible. Groups of readings may be styled "seasons" because they cycle through the solar rounds as natural seasons do; but they have no such reality as Winter and Summer have.

Christians and Jews commemorate ancient events by reading scripture together, and recall most without reenacting them. Twentieth-century liturgist Gregory Dix labeled such purely mental recalling *anamnesis*, by contrast with *mimesis*, the imitative re-enactment characterizing parish Christmas pageants.[3] Typical parish Christmas festivities feature both kinds of remembering in a single service. Following Dix, reformers stress *anamnesis* today as liturgy's proper core action, leaving *mimesis* to folk custom.

For at least one week of the year, nevertheless, liturgical churches follow mimetically the Bible story of Jesus's Last Supper, arrest, trial, and execution. Some Western villagers reenact Passion plays throughout Lent. *Penitentes* of New Mexico vie for the honor of physical crucifixion at one of those. Popular *mimesis* began in fourth-century Jerusalem, with crowds tracking Jesus's footsteps from place to place daily, as a conflated passion story might dictate, and meditating with deep emotion on acts they heard recounted at every station. We may contrast enacted Passion Week *mimesis* with Jewish synagogues' *anamnesis* of salvation at Purim. There raucous ratchets drown out hateful Haman's name every time the reader speaks it; and afterwards all munch tasty three-corner cookies representing his hat; but only schoolchildren replicate the Bible story.

Mimesis flowered in ritual worldwide. Late Byzantine Good Friday worshippers began processing beneath the prone *kouvouklion* icon of a dead Christ, before burying him at the altar table. Local Christian lectionaries differ, and Passion Week is no exception. Unlike the worldwide synagogue custom of reading the Torah straight through every year, early church plans scattered like farm hamlets over a sprawling Mediterranean estate. A readings vine brought out of Egypt,[4] and suckered in Palestine, sprouted odd shoots everywhere. Syria's stock spread fruity branches eastward across Asia and India. Georgian and Armenian documents show how cathedral and monastic meadows cross-fertilized each other. Fourth-century Jerusalem, a pilgrimage center, hot-housed innovations. And as pilgrims returning home transplanted Jerusalem's mimetic

---

3. *The Shape of the Liturgy*, 1945. Hellenistic usage may not have distinguished these meanings so sharply as Dix did, but liturgists separate them thus today.

4. Psalm 80:8, Numbers 23:22, Hosea 11:1, Matthew 2:15.

Passion memorials abroad, Constantinople baled up the four gospel passions into one day-long Good Friday service. Elsewhere hardy hybrids took root.

Planting an orchard-like alternative, Rome's Christians had long been reading Matthew's Passion on the Sunday before Easter; so now they grafted on Jerusalem's new lection about Jesus's entry to Jerusalem, thus hearing two starkly contrasting pericopes in one Sunday liturgy. Some Renaissance Reformers pruned their reading back to St. John's gospel alone on Good Friday, with a lengthy sermon. This simpler husbandry allowed German baroque composers to wrap the gospel trunk with beauteous motets like flowery clinging vines. Originally performed with public prayers, these "Passions" are too long for modern congregational taste, and are now performed professionally outside church worship.

After centuries of diverse growth, the twentieth-century ecumenical movement reseeded multiplex strains into one three-year lectionary, published at the Second Vatican Council (1962–1965) so that denominations might share their weekly worship experience. As a *peritus* (theological consultant) to that council, Episcopalian Massey Shepherd reported that planners envisioned two (not three) Sunday readings: the first chosen from either of two lists offered from both Testaments. Variants since then have chiefly re-sorted those first options, leaving the gospel pericopes ecumenically shared.

At most Eucharist services, the gospel reading follows the rest. This tradition arose not to show honor, as some suppose, but because the four canonical gospels took shape by gathering early sermons upon other scripture. Hence, their concluding placement is hereditary, and endures even in modular plans (medieval Syrian or modern Western) where the first reading actually sets the day's dominant theme, and the day's gospel is chosen to match it.[5]

God Speaks to the Church

However diverse, all scripture calendars serve one salvific purpose, and Armenian worship declares that clearest. Before chanting a gospel passage at any service, deacon and choir cry: *Aseh Asdovádz!* "God is speaking." That interjection points obviously enough toward sayings about to be read aloud, which early gospel editors attributed to Jesus. Yet beyond biblical literalism, the Armenian rite makes a broader claim. As Roman Catholic liturgist Ralph Kiefer said,

5. John Moolan, "Yearly Gospel Encounter in the East Syrian Calendar of St. Thomas Christians in Malabar," *Studia Liturgica*, vol. 40, 2010. *The Period of Annunciation- Nativity in the East Syrian Calendar* (Kottayam, India: Oriental Institute of Religious Studies, 1985).

"The Word of God is not the Bible. The Word of God is what God says to the Church when the Bible is read."[6]

Kiefer's definition tells why good lectionaries matter. Paul's final letter to the Roman church argues that God's plan was already saving humankind before Christ fully revealed it, if only people responded with faith.[7] That is why the Bible chiefly reproves not feckless blundering, but lies. Today's worship planners favor the cheery promises of Isaiah, which earlier lectionaries too long overlooked. Yet Isaiah himself rebukes untruthful despair, whether in his king or his public. Deceit and self-deceit pervade our social life. Dacher Keltner[8] reports studies showing that people with more power break more rules, all the while inventing false reasons to entitle themselves. Yet equalizing power will not end falsehood, which is no monopoly of the powerful. Lying lures everyone because people unreasonably like it: as Elizabethan essayist Francis Bacon wrote *Of Truth*, "A mixture of a lie doth ever add pleasure."[9] *Psychology Today* magazine reckons that the average North American tells hundreds of lies a day, many "polite" or tactful.[10]

Love of lies corrupts government proverbially. Persian emperor Darius I claimed one qualification to rule, under constant self-discipline: "What is right, that is my desire. I am not a friend to the man who is a lie-follower."[11] The Bible's histories rebut treason with truth-telling. The prophet Nathan tempts King David into royal rage against an unnamed murderer, then declares, "You are that man!"[12] At Jesus's trial, Pilate repeats sedition accusations that religious authorities have brought, and Jesus answers, "Who told you that? You may say such stuff, but I came to speak up for the Truth."[13]

Science and politics philosopher Sir Karl Popper wrote, "It has been said that a race is a collection of men united not by their origin but by a common error in regard to their origin. In a similar way, we could say that a nation in Hegel's [modern] sense is a number of men united by a common error in regard

---

6. Address to the Association of Diocesan Liturgy and Music Commissions, San Juan Bautista Conference, 1988.

7. This is the lengthy burden of Romans 1–8.

8. Keltner, *The Power Paradox*.

9. Francis Bacon, "Of Truth," *Essays or Counsels Civil and Moral*, Richard Foster Jones, ed. (New York: Odyssey, 1937), 4.

10. *Psychology Today* 2006. See chapter 1, above.

11. Wiesehöfer, *Ancient Persia from 550 BC to 650 AD*, 33.

12. 2 Samuel 12:7.

13. John 18:34–37. Author's translation.

to their history."[14] Archaeological and historical researchers prove that the Hebrew Bible promotes national errors. Despite prophetic and priestly protests within the Bible text itself, readers around the world have used those errors to rationalize imperial expansions, exclusions, persecutions, rapine, and quiet domestic violence. Selective reading helps, of course. Demagogues can trumpet Genesis's promise to give Abraham other nations' lands, while they silence Amos's declaration:

> Aren't you just like the Ethiopians in my eyes, people of Israel?
> I brought you up from Egypt,
> but didn't I bring all peoples up
> —including your classic rivals, the Philistines?
> I brought them up too![15]

Every army in World War I professed a divine commission to End All Wars by a war all pursued to Pyrrhic exhaustion. Propagandists slandered each other using biblical epithets first coined against Israel's foes.

Aseh Asdovádz! From the world's beginning God's Word has shattered every fond falsehood, including biblical fundamentalism.[16] Abolishing slavery showed that. Hebrew and Greek scriptures never question slavery, but accept it as Confucius, Cicero, Celsus, Caliphs, and Christian champions all did. Then Dominican bishop Bartolomé de las Casas persuaded the Spanish court not to impose it on Native Americans. His Queen Isabela I wore the first European crown that banned slavery's expansion by royal decree, even while African slaves worked her Bolivian silver mines. In England next, from three centuries of hearing scripture read aloud in church while Anglican bishops fattened off slave labor on their Caribbean estates, non-conforming Quakers, Methodists, and Evangelicals resolved that the Bible's God called them to end slavery wholesale. Abolition spread through the Protestant world, until in 1880 Brazil's Roman Catholic emperor Dom Pedro II joined up. Today slavery endures criminally through human trafficking, but with no open state sanction anywhere. And public Bible-reading also endures. So whatever our slanted text choices, whatever our deafness, whatever deceits we prefer, the returning worship year renews one clarion call: *Aseh Asdovádz!* God is speaking.

---

14. Karl Popper, *The Open Society and Its Enemies* (London: Routledge & Kegan Paul, 1945), ch 111.

15. Amos 9:7, author's translation.

16. See chapter 4, note 37.

This book does assay some errors propounded in church schoolbooks and it proposes some practical steps, such as the hymn table in the Appendix following. But those can only broaden and freshen the conversation we have long had. Since Maximus the Confessor's seventh-century writings,[17] the Divine Liturgy's chief function has been not humankind's rescue from sin (already accomplished in Jesus's incarnation, ministry, and death) nor ecstatic experience (always treasured) nor ethical simplicity (day by day) but our education: whoever we are, wherever we have come from, when we enter a church together. Hearing inspired writings read—particularly though not exclusively the Bible—is God's principal medium for conversing with most of us, just as historical criticism, physical investigation, and social science are our principal media for conversing with each other. Combining these makes for endless change and progress; stopping for an instant, we would fall away from God.

In all our turbulent conversation, only one speaker is constant. *Aseh Asdovádz!* Those two Armenian words declare the whole purpose for Christian worship services: why we read ancient texts and recall the past by *anamnesis* or *mimesis*; why we rewrite prayers to speak our faith clearly; why we welcome the world to join our work; why our artists and composers beautify the experience of all who come, whether believers or not. Our purpose is not to warn sinners of punishment; nor to gain new church members; nor to resolve opposing views; nor to pursue peace by balancing bankrupt accounts; nor to reassure ourselves that we are right—or at least more nearly right than otherwise. Our Eucharists, daily offices, reconciliations, marriages, and burial liturgies all declare the same good news: *Aseh Asdovádz!* God is speaking now the same love and truth spoken always to *homo sapiens sapiens, homo neanderthalensis, homo ergaster, homo habilis* and the rest of us, and will speak until calendars and the universe end together. The ancient Hindu Rig Veda sang from hymns even older:

Truth is one.

Sages call it by various names.[18]

---

17. See Wybrew, chaps. 3 and 4, *The Orthodox Liturgy*.

18. Rig Veda 1.164.46, compiled 1400 BCE. Srinivasan, *Crete to Egypt*.

CHAPTER TEN

THE CREATOR'S SIGN:
BEAUTY

Cellist Pablo Casals was asked "Why are you still practicing in your eighties?" And he answered "Because I can still hear some room for improvement." That's what's so great about the therapy field we practice in. There's tremendous room for improvement. When I expected we would talk about beauty today, I was thinking about how much meaning I find in the beauty of Nature. But relationships are nature. There's that endless complexity! It's so meaningful to me how it all fits together. It can be the relatively static beauty of the landscape or the beauty of a peregrine falcon trying to drive off a red-tailed hawk; watching that sort of thing is beautiful. And I don't know why, but I'm glad that our brains are such that the way the world works is just so beautiful.

—TERRENCE BECKER, CLINICAL PSYCHOANALYST

Poets have stood in awe before nature's landscapes, sunsets, stars, comets, and eclipses; storytellers have summoned awe before heroic human acts. All created beauty inspires awe: landscape painter Olivia Kuser switched to figure painting and now declares, "I've never seen a human body that was not beautiful."[1] Gregory of Nyssa finds God's image in the human race as a whole, since we all descend from Adam and Eve.[2] Hence our common human pleasure in beautiful things reflects God's love for all. Our response to beauty begets love, which is God's own life shared in our human life. Love provides humanity's most powerful motive for service to our fellows, and to our natural world. Mystics of many faiths have discovered here an immediate revelation of God.

---

1. See interview below.
2. Genesis 2.

160

Torres del Paine, Patagonia

On the other hand, skeptics since the European Enlightenment have countered that human religious ideas are mere projections from our emotional experience, especially childhood experience. Worse, they are alienated—that is, falsely attributed to God, rather than acknowledged for their human origin. To replace such concepts, nineteenth-century anthropologists and psychologists crafted new taxonomies based upon experimental research, much as physics, chemistry, and astronomy had become centuries before. That earlier scientific revolution had already divided religious authorities: Anglican bishops and Jesuits fostered it, while Dominican inquisitors and Martin Luther alike condemned it. Since their era a presumptive opposition between religion and science, if not shared by all practitioners, has impoverished learned discourse. It allows writers from either side to debate evolution, for example, with less rigorous care than their colleagues demand over other questions.

To bridge that putative chasm between religion and science, scientists have taken the lead. Michael Polanyi's *Personal Knowledge: Towards a Post-Critical Philosophy* (1958) upended commonplace understanding of scientific method, and objective versus subjective knowledge.[3] Students had been taught that science progresses by objective evidentiary steps, which corroborate one explanation

---

3. Michael Polanyi, *Personal Knowledge: Towards a Post-Critical Philosophy* (Chicago: University of Chicago Press, 1958).

and rule others out. Instead, Polanyi observes that among the greatest discoveries by Einstein, Newton, Harvey, Galileo, and other famed scientists, revolutionary explanations were offered—and many were published—long before evidence could be gathered. Einstein twice changed his relativity theory, and then revived an early version, all from inner reflection before planned testing could be done. Often proof required mechanisms that the visionary innovators lacked, like electron microscopes, cyclotrons, and supercomputers. At this writing, experimenters still test hopefully two "laws" Einstein proposed in advance of evidence: his description of gravity; and his conviction that a unifying factor links quantum mechanics with relativity—a match whose evidence does not yet add up.

So scientific ideas arise much the way great social and religious ideas do, as creative minds recognize patterns in the universe. This recognition process is intrinsically personal and "subjective," and fosters language that poets trust, but logicians may not. Therefore Polanyi proposes augmenting standard writing with symbols that communicate researchers' own seeing and believing, so that a reader can weigh their commitment along with data offered or still sought. Polanyi's scheme of symbolic logic signs has not received scientists' acceptance. But his goal is familiar to modern historians, who have learned to mark their own attitude to ancient or culturally distant source materials.

Patterns can have beauty. Today's scientific term "elegant" describes beauty in theories. Patterns can also persuade before proofs eliminate alternatives, because humans give "subjective" weight to coherence, which must be explained otherwise if a theory fails. Indeed, scientists often work with partial evidence where ultimate proof looks unlikely. Joan Roughgarden's *Evolution's Rainbow: Diversity, Gender and Sexuality in Nature and People* rebuts neo-Darwinian orthodoxy, which affords little room for questioning.[4] Unlike Victorian social Darwinists, Roughgarden finds that collaboration is at least as potent an evolutionary force as ruthless competition. Furthermore, she traces diverse behaviors arising in many species without genetic winnowing. Her portrait of sentient life implies evolutionary power for beauty and a desire for beauty.

It is hardly surprising that the Bible is filled with beauty's praises. Concordances list some four hundred Hebrew texts extolling the grandeur, glory, splendor, and beauty of God and God's creation. Plato and other Greek pagan

---

4. Joan Roughgarden, *Evolution's Rainbow: Diversity, Gender and Sexuality in Nature and People* (Berkeley: University of California Press, 2004).

writers likewise admired and emphasized beauty. Words in both Hebrew and Greek (*yapheh*, *kalos*) mean "good" and "beautiful" at once. Needless to say, those qualities are projected from their authors' subjective insights, in much the same way that Newton's gravity or Einstein's relativity actually arose.

On the other hand, the Greek New Testament yields barely fifty beauty texts, few mentioning art.[5] While Hebrew writers extol singing and dancing, for example, the sole musical saying attributed to Jesus chides his opponents for behaving like children who will not join in.[6] In that saying, Jesus's adversaries oddly prefigure his future church. Hence Greek theologians turned habitually to the Old Testament instead.

> These things concerning the perfection of the virtuous life . . . we have briefly written for you, tracing in outline like a pattern of beauty the life of the great Moses so that each one of us might copy the image of the beauty which has been shown to us by imitating his way of life. What more trustworthy witness of the fact that Moses did attain the perfection which was possible would be found than the divine voice which said to him: *I have known you more than all others?* It is also shown in the fact that he is named the "friend of God" by God himself. . . .
>
> As your understanding is lifted up to what is magnificent and divine, whatever you may find (and I know full well that you will find many things) will most certainly be for the common benefit in Christ Jesus. Amen.[7]

Like his universalist ethic, Gregory's exaltation of beauty put him at the head of a longtime Christian minority. Later preachers warned against beauty's fleshly allure more than they urged us to contemplate it. If churchmen esteemed Moses's legislation, few saw his life as a "pattern of beauty," or bade us shape our lives beautifully in turn. Even so, for ages churches have practiced beauty to the public benefit. Wondrous music, architecture, and art have drawn converts into sanctuaries and inspired hours of mystical contemplation—not to mention the intense personal fulfillment artists have experienced creating them. Why then should theologians and apologists sidestep these? But too many do.

---

5. David Bentley Hart counts *kalos* forty times, *horaios* only twice translating Hebrew. *The Beauty of the Infinite* (Grand Rapids, MI: Eerdmans, 2003), 212.

6. Luke 7:32.

7. A. Malherbe and E. Ferguson, trans., *Gregory of Nyssa: The Life of Moses* (New York: Paulist Press 1978), 136–137.

For example, churches have lately launched a renaissance of lay ministry, something planners want to empower in worship and the working world alike. In the United States, lay ministry articles fill Episcopal publications issue by issue. We may wonder, therefore, over our world's most famous Anglican lay minister: an active churchman whose creations thousands cherish at home and abroad, who encourages popular zeal for humane causes, who consults with political leaders in crises, and whose admirers include countless faithful, ordained and lay. This lay minister has appeared on covers of the *New York Times Magazine*, *Time*, and other secular journals—but never once on Episcopal Church covers, which prefer uncrowded sanctuary buildings and hierarchs in pointy hats. This faithful modern Church of Ireland spouse and parent, baptized Paul David Hewson, composes and sings worldwide under his professional name: Bono. The members of Bono's band U2 have performed loyally with him longer than most symphony conductors can boast. And Christian clergy worldwide celebrate "U2 masses" assembled from their favorite songs. As a poster child for Anglican lay ministry, however, Bono might as well be unborn.

> I am holding on to the idea that through wisdom, through experience, you might in some important ways recover innocence. I want to be playful. I want to be experimental. I want to be useful. That is our family prayer, as you know. It is not the most grandiose prayer. It is just, we are available for work. That is U2's prayer. We want to be useful, but we want to change the world. And we want to have fun at the same time. What is wrong with that?[8]

Perhaps church publicists bypass Bono from anxiety about his unruly young fans, who would swamp our dry worship if they flooded in—and even worse, voted at our legislative gatherings. Church growth studies show that most newcomers decide whether to stay within three minutes of entering for services, and chiefly in response to a church's music. That might offer threat enough! But this dysfunction is deeper and older. It discloses a longtime contradiction within Christian institutional life: the love and fear of beauty itself. Lately such writers as Dorothy Sayers, Hans Urs von Balthasar, Richard Harries, David Bentley Hart, and Natalie Carnes have refurbished the eminent palace that Gregory of Nyssa once built for beauty. Moreover like the inspiration of biblical priests and prophets, beauty speaks up for itself, and humans

---

8. Bono quoted by Jann S. Wenner, "The Rolling Stone Interview: Bono," *Rolling Stone*, January 11, 2018, 32–41.

Modern Anglican Composers Beloved in Worship: Harry T. Burleigh & U2

respond everywhere: *Vox Populi Vox Dei!* Critics miss their mark who charge that beautiful churches make costly museum objects, lacking ties to popular culture. Even more than churches, on Sundays the art museums are *full*.

A Metaphysic of Beauty?

Ours is a revisionist epoch, and recent revisions within science must eventually transform our talk of beauty. Whitehead quipped that Buddhism is a metaphysic in search of a religion, while Christianity is a religion in search of a metaphysic.[9] Buddhists collect theories: Tibetans faithfully teach all that have ever reached their mountains, where monks debate daylong in monastery courtyards. On the other hand, the *Prajña Paramitra Sûtra*, beloved of Chan (Zen) meditators, might be summarized: "There is no metaphysic, and also no extinction of it." Such Buddhist iconoclasm challenges the western lust for objective reason above subjective insight. When the eighteenth-century Irish bishop George Berkeley proposed that human experience is a mental fabrication, like revelation, Dr. Samuel Johnson kicked a stone and shouted in awful gouty pain, "Thus I refute Berkeley!" But now for a century from Nietzsche to Derrida an ascendant school holds that values in history, in ethics, in literature, have no intrinsic reality. Human experience means just what we say it means, and no more. Hence language is all we can discuss. Beauty remains an individual inward judgment, impregnable to critical attack; as a popular canard has it, "Beauty is in the eye of the beholder."

---

9. A. N. Whitehead, *Religion in the Making* (New York: Macmillan, 1926). Based on the 1926 Lowell Lectures.

And yet while some thinkers might prefer objective useful talk, linguists have discovered no human tongues without values. Indeed, as the range of species credited with language spreads beyond mammalian and avian neurology to include bees and ants, their social values commitment appears among the strongest, and includes existential self-sacrifice. Therefore labeling our most primitive brain cells the "reptilian brain" shows human values projection wholesale. To learn how actual reptiles or even *Caenorhabditis elegans* roundworms actually think, we must learn their languages: a riddle that zoologists have so far declined to answer.

We have seen how Polanyi upends the scientific reign of objective evidence above subjective insight. His reverse discovery process is now presumed as standard among scientists, if not yet among philosophers, historians, or literary critics. When scientists call a theory "elegant," more than complimenting its aesthetic, they claim its economy suits the natural universe.

Historians of science shatter another graven image, that of the lonesome pioneer struggling with feckless servants and myopic opponents. Patience Schell finds that "science is constructed in a moral field" of "mutual trust and good manners . . . For naturalists, in particular, science was sociable."[10] Colleague friendship makes for mentoring, and especially for invited opportunities to common discovery. Charles Darwin's work prospered from his singular skill at making friends. "When Darwin's Theory of Evolution was first made public, it was his friends like Thomas Huxley who became its dogged champions." Moreover "like Darwin's assistant, Syms Covington, 'servants' were in fact highly skilled workers vital to specimen production."[11]

If the Western relation between religious and scientific knowledge today resembles an estranged marriage, though not a divorce, religious reaction bears the greater blame. Protestant Patience Schell relates how Darwin's Chilean and Polish Catholic colleagues welcomed "a broader view of God's creation"; and Prussian Lutheran Rodulfo Philippi extolled "a more perfect idea of the Supreme Author." Philippi concluded: "The study of nature, the contemplation of its various products will always be an unending fountain of enjoyment that will never leave remorse and never awakens miserable passions."[12] But on the contrary, despite centuries of Anglican support for science (including the

---

10. Patience A. Schell, *The Sociable Sciences: Darwin and His Contemporaries in Chile* (New York: Palgrave Macmillan, 2013), 6–7.

11. Schell, 140.

12. Schell, 170.

youthful Darwin's clergy mentors), English evangelical zealots debased evolutionary debate with verbal and even physical violence. To answer a mean family mockery from Oxford's bishop Samuel "Soapy Sam" Wilberforce, Huxley needed only turn the tables: "Would I rather have a miserable ape for a grandfather, or a man highly endowed by nature and possessed of great means and influence and yet who employs those faculties for the mere purpose of introducing ridicule into a grave scientific discussion? I unhesitatingly affirm my preference for the ape."[13] As a far sadder exemplar, aristocratic Patagonian explorer and meteorologist Robert Fitz-Roy was young Darwin's "idol," host, and captain for five years aboard the *Beagle*. Fitz-Roy converted to evangelical fundamentalism and remorsefully repudiated occasioning Darwin's research. Then he kissed his sleeping daughter, Laura, and with his own razor tragically slit his throat, leaving his family "with nothing."

Engaging the process of discovery so personally, scientists can hardly be more objective than other humans. Subjective insight births both our new notions and our hard learning about physical realities. To what reality then does the hunger for objective truth scrubbed clean of cultural values apply? Is that not another projection like the rest? Cannot Bach's gorgeous melodies, or the chant "Om," resonate with vibrating black holes? Cannot the hidden curves of Athens's Parthenon show how human art evolves from the whirling galaxies? Cannot Shakespeare's sonnets be reasonably rocketed aboard time capsules for other worlds to read? Cannot one existential sacrifice by one *praüs* Palestinian healer to save his friends reveal "the love that moves the sun and the other stars?"[14]

Ethiopian Christians dance today at nearly all worship services, all year round. Hellenistic pagan worship centered on communal song and dance.[15] Christian celebrations fostered both at first, as Gregory Nyssen, Gregory Nazianzen, and their allied Cappadocian preachers prove—but only for a time. Fifth-century Latin bishop Augustine's oft-quoted "whoever sings prays twice" actually apologized for giving his congregations some business to do in church, instead of chattering noisily while the clergy preached or prayed. Christian bishops, increasingly celibate, opposed dance as sensual and issued fifteen centuries of conciliar prohibitions. Such repetition proves dance's hardy endurance, of

---

13. Schell, 175, citing J. Vernon Jensen in *British Journal for the History of Science*, 1988.

14. "*l'amor che move il sole e l'altre stelle*"; Dante's *Paradiso* ends with this poetic line.

15. Ramsay MacMullen, *The Second Church: Popular Christianity A.D. 200–400* (Atlanta: Society of Biblical Literature, 2009). See chapter 4 on dancing the mystery, above.

Ethiopian Girls Dancing at Christ's Baptism Feast

course. Western cathedrals featured festive dancing outside the Mass; and medieval university divines danced publicly when new doctors of divinity were added
to their number.[16] But Eastward, bishops and other monastics still refrain today,
and their villagers dance only outside sanctuary buildings. Eighteenth-century
English Methodists eventually forgot their dances in America, where Shakers
carried on alone until their dancers died out. Today some "conservative" Christian preachers inveigh against all dance, church or secular.

More revealing yet, music composers are nearly missing from calendars
of saints. Conservative Roman Catholic bishops had hoped the sixteenth-
century Council of Trent would condemn Palestrina's new polyphonic
style. To their dismay, the Council canonized his music instead—but never
Palestrina himself. Baroque composers popularized both Reformation and
Counter-Reformation preaching services; yet for all their devotion they were
never beatified as those preachers were. Consider the raptures of Protestant
visionaries Bach and Handel—who said after writing his Hallelujah chorus,
the most widely beloved composition in human history, "I did think I did see
all heaven before me, and the great God himself . . . Whether I was in my
body or out of my body I know not. God knows it!"[17] Such mystical experience

---

16. See chapter 4, above.

17. As quoted in early nineteenth-century biographies. Original source uncertain.

would have promoted baroque Spanish theologians to cult. Instead, these inspired composers remain un-venerated by Western ritual.[18] Eastern musicians fare little better. From Ephrem Syrus, John Damascene, and Romanos to Rachmaninoff and Tavener, their lyrics are honored for enhancing orthodox thought while their tunes fade before fickle fashion. Eastern church calendars exalt countless theologians, missionaries, and martyrs; but by contrast a bare half dozen composers from Ethiopia, Armenia, Georgia, and Greece enjoy annual feasts.

And as one married Greek Orthodox liturgist laments, those few sainted composers are exclusively monastics. The Christian monastic movement has raised up great scholars, artists, missionaries, and servants of the poor, who serve God heroically in disciplined communities, and have repeatedly captained church renewal. The nineteenth-century Anglican monastic revival has enriched far more than worship reform. This book was suckled at the paps of our one monastic seminary, the College of the Resurrection at Mirfield, UK, and shaped by outstanding vocational celibates: Benedict Green, CR; Paul Wessinger, SSJE; George McCauley, SJ; scholar Richard Norris. Claudio Monteverdi and other devout creators of beauty embraced celibate priesthood when widowed, to the benefit of further centuries. Their many vocations involved noble existential sacrifice. But a church that requires such sacrifice by all its leaders suppresses the sexual desire for beauty that drives most Christians' life decisions, and that moves each human and animal race to do as God commands and blesses before all else: "Be fruitful and multiply and fill the earth and govern it."[19]

Confucius's *Analects* taught that rites and music are core exercises for healthy statecraft.[20] Most parish teams include a lay member who swims weekly in strong creative streams, but may be consulted less often for pastoral talent. Whether conservative or innovative by taste, parish musicians devote hours to introducing, persuading, and teaching: skills all leaders require. Fashions do shift along with secular culture: for example, early Western music has become a surprise leading edge among younger artists. Denominational planners may yet devalue beauty as frivolous frosting upon the real Christian faith cake. But as habitual religion ebbs, the arts bring a rising proportion of worshippers into

---

18. The Evangelical Lutheran Church in America has placed some names on the calendar, but without readings or prayers for ritual commemoration.

19. Genesis 1:28.

20. *Analects* throughout.

church, and motivate more to stay and work. Here arises an important ascetical, as well as a practical opportunity.

> God creates Life;
>
> Life beholds Beauty;
>
> Beauty begets Love;
>
> Love is the Life of God.[21]

Recent decades of revision have freshened our knowledge of classic architecture and iconography.[22] We are recovering the artists' first intentions from
beneath later overlays. At the same time, physical science unearths new understanding. Neuroscientists discover that music alone engages the whole human
brain, from the earliest levels to the latest evolved, and can revive synapses lost
to elderly or injured minds. Music connects humans with non-primates too:
dancing parrots, elephants, and some whales rehearse melodies as humans
do, and can imitate tunes and rhythms we share with them.[23] Their readi-
ness to learn human music implies that some animals can love beauty consciously, as we do.

Here is chiefly why St. Gregory's Church places the collection of money
after Communion. Instead of implying prepayment, it fosters worshippers'
response to many beauties known during the service: sublime music; rich colors
and fine art; joy of singing; fragrant incense and flowers; enlightenment from
scripture and sermon sharing; growing affection in company; and above all, the
ecstatic experience of Communion. People engage these at different times, but
giving thanks for them is always a pleasure in itself. Evangelical bishop Colin
Buchanan argues this is the earliest order for Anglican worship.[24]

So in place of metaphysic, this book offers the following symposium, as ten
lay ministers tell us plainly the beauty they hear and see in their work.

---

21. Hymn lyric by Scott R. King (2001) versifying Gregory Nyssen's *On the Soul and Resurrection:* "For
the life of the Supreme Being is love, seeing that the Beautiful is necessarily lovable to those who recognize
it, and the Deity does recognize it, and so this recognition becomes love, that which He recognizes being
essentially beautiful." Fromberg, *The Art of Transformation*, 37.

22. Thomas F. Matthews, *Byzantium from Antiquity to the Renaissance* (New York: Abrams, 1998).
David Stancliffe, *The Lion Companion to Church Architecture* (London: Lion Hudson: 2009).

23. A. D. Patel, *Music and the Brain* (Chantilly: Great Courses, 2015), 83.

24. Colin Buchanan, *The End of the Offertory: An Anglican Study*, Alcuin Club, Grove Liturgical Study
14 (Bramcote, England: Grove Books, 1978).

Lay Ministers' Symposium on Beauty

1. *Aldo Billingslea*, *African American Shakespearean actor, professor of theatre arts at Santa Clara University; interim artistic director of San Francisco's Lorraine Hansberry Theatre; advisory board of Gritty City Youth Repertory Theatre; vice president of the 100 Black Men of Silicon Valley, interracial husband of photographer Renee Billingslea, and father.*

It's a gift to be able to speak—to act is a gift. And to do the work of Shakespeare is a gift. Everyone wants to do great scripts because then you can tell great stories, and you can strive for greatness, and you can't do that without a great story; and so many of Shakespeare's stories are great.

What is the essence of "beauty?" For me, it keeps coming back to art. I've always defined art as man's reaction to the work of God. In God's work there's beauty and we want to replicate that somehow. Whether it's the photographer or a painter that sees the work of light on something and they try to capture that somehow—the filmmaker with light; the designer in the theater, trying to craft and carve with light. You try to capture the essence of that beauty which, like art, connects us eventually back to God. The things that allow us to recognize humanity in the world, and God in our self, take us to an emotional place: that's what beauty is. Landscapes have constant beauty: even in their decay and destruction you can see beauty, and feel its power. You can do that with people, too: you get to see beauty in the face of a 102-year-old person. Being able to see it, recognize it, that's beauty too. It strikes that chord of humanity in you, to see in that person's eyes some of their story, and that's that moment of beauty.

To stand onstage and deliver beautiful language allows me, for that moment, when those words are coming from me, to feel—"I'm beautiful." It's me that gets to be the vessel of that beauty. It's really the flower in the vase that's gorgeous, but right now I'm looking at both. And in that moment, if I can do those words justice, if I can get out of their way and deliver those words and use the timbre of my voice and my own breath and my own vibrations, matching to those words that are four hundred years old, it adds to the beauty, framing it. So you become connected to that history, and that symbiotic relationship is beautiful.

In seventh grade at a new school I was the only black kid, and the kids around me didn't know the answer to a science question, but I did, and the teacher said "You are just like a walking encyclopedia." And I said, "a good-looking encyclopedia." But by October of that year, my Halloween costume was a superhero called "Captain Ugly," because I felt I was ugly. And both of those kids are still inside me somewhere. But to be the person that gets to hold beauty, is just a wonderful experience. I get to share my humanity with other people, move other people, have other people sigh, laugh, weep, because I get to use this language; that experience is a wonderful thing, and like a lot of other aspects of beauty, it validates my humanity.

There's beauty in a painful moment. Between five *Othello* productions, I have died numerous times and killed numerous Desdemonas, and when it's well done, her death—and mine—may have elements of beauty in them. I watched a production where I was sitting next to a high school junior who, as Othello's being duped by Iago, was biting his bottom lip and shaking in his seat, trying to keep from crying out loud. As the tears are rolling from his eyes, just knowing that it's wrong, and he's shaking in the seat beside me—and in that pain is beauty. He is feeling, having a sympathetic reaction for another human being, knowing full well that this is all make-believe. Yet his emotion is absolutely genuine, and his pain is absolutely genuine, and there's beauty in that. Some people who believe that beauty is a rigid form wouldn't find beauty in pain, but there's great beauty in that moment when this person is feeling for another human being so intently. I thought: please don't draw blood; he's biting down so hard; he's almost willing to hurt himself because he's so into this moment right now. And there's great beauty in that.

What makes beauty so difficult is that it comes to each of us in a different way, and it affects our heart in a way that sometimes is not logical; there's not a cerebral path for the course of love. "True love never did run smoothly," Shakespeare says in *Midsummer Night's Dream*, "Therefore is wingèd Cupid painted blind," because it doesn't make sense that you would fall for this or that person. I had ideas about what my love would look like. But the reality was: I'm falling for this person so deeply, so quickly, that it's beyond my control, which is very difficult for a control freak like me. I decided I wanted a black woman, but I also wanted someone who could help me financially so I wouldn't bring them down, by saddling them with all my debt and making their life more miserable. So I called Renee to say we were broken up—and instead we got back together, thank God.

Now you've got me thinking that love and beauty are not all that different. An actor might want to speak beautiful language and tell powerful stories, in a way to be a better human being. That's one thing I felt about Renee. I wanted to be a better person for her. I just found her extraordinary, and recognized choices I was making to be a better person, more worthy of someone I thought so highly of. Love is not unlike beauty in some ways: it made me more connected to humanity, made me more appreciative of this gift that God had made and had given me. That's one of the reasons that we were looking at St. Gregory's immediately when we got to San Francisco. We'd been searching Ashland for a church home when I thought I was going to be there long term. Then we discovered we were coming down to the Bay Area. So for years we drove eighty to ninety miles roundtrip every Sunday to get to people who seem to appreciate us, where we find beauty and a connection with a higher power that makes us more alive, makes us want to be better people—all those things.

> 2. ***Olivia Kuser,*** *landscape artist turned figural painter; artistic committee for St. Gregory Nyssen Church's prize-winning sanctuary building. The church's principal project (by African American iconographer Mark Dukes) depicted eighty-five life-size saints, chosen by the congregation from all nations and eras, dancing in circles above the altar.*

> 3. ***Alfred Bay,*** *residential architect, champion pole-vaulter and New York modern dancer, Olivia Kuser's husband.*

Olivia: I've been a landscape painter all my life and I've just started painting figures, and discovered that I have never seen a human body that was not beautiful. Once people take their clothes off and you're no longer dealing with what the cultural ideal of what beauty is, as communicated by clothes, and you just look at their bodies, every body creates its own world. And to me, once you enter that world, you see there are repeated patterns of proportion: the length of the thigh compared to the length of the calf, relates to the length of the lower arm to the upper arm, and that proportion, that ratio in every body is different, but once you enter that world, it all looks beautiful.

And you see that the body explains to you what that world is and it explains it through proportion—every body creates its own sense of ratios and its own proportions; and it's your job as the artist to look for that. And looking for that is pleasurable—it's fun; there's no other word for it; it's fun; it's delightful. And also working from the model, I've always just felt like it was an incredible privilege to see somebody without their clothes on, who you were not in love with. It's a gift. So that in itself was beautiful.

Alfred: One of the difficulties of proportion in architecture is that they're always trying to simplify everything and make it neat and clean and efficient, which nature never is—and the context of nature is always so complex, there's always so much information that I think proportion responds to the context and the surroundings, so that an exact equation doesn't work except in a square on paper.

Beauty is something that takes me out of my narrative; out of my naming things, out of my giving things meaning, out of my giving things identity, and puts me into the community—into the same structure—of whatever it is I'm engaged in. I imagine what the goal of meditation is, but I can never find it in silence and darkness; I only find it through sensory input. And so when I say, "Oh, this is beautiful," what that means is I've just experienced being part of something outside myself, of being outside myself, which I see as God. It's always infinitely complex and at the same time, incredibly simple; together. And without both, it doesn't get me. So beauty mostly gets me unaware; I forget who I am.

Olivia: I also get to draw old people. Not often—not often enough. I worked from one model for about a year with two other women artists. She herself was talking care of an old woman, and was somewhat bored. She must have been in her upper sixties when she was modeling for us. It was wonderful to work from one model, one body, and to get to know that body so well, week after week after week for an entire year. And that kind of familiarity also felt loving after a certain point; her body became beloved to me because it was so well known and so well looked at by me.

Alfred: Olivia's mother had diabetes, and she came to visit us and she had these lesions on her legs—and one thing I did for her was dress her lesions a couple of times. And so I'm cleaning out her wounds one day, and I got into it, and then I'm just looking into the wound, and it was just like Yellowstone lava pits. All these colors and all these variations of red, all these cells and white and yellow pus and it was like a pizza or lava flow—it was like not a wound, and not diabetes and not her mother. And I just really got into cleaning it out and looking at it, and that is a beauty experience for me.

Olivia: One day when I had been working in the studio really hard all day, I was gazing out towards the bay just to rest my eyes, to rest myself, and I saw a bird on a branch, and it just struck me as, "What is this bird? This is gorgeous! What is this bird?" Finally, I look at the bird and I realize—it *is* a robin! I was only looking and not naming, and not intellectualizing that I couldn't even identify a bird I was completely familiar with, but I saw it as an entirely new bird to me. It was just gorgeous—I can hardly tell you how beautiful this bird was, and how it just stood there to be looked at, and I couldn't identify it until I got back into the studio and was reading over my notes, and I just thought, "Well, that was a robin!"

Alfred: For me, beauty is a physical experience of relief. I'm more comfortable and more in the world and it's a pleasure.

I think the challenge in architecture is that what you're doing is so complex; it has to serve so many masters, it costs so much, it has to last a long time, that I think really when you *try* to make beauty, it doesn't work. So I think the best that can happen as an architect is to make an opportunity for beauty to happen in and around your space. So I see buildings that I think are very conducive. For example, the Golden Gate Bridge. In context and from different views, and you see it from this way and that way and this way and you go, "Oh, that's beautiful with those mountains," "Oh, that's beautiful against that sky," "Oh, that's beautiful"—in relation to whatever.

But as for buildings themselves being beautiful, I've seen a few—the Hagia Sophia—but pretty rare. I was sixteen, and had had just been to the Munich Olympics; I was in Constantinople, with a Turkish family, and I knew nothing about the Hagia Sofia; never heard of it, and we just walked in, and I was dumbfounded. It was like being inside of your brain. It was a spiritual experience. That seldom happens with buildings—for me. And so I was caught totally unaware; I had no expectation.

Olivia: The Grand Canyon of Yellowstone has a famous waterfall that Thomas Moran painted; lovely painting. I wanted to see the waterfall because when you're down on the canyon floor, there's a natural rainbow when the sun goes through the waterfall. I really want to see this waterfall. I really want to see this rainbow effect. We get a couple of hundred feet down the trail, and I am trembling with fear; I got to the bottom. I did see the rainbow, and it was really beautiful. Alfred took a photograph of me there, and I look fifteen years older from fear. But that something more beautiful I wanted to see was more powerful than my fear. I had to simply push through the fear to get to the thing that I really wanted. And the beauty was the magnet. The beauty was the pull.

Alfred: People tell me when we'd go out, my friends would say, "Oh God, Olivia is so gorgeous; she's like the most beautiful woman I know." So Olivia used to ask me, "What do you see in me? Why do you like me?" And the real answer I could come up with was that you explain the world to me. I know more of the world, I see more in the world, I understand the world better in your presence.

And part of that is her looks—and her physical presence. See this hand here? So *that* to me is quintessentially Olivia; the way her hand is hanging there. And *that* is very beautiful to me; it's that drape. If I saw that in a crowd of a hundred people, I'd know that's her hand. So it's things like that, again, that catch me unaware that really move me.

Olivia: I would like to draw another picture of Alfred. And it would be a very different experience now to draw him in his sixties versus when I was drawing him when we first met in our twenties. Partly because I have now forty more years of drawing experience, but also just having known his body through looking at it and through touch for forty years. So I have a different apprehension of this body now.

Alfred: When I see photos of us young, I think, "God dang! We were good looking!" But it doesn't look like Olivia. Now I see you with your clothes off, and you say, "Oh, I'm fat and I've gained too much," but I do see you and your body, still beautiful to me.

Olivia: One thing I have always said about beauty is that beauty is its own excuse. It doesn't have to have any other explanation or meaning. It's sufficient unto itself. And that's what I feel when I'm drawing.

Alfred: It's necessary. It's necessary to us—to maintain sanity and health and anything. I'd be a very miserable person if I was not always trying to access it.

Olivia: Absolutely. It's not a luxury. It's not an add-on. It's an essential thing.

> **4. Daphne de Marneffe,** *psychologist and author of the best-selling* Maternal Desire *and* The Rough Patch: Marriage, Midlife, and the Art of Living Together.

> **5. Terrence Becker,** *Freudian training psychoanalyst and nature-lover. Husband of Daphne de Marneffe and father of their three children. Like many practitioners, both Terrence and Daphne say that psychiatry is an art as much as a science.*

Terry: People mattering to each other is one of the really meaningful, moving things in the world. And that's something that you get so strongly from children. In even trivial things, it matters so much.

Daphne: There's nothing quite like the *way* you matter to your children—especially when they're very young. The love is incredibly fulfilling when they're little. In terms of beauty and parenting, I acknowledge our clergy

Rick and Donald because my thinking about desire this way was affected by hearing them talk at church, about our relationship with God being about desire. That helped me think about what moves people, really. To hold desire outside your relationship with God seems weird—like the love thing; it's physical and emotional and we have it for children and we have it in marriage. So there's an early childhood piece of love and desire and pleasure and beauty.

Terry: But even there, you're trying to see who they actually are, what actually interests them, while you're sharing what interests you about the world: "I think you're going to like this." That's initially influenced by what you like—but then it becomes a shared pleasure. Are you really thinking about *them* and who *they* might become, as distinct from who *somebody* might become? "Oh! this is the kind of thing *you* like, and it's fun to do this with you. What do you want to do? Go to the zoo or hike down to the beach?" One of the wonderful things about small children is being able to share the beauty of the world—to look at those monkeys at the zoo, or look at the ocean, or look at the moon. It's neat to see somebody else start to take in parts of the world that you find beautiful.

Daphne: It's in parenting, and it's in our work because we're therapists: "Who *are* you? And can I understand who you are?" And that's in marriage, too. I see a lot of couples in my work—and the beautiful position is "I want to understand you, and love *you*." The more dysfunctional position is: who's right, who's wrong. That usually comes from the way *they* were treated. But the beautiful thing with children or with a spouse or with a patient is: "Actually who *are* you?" If I love *you*, I'm highly aware and attuned to who you are as a personality I try to gratify, or satisfy, or harmonize with, or accept.

Terry: And on the other side (I'm thinking from both sides—I'm both a child and a father) the feeling of being given to. I've been thinking about the last thing that my mom said to me. Before I went to the airport, I came into my folks' bedroom, knowing it could well be the last time. I was crying and telling her how grateful I was for her being my mother: "Thank you so much, Mom, for everything you've done . . ." and she just looked at me and smiled and said, "I'll see you in my dreams." I'm part of her; we'd become part of each other. Somebody's gone and you think about them, you get this feeling of timelessness. My mother's always part of me, and even when I left for the airport, I was part of my mother.

Daphne: One thing we both find beautiful about our work is that it is above all at peace with our life. The stuff that matters to our work is central to what matters.

Terry: You're helping people matter to each other.

Daphne: And you're letting them to matter to you, and you're mattering to them—and what else is there, really? I feel incredibly fortunate that we got to do that.

Terry: I don't know exactly how to distinguish between curiosity and following beauty, following meaning, following interest, but all of those are involved, and you get to see them when you talk to people about their experience of meaning or meaninglessness, or relationships, or the particular suffering they have.

Daphne: In the last ten or fifteen years, the clinical work of being across from people in the room and doing the therapy has been the source of beauty. Before that, I think it was much more writing. With this guy Jesus: it was your life path, and he represented someone who followed that. But I have the same feeling with writers: you *get* it, you talk to me. There's something intimate and truthful and beautiful in what you're saying, that draws me and helps flesh out what I'm trying to do. Those are a huge part of beauty. And you must have this all the time in music. Bach seems like one of those guys—even to me, and I'm not a big fan—oh my God, you get it! You're doing something so profoundly that—it just matches some need or desire of mine.

Terry: As a college kid, when you talk to friends you start to hear about other people's struggles, and it became more interesting to me. How do people solve these things? It's a relationship also, which I find most compelling. It's a relationship that you're trying to think about as best as you can, knowing that you're always imposing your own view of things, but trying to *get* somebody else, because there's something really helpful about being gotten.

Daphne: Comparing art and science—with therapy, like everything else, you have to develop technique and then you can soar at moments; you have to have the basic tools, and know how to use the paintbrush. With some people the therapy relationship becomes a creative space. You're on all levels of your own registers: the poetic level, the dream level, the emotional level, the intellectual level; it's all working, together. And you feel creative joy that something is happening that feels real and aesthetically beautiful and true. At those moments it feels humble you're in that place, whatever that place is—and it feels beautiful; it feels fully humanly satisfying to be there. That's often how it feels in the great moments of parenthood: I'm all there. And in the great moments of marriage, too—or singing—like every part of you is engaged.

I realize with age that everyone is sort of driven in different ways about beauty, and that's okay. Everyone can have their own version of it. And when I'm around Terry in nature, he's just different from me. I benefit from having him point out things to me; I benefit from his noticing this tiny little bird up in a tree that I would have never seen. That's the wisdom of age, that we're all different, and we all have something to add, and we all have our own aesthetic compass.

Terry: When we walk over the little wooden bridge that spans the estuary there, I always make Daphne stop so we can watch the jacksmelt jumping.

Daphne: And he's so happy! And I appreciate that he sees it, because I wouldn't otherwise.

Daphne: I found a surprise. With the work we do, we have to really get involved. And I have a highly ambivalent and confused relationship to God, but whenever it gets very painful, I start praying and reading scripture. The surprise is that if you're going to be involved with life or people, there's going to be complicated suffering. And if you're really going to be involved, you're going to get into the soup. A Christian perspective matters to me, as it treats suffering. I know Buddhism does, too—but there's a more personal relationship in "it's okay that you're suffering, it's part of it to be suffering, and there's help for suffering." The surprise is that to be alive, you keep feeling a lot, and you don't get over that. You might get perspective, or you might recognize it's not your problem, or you might say my child has to figure it out by themselves, or you might have all sorts of reasonable, wise things you say. But if you're alive and you're involved, you're going to feel. And that's going to be beautiful and hard. And that's what it is.

Terry: Oh! There's beauty—that's the way things fit together. Look at Chimney Rock beach in Point Reyes: if you stand there long enough, you'll see an elephant seal cow lying there on the beach. Then a dozen gulls all of a sudden land all around her, and you say, "Oh, wow!" because they smell that she's about to give birth. And then you'll see a blossom of red on the sand, and a little pup there, and then all the gulls are there saying, "Can we have the placenta?" I mean, those things are amazing.

6. *Helene Zindarsian, choir director and soprano at San Francisco's St. Gregory the Illuminator Armenian Apostolic Church. Sings baroque reper- tory for professional choruses, European concert tours, and CDs.*

What I find so miraculous about the human voice is that each one is so individ- ualistic. When we think of someone we love, especially if it's someone we hav- en't seen in a while, it can be very emotionally touching to recall their voice. Or their laughter. That's something so unique: that sound! When someone enters a room and laughs or speaks, even without seeing them, you know exactly who it is. That's something really magnificent and beautiful, the individuality of the human voice.

I do a lot of professional choral singing, which is quite a different experi- ence from when I sing as a soloist. In a chorus, there's some miracle by which another kind of beauty comes forward; a collective beauty out of all the indi- vidual beauty. While we don't subjugate or abandon our individuality to bring this cohesive sound about, we do need to empty ourselves somewhat to make room for a collective beauty. And every group is different. I don't blend the same way in one chorus as I do in another. It's a mysterious process, and yet, we're all doing it somehow side by side, simultaneously.

I had the opportunity to experience Janet Cardiff's "Forty-Part Motet" exhibit (playing a recording of Thomas Tallis's *Spem in Alium*) where each of the forty voices is isolated through a separate speaker. You could get really close to each voice and hear its individuality by walking around the room; then you could step into the middle of the room and hear the whole. The experience was so moving because it demonstrated how incredibly beautiful the whole can be, but how the whole beauty is impossible without each individual part.

Recently, I was in Zion, Utah, hiking through The Narrows. What struck me even more than the obvious natural beauty was the realization that no one person's path through the river is exactly the same—where you're going to cross, which rocks you're going to step on, all the endless combinations of tiny little decisions and individual choices. Just like in the music—there's a through line; everyone's going in the same direction, but the way we manage to get there is completely different, and I find that incredibly freeing and beautiful.

Beauty is often a surprise. It might even happen when revisiting a situation or a place or a person; like on a second hearing—listening to that singer, for example, that someone found beautiful although you didn't agree with them at the time. And then you listen again, and then, *then*—there's something sur- prising there; something that you didn't hear the first time, or you didn't see

THE CREATOR'S SIGN: BEAUTY

the first time. The through line there would be that no, it's not surprising that there's more beauty. And you kind of have to laugh at yourself a little that you didn't see it the first time. It's like the feeling of "of course—." It's still a surprise, but of course—of *course* there's more beauty. That part is not a surprise.

When we appreciate something beautiful, it's restorative. It restores that original state prior to our disillusionment; it restores our sense of wonder. No matter how virtuosic or technically "perfect" the performance, my main criterion is, "Does it move me?" Did it feed me? Did it help restore or fill this hungry reservoir of wonderment? During Robert Schumann's glorious Year of Song in 1840, he wrote two beautiful song cycles—one is *Dichterliebe*, which is told from a man's perspective, and the other is *Frauenliebe und Leben*, which is written from a woman's point of view. But so much of the story is the same. Disappointment, pain, joy—these are things we *all* experience. And I think beauty is the same way. We *all* experience it—whether we acknowledge it or not, there's no doubt that it is there. But if a person's nature is oriented towards looking for it, or pursuing it, or acknowledging it, then I think those are the people that will find it more often.

I sing in an Armenian church. The service is a centuries-old tradition, a lineage dating back to the fourth century. Since we don't have a large choir at our church—and I'm only half Armenian!—I feel a great deal of privilege and responsibility to help carry on the tradition. When I sing as part of a church service, I am also aware that there is a different audience, so to speak. I feel the need to create an atmosphere and an interpretation that is both as beautiful—and as unobtrusive—as possible. In order to do that, I need to be present, and yet completely out of the way. There's an interesting balance there. When I'm singing someplace else, though, there isn't the need to acknowledge a higher power in quite the same way—well, maybe except for the conductor!

7. *Jacob Slichter,* *church musician and drummer in prize-winning rock band Semisonic; authored* New York Times *best-seller* So You Want to be a Rock Star! *Earned A.B. degree in African American Studies at Harvard and teaches creative writing at Sarah Lawrence College in addition to bookless congregational song at Music that Makes Community conferences. Husband of poet Suzanne Weiss.*

One thing about beauty is that it's beyond our control. I can practice or write regularly, and the more regular I am, the more likely it is to show up. And I've learned certain things like [to] relax, or not try to be over-determined, and it's more likely to show up. But in the end, it's all beyond my control. And I think that is the really frustrating and beautiful—or wonderful—thing, that beauty is beyond us, and that's why it so captures our attention. And I think this is one reason why churches have trouble with it, because it's something they can't control. They want to bring the people in and give them a great show. And they dare not involve the people in the creation of that show, but they want to blow people away with high-quality product. And that is exactly what gets in the way of beauty at church.

Usually it surprises people when it surprises me, so I can't have beauty up my sleeve. I'll give you an example. At St. Lydia's, I play the doumbek, which is a Middle Eastern drum. I play that drum underneath the Eucharistic Prayer. It's just improvised, and Emily, who is usually presiding, sings over it, and she's not attempting to be in rhythm with the drum; she's just singing, and the drum is creating a sense of time underneath her rubato singing, and often really beautiful things happen. Having the drum underneath the singing does something to the experience of listening to beauty, with aesthetic experience, and that is deeply meaningful to people.

Most of the workshops I do are for people who are creating. People with hardly any musical training are surprised that they actually have deep musical intuitions, because musical intuition is deeply wired into us. And when you set them loose to write a melody, their first efforts are surprisingly good. Their ears, of course, are far beyond their abilities as composers, but they recognize that what they did right out of the box is interesting, and reveals a part of themselves that they have never let out.

Experience really teaches people much more deeply than all of the words I could ever tell them. So I get them making melodies as soon as possible. Within a minute or two of a song writing workshop, I want the participants already engaged, trying and maybe failing, but maybe succeeding; and learning how to talk about it. I do the same thing when I teach creative writing at Sarah Lawrence College. I talk to people about capturing their experience of what writing did to them. By the time we're actually having material from the students, we've practiced the art of talking about the writing already. Because their own experiences really stick with them.

When I teach music or writing or drumming workshops, I'm trying to awaken the learning of the students, because they'll be able to put it together for themselves in ways that I don't necessarily know how to do. Everybody has different learning strategies, and you've got to give them an experience so that they can engage those strategies.

I grew up listening to soul music, and it just got to me—especially the emphasis on rhythm. And a lot of the black pop artists of the early '70s were singing about social issues, and though I was only a kid at the time, that particular spiritual awareness spoke to me. Before I was going to church, I secretly had my own little religious experiences, and soul music was a place where I could find a sense of communion. There's a powerful communal music-making experience alive in African American musical traditions, and it got to me at a very young age and has stayed with me ever since. Black culture is gigantic and vast, and I am so ignorant of most of it.

The Stevie Wonder albums of the early '70s were albums where he played everything himself. Those were my all-time favorite records. He went off and just explored—when you listen to those records, you really feel you're listening to Stevie Wonder off in his very own corner of the musical cosmos. It's nothing I ever could have ever dreamed up, and every time I listen it sounds brand new and discovered all over again. It's not perfectly played, but it's so soulfully felt. The fact that it isn't perfectly played is one of its most engaging aspects. He's focused on channeling music—or feeling!—out into the world. There's so much more beauty in Stevie Wonder's sloppy drumming than in all the neat-freak drumming in the world. He's absolutely one of the best drummers; not as a technician—unless you define technique a little more widely, as I think we ought to. He is going after something more important. Too many drummers focus on speed and execution, as opposed to just channeling music and expressing.

Here's one thing that I've learned, that's relevant to churches. I learned that what really makes a rock show is the crowd. A great band helps the crowd figure out how to *be* the show. You can't have a great rock show if you're only one person seeing the world's greatest rock band. It's just not going to be what rock and roll is supposed to be. So many churches say: we've got to give them a great show, with the best music, and blow them away, and send them home with the best preaching, and the best coffee and all of that stuff. Well, I think that's missing the point: the really most amazing things that can happen at church can come out of the congregation. I discovered this at St. Gregory's, when I noticed that the beauty of the sermons was actually a collaboration. The preacher would preach, and then a moment of silence, and then people would stand up and share their own experiences that came to mind during the sermon. Not that their experiences proved more interesting, but the experiences allowed me to see the size of what had been discussed. When I'm playing the drums on a stage, I'm playing my beat, and people are shaking their hips. But those hips are so much bigger than the drums in terms of the energy they create, even if they're doing it very subtly. That's what happens at church—and at rock shows. The crowd takes the band and makes it huge. And it's the same principle at church. I'm sure you've found as a preacher that you think you have your sermon together, but only once you're in front of people, does the thing actually come together and become what it's supposed to be. There's something about having people in front of you that helps your own creative process reach the thing it's got to reach. That's what I meant earlier, that beauty and creativity are all beyond our control.

Noam Chomsky says that one of the biggest misconceptions people have about language is that it's designed for communication. Language is far too complex, and human grammar capacity creates structures that are much more complex than we would ever want if all we really needed to do was communicate with each other. Language is really designed for thought. And I think there's something analogous with creativity. We think of music as expression, but it's more. If you bring a powerful musical experience into church, you don't know where it's going to end up, because people are going to be thinking and feeling and discovering something as they make music together. And you can't know what it is that they're going to discover.

> **8. *Nicolas Elsishans,*** executive director of San Francisco Parks Conservation Fund and finance officer of the Art Museums of San Francisco; also Julliard graduate in music composition.

> **9. *Christopher Hayes,*** chancellor (legal counsel) of the Episcopal Diocese of California. Classical instrumentalist and concert-goer. Husband of Nicolas Elsishans.

Nicolas: For me, growing up in the Roman Church and coming to the Episcopal Church, I grew up very lucky to be preached to and taught by Franciscans. And Franciscans spoke to me specifically about the most important part of liturgy, on occasion, is the music alone, because that can speak to you in a way that the confusion of the human mind cannot penetrate. And because I am so in tune with both listening to great liturgy, hearing great liturgy being celebrated, hearing great homiletics, as well—I need all of them. I need the whole thing put together.

Chris: I did spend my teenage and some young adult years as a Unitarian: it has something of the austerity of reason alone, and I don't think I realized what I was missing. But my first day at Grace Cathedral with Nicolas it happened to be All Saints' Sunday, with baptisms and smells and bells. And here I was saying this Creed—no one was compelling me to say it. But something internally was.

Nicolas: I believe my experience of musical beauty doesn't matter if it's in a church context or not. We will be going to the symphony tonight, listening to a Mozart piano concerto played by Emanuel Ax, and then *La Mer*, one of the greatest pieces that changed the concept of the symphony orchestra. I will not be thinking when I'm listening to Debussy, I will be absorbing. It is not unlike a spiritual connection with the Holy Spirit, when you're dumbstruck. Its repetition and perpetual accessibility is one of the most important things in my life. I can have that spiritual experience in Davies Symphony Hall or in Grace Cathedral.

I do have an undergraduate degree from Julliard, and master's degrees in finance and administration, and in music. So the background is there. But my pure experience of musical beauty is as a worshipper. And it doesn't matter if I'm worshipping God or the music of Debussy.

Chris: I picked up a few different instruments in high school—saxophone, baritone horn, every variety of clarinet there is—and I was in the Stanford Symphony, so I kept it up through college. I would say that the Baroque era is what first drew me into the real love of music, and perhaps maybe because it is governed by rules that are fairly obvious to the listener. At least it's obvious to the listener that there are rules; even if the listener doesn't know what the rules are, a good Baroque composition has them on display.

Nicolas: Palestrina and Bach were capable of creating absolutely transcendent music supported by the rules, not hampered by them. Debussy is just one more example, aesthetically approachable. I would find it very easy to fall in love with Debussy in the first three minutes of the composition. I can find that in more complex music, from a contrapuntal or harmonic perspective—but it is nevertheless a distinctly profound message, specific to Debussy.

Chris: You know, some people have their air guitars. Well, I have my air clarinet. It's not quite dancing, but there's some kind of physical interaction with the music.

Nicolas: And not to be terribly metaphysical, but I tend to leave my body and feel it in a spiritual body. And if there's dancing to be done on that plane, I am dancing. And I find myself rather stationary in my seat at Davies Symphony Hall; nevertheless, I'm dancing elsewhere.

Chris: I'd never even set foot in California before; I arrived to live here for college. The beauty of this part of the world has never left me. I moved away for a couple of years to live in New York and I moved away for a year to live in Germany, but I was always drawn back. And I never get tired of the beauty of this place, even as familiar as it is.

And our marriage was love at first sight.

Nicolas: We saw each other and, quite literally, fell in love immediately. I was completely attracted to him, and he was completely attracted to me, and that has not stopped in twenty-three years. There's a certain buoyancy to that; a certain just sheer joy. I had placed a personals ad that was reflecting on a year or two of dating which was disastrous. And I received a letter from Chris: extraordinarily well-written; very thoughtful; very clear, but also very earnest. We decided that we would just meet and talk for dinner for about forty-five minutes to an hour. I think we talked for six hours going into the next morning, and that was it. It was as if God said, "Door's open, walk through or not." We walked through, door shut—

Chris: That's it. I think of all the beautiful things we did that same weekend. We went for a walk in Golden Gate Park, and we found this little dell where we talked about what our life together would be like. We've gone back and tried to find that place, and we can't find it. It's like the Brigadoon of Golden Gate Park. But it's a thing of perfect beauty in my memory.

Nicolas: The story we just shared with you—as if I'd thought on Monday that by the next week I'd be essentially married—came as a surprise. Probably the greatest of my life. That something could happen so quickly, and so absolutely, and so surely.

Chris: I had been totally persuaded that love at first sight was a myth that sold Hollywood movies and romance novels. I didn't think it could actually happen! We have told the story of our relationship over and over and over again. But I hadn't thought about it from the perspective of moments of beauty that came along. So that's a surprise to me, to think about it that way, because it has more importance than I would have thought.

Nicolas: I was the chief operating officer of the Fine Arts Museums of San Francisco before my current job [for the Parks Conservancy]. So my exposure to the visual arts, albeit from a business perspective and a negotiations perspective, was intense.

Chris: You were also walking through those galleries every day.

Nicolas: That's the point. I found that there were works—particularly abstract Expressionist works—that appealed to my ethereal sense of joy and expression. So anything from a Kandinsky print that I had in my office, and we still have in our home, to California Diebenkorn, to Matisse . . . they were able to speak to my sense of almost inexpressible joy and experience. And "modern art" has the distinct advantage that it has a vocabulary that can speak to those things that can't be put into words.

10. *Joan Roughgarden, transgender Stanford professor of biology emerita, author of* Evolution's Rainbow *and* Evolution and Christian Faith. *Born the child of a construction engineer working for the Episcopal Church in Zamboanga, Philippines, and working for the United Nations in Bogor, Indonesia, she is also the wife of marathon athlete and professional chef Richard Schmidt.*

I was a philosophy major as an undergraduate, and there was quite a bit of question as to what beauty was, and whether beauty had anything necessarily to do with art. We discussed whether the purpose of art is actually to broadcast a message. But even if the intention of the art was propagandistic, if you looked at it from a certain angle, sometimes you could discern an artistic perspective. Some attempts at beauty are trivial. Early in my instruction, I questioned the centrality of beauty in art, and the irrelevance of beauty to what constituted art; that art could subsume beauty, but it didn't have to. And nature could be beautiful, and yet not be art. Because art does have to be made by a person. Or extracted from nature, and presented by a person. So art is not documentary.

What motivated me has been primarily curiosity. And a sixth sense for when some angle is being deliberately overlooked, when I sense a spin or a cover-up. That is what I definitely experienced when I started the research for my book, *"Evolution's Rainbow: Gender and Sexuality in Nature."* I felt that the biology being taught amounted to a cover-up. What's called the theory of sexual selection was part of Darwin's writings. It envisions stereotypical gender roles, very heterosexist, and focused on the nuclear family and pair bonds—as though written by one of the right wing quasi-Christian organizations. It envisions the male as the captain of the nest, and the female as subordinate. Not only is this picture inaccurate, but its rationale is problematic, because there's a "genetic classism" involved. The best male gets the female, and the males compete with one another. And the females are content to choose the victor according to the Darwinian account.

And that's just not true of nature. Yet there's no willingness among the biological peer group to confront the depth of the problems in sexual selection theory. A lot worship Darwin as an almost Jesus-like figure in biology. So criticizing him is truly a heresy, an abomination. I wasn't really led into all this by considerations of beauty. It was more by curiosity, and smelling a rat. The various colors and shapes that animals have, which are normally explained in terms of a male advantage in sexual selection terms: I have suggested that these are a form of communication. Look at dogs and cats, they wag their tail or use their tails in ways that are very expressive. So a lot of communication is through body posturing and body colors.

It's just my suspicion, not evidence, that whenever traits are ascribed uniquely to humans, such an attribution is usually wrong. We're not the only tool-using species, nor the only ones who feel empathy; we're not the only ones who have a sense of morality; we're not the only ones with a code of conduct; we're not the only ones that work in groups, and on and on this goes. So to suggest that there is no sense of aesthetic in an animal mind is probably wrong. You can make a pretty data-driven case that animals feel pleasure. And if they feel pleasure, then they would be motivated by pleasure. And again, over the last decade, it's just now understood that animals can make choices. They learn, and they weigh pros and cons, which you could say is also functional. So if they can feel pleasure, then undoubtedly pleasure would be one of the considerations they would take into account when making a decision.

There's a lot of argument as to how rational animals are, even in a functional sense. It parallels discussions of human rationality and economics. A lot of behavioral economics challenges the earlier rationalist view of the wise consumer that acts in their own best interest. People don't understand probabilities well, so they screw up the right decision when it comes to probabilities. The problem with animals is that we'd like to assume that an animal does what it set out to do, but we know based on humans, that they would make mistakes sometimes. Do you assume that they don't know what they're doing? That's wrong. Or that they know exactly what they're doing? And that's wrong too, a little bit. You have to come in at it from both angles, and narrow in on just how smart they are.

I'm drawn to truth. It's the truth that has been fascinating. Yes, what's really going on. What's the real story? And that's fun to find out. That's very satisfying to discern. It's the real truth. You couldn't make it up.

The history of my own gender transition is that I'd been fighting it for quite a while. So I started seeing therapist Millie Brown, who wrote a book called *True Selves*. And I felt like she had a mirror in my house and throughout my life, and she completely characterized what people who are trans go through, from the time they're children up until the time when they're adults. So once I realized I was trans, I didn't waste any time. I said: the sooner I transition, then the longer a life I can have living as Joan. That involved systematically coming out to the people you had to.

So I went to Condoleezza Rice. She was the Stanford University provost, and it was her portfolio to cover the faculty in academic matters. I had heard her commencement speech at the local high school when my son was graduating, and her own story is very compelling. Growing up in the South, she became a Republican because the Dixiecrat Democrats wouldn't have her. And also as provost, she was instrumental in bringing women into positions of leadership and consulting with them, so that the woman's voice was heard. And she also was fearless in taking on a lot of the powerful male academics. They would badmouth her to no end, but that's just because she was not folding under their pressure, she was not trying to kiss up to them. And so I felt comfortable going to her. She was remarkably empathetic and helpful, and not at all taken aback. So there was a lot of support, and I thought at the very beginning that everything was going to go very smoothly.

The problem that someone in any minority feels, though, is the pressure to conform. When I first transitioned, a lot of biologists just said: Oh, well that's great. But when I got into looking at sexual selection theory, and took a contrarian view, the initial reaction to my critique of sexual selection theory was, this was just the gay agenda. So they used my coming out to discredit what I was saying. Just the way a black professor would be criticized for being biased if they said something different about the black experience. There is an attempt to normalize gay and trans expressions as a medical anomaly. So if you adopt a medical explanation of yourself, then you buy yourself acceptance. But I call this self-pathologizing. Of course, in previous decades gays would do that. They would go and try to get themselves cured. And the trans people are still in this, to a large extent. A fairly large number consider themselves actually to have something the matter with them biologically or medically. And that's why my book *Evolution's Rainbow* was important, because it showed how diversity is widespread throughout nature. I think I have made a difference. And it's just not imagined that somebody my age would still be able to do this, or have anything to say. I'm out to pasture now. So I'm flattered that you're interested.

CHAPTER ELEVEN

⁓

A FITTING END

Religion begins in awe, and ends in affection.

—THOMAS AQUINAS

British historian Geoffrey Moorhouse was one of the first Europeans to attempt crossing the Sahara Desert from west to east.[1] Leaving Moroccan villages behind, he journeyed in company with Tuareg camel riders until hardships terminated his pilgrimage halfway, in the Hoggar Mountains. By then he had learned that contrary to legend the Tuaregs travel by dead reckoning, not celestial navigation, and are often lost in the desert. Near nightfall when one Tuareg spies another approaching a well or oasis from the opposite side, both riders dismount and throw sand into the air in patterns identifying their clans. This custom prevents tribal opponents from accidentally dining together, since having once shared a meal, Tuaregs may never fight.

Many African Christians gather hours before a stated service time, and continue long afterward sharing food and dancing while travelers depart for home. By contrast, first-world services end abruptly on purpose. Over centuries European church rituals multiplied beginnings and endings, which reformers now prune at both ends to nourish the central action. Clergy try to start smartly on time, using formulae anciently designed for crowds—but must therefore imagine mass participation while laypeople actually arrive more slowly. Ministers likewise manage a "recessional" hymn and dismissal, leading swiftly to farewells by the parish doors. Layfolk wishing actual conversation must remove to a different building counted less sacred, where clergy may attend or not.

Such ax-work dismembers the natural community among people who share a sacred meal. Moreover, as a visiting preacher I sometimes find wealthier churches offer less generous hospitality, while their clergy retreat into privacy,

---

1. Geoffrey Moorhouse, *The Fearful Void* (London: Faber & Faber, 1974, 1989, 2011).

or into closed meetings for vestry and committees. One California seaside parish even substituted an invitational home sherry hour to filter hippies and weekenders from influence. No wonder such churches do not grow! In John's gospel's Last Supper story, Jesus gives a sop to Judas saying, "What you do, do quickly," and Judas leaves at once to betray him.[2] That story echoes when Christians scatter quickly after worship without stopping to share affectionate company with fellow parishioners of all classes. Is not economic classism the dirty secret of American society?

Food Pantry Volunteers Distribute Groceries from St. Gregory's Altar to the Needy

Parish "coffee hour" importantly extends eucharistic feasting upon Christ's body and blood, as does distributing victuals to the poor. St. Gregory's Sunday liturgy closes with coffee and simple foods laid out upon the same eucharistic table, where worshippers linger to converse with new friends and old. (Meetings are postponed awhile.) Each Friday, groceries are piled upon that very altar table and others around it, while the poor pass by receiving staples for the week. Many recipients return to help hand out foodstuffs in future.[3] Thus Jesus's table continues welcoming in every way the gospels describe. By contrast, removing coffee drinkers to a supposed less sacred space contradicts church theory. It is

---

2. John 13:27.

3. Miles, *Take This Bread.*

the people, not the sanctuary or its furniture, whom Christ hallows with his presence, which the bread and wine effectually symbolize. Historian E. C. Ratcliff concluded from ancient prayers that the *epiclesis*, a third-century prayer innovation, called first for God's Spirit upon the *people*, and only later upon the bread and wine as well.[4]

Pastoral care at "coffee hour" is crucial for the day's presider and for any visiting preacher, however exalted, to join in. Six years ago, Lebanese New Testament professor Fr. Jack Khalil invited me to his struggling Orthodox parish in a hostile Hamas neighborhood at Tyre. After liturgy he spoke warmly with every single worshipper over coffee. Two told me they faced family shunning and death decrees after converting there from Islam. Within months the Syrian war made my return visit impossible. I wrote my thanks—but got no reply—and I continue to pray for them all: so enduring was the community their hospitality made me part of, overcoming deadly human boundaries.

So I will close the way every Chinese schoolchild memorizes the couplet opening Confucius's *Analects:*

<blockquote>

Is it not a pleasure studying long and hard?

Is it not a pleasure having friends come from afar?[5]

</blockquote>

<blockquote>

學而時習之，不亦說乎？

有朋自遠方來，不亦樂乎？

</blockquote>

---

4. E. C. Ratcliff, "The Sanctus and the Pattern of the Early Anaphora," reprinted in *Liturgical Studies*, ed. A. H. Couratin & D. H. Tripp (London: SPCK, 1976).

5. Confucius's *Analects, fifth century* BCE. Annping Chin, *Confucius: A Life of Thought and Politics* (New Haven: Yale University Press, 2007, 2008).

GRATEFUL MEMORY

M y heroic yokefellows Donald and Ellen Schell have teamed with me for half a century. Joining first at New York's East Harlem and then Yale's Episcopal Chaplaincy, together we planned, seeded, and cultivated St. Gregory Nyssen Church in an open San Francisco neighborhood field. Their ideals and insights glisten through every chapter you have read.[1] Eight years' shared householding put their four children into my single gay life, a joyful influence on this book. What a blessing that their friendship with God embraced me too, and for how long! With our families and friends and a hundred generous church members, we built a prize banqueting house[2]

St. Gregory's Church (Elevation)

David Sanger

---

1. St. Gregory of Nyssa Church website offers "Worship at St. Gregory's," a liturgical customary emphasizing lay ministry, as well as the original Plan for St. Gregory's Church, adopted by the Diocese of California in 1978 (*https://www.saintgregorys.org/articles.html*).

2. Song of Songs 2:4. American Institute of Architects' Religious Architecture Design Honor Award 1998.

by John Goldman that victuals and provisions spiritual pilgrims still. Earlier books have told how Providence called lay and ordained ministers Sarah Miles and Paul Fromberg to create model Christian service and teaching for our age. Sanford Dole and Fred Goff filled the house with singing, while All Saints Company's contributors still publish volumes, and Music that Makes Community spreads congregational song. It is only my grateful duty to rejoice over such wonders here.

A half dozen Episcopal clerics—always men in those dim days—led me up the path toward this book. Benedict Green, CR, and Richard Norris appear repeatedly on these pages. Eugene Blankenship enfleshed a priestly ideal I still try to copy. Benedict Green forced me (alarmed at first) into historical text criticism; Richard Norris introduced me to Gregory Nyssen; and Old Testament professors Judah Goldin at Yale and Robert Dentan at General Seminary guided me through Gregory's favorite books. Those teachers' labors produced whatever good my readers may find here. Indeed, the longer I live and work in a parish, the more Gregory of Nyssa's seems the only classical Christianity that makes sense. Lacking his taste for metaphysic, I must thank historians at the North American Academy of Liturgy, *Societas Liturgica*, and the Society of Oriental Liturgy for slaking my scholarly thirst year by year.

Chinese Studies—I was one of Yale's first two undergraduate majors—opened a radical perspective on our Western norms. Yale's Nelson Wu and San Francisco's Jungying Tsao infected me with their passion for Chinese art, which I have collected since. A Paul Mellon Fellowship at Clare College, Cambridge, informed my history teaching at Yale's Saybrook College and the California School for Deacons. Clinical Psychoanalyst Richard Greenberg directed my inner steps until Yvonne Rand, Jonathan Dunn, and my loving husband Stephen Holtzman took me up.

The monastic Community and College of the Resurrection at Mirfield, Yorkshire, realized a modern common worship life for me. Mirfield would shape my Yale Chaplaincy and later our plans for St. Gregory's Church. We monks and students sang plainsong services daily. Composers Maury Yeston and Elinor Armer later pressed me into counterpoint, while Richard Rephann and Corey Jamason taught me at the harpsichord.

Then San Francisco surprised me with athletics: three charity AIDS Rides tandem-bicycling to Los Angeles, twenty Gay Games swim medals, and thirty years of snowboarding. My family, Francis, Gretchen, Jennifer, and Michael, have steadfastly supported a journey that wandered from their own. Karl and Joan Stockbridge kept us all working together as only devoted friends can do.

When folks ask for divine visions, thank Heaven I saw one, the night the Royal Cambodian Ballet danced at San Francisco. Classical dancers had been top targets of Pol Pot's genocidal revolution (1975–79). A lone surviving choreographer gathered refugees from camps worldwide and composed a dance to thank God who had saved them from the "killing fields." Tragically on the tour's opening night, the choreographer was killed by a truck outside Washington, DC's Kennedy Center. So his troupe danced his thanksgiving piece to end every performance in his memory.

Now the drums and gongs began rolling waves of rhythm, and the curtain rose above a young man sewn into a divine costume with a troupe lined up behind him, their many arms forming an Asian image of God's countless powers. Advancing toward us, his fellow dancers split off like crowds of worshippers. They wove graceful lines with lamps in both hands, while the deity moved among them, blessing his followers. At last he reappeared and moved downstage again as his fellows rejoined him, forming a unified figure of God— smiling, blessing the world with thirty moving arms, and coming to greet us. I could not keep my seat; I jumped up shouting! We thousand watchers were all electrified. I have never caught a more powerful emblem of God's loving providence.

Iconographer Mark Dukes and photographer David Sanger have beautified St. Gregory's Church and this book with our shared vision of what will greet us after this life. Some friends and teachers named herein already enjoy it. My tireless editors Victor Gavenda and Nancy Bryan practice to conduct their chorus dance one day. Meanwhile for us, the rabbis say,

To remember the righteous is a blessing.

זכר צדיק לברכה

APPENDIX

HYMNS OF CHRIST COMING IN OUR WORSHIP NOW, FOR THE EUCHARISTIC PROCESSION

(See chapter 2, The People's Sign: Giving Authority to Christ.)

A. THE FIVE EASTERN HYMNS FOR THE EUCHARIST PROCESSION

Earliest among these five is the Psalm 24 chorus. The refrain "Alleluia!" sung thrice enabled congregations to sing along without books. Armenians still chant this chorus and refrains on Sundays. (Before the twentieth century, Psalms were sung only in segments for the Eucharist. Ancient proper melodies are lost, although Western plainsong preserves very early psalm tunes.)

Psalm 24, OPENING VERSES [The earth is the Lord's and all that is in it,
(not sung) The world and those who dwell therein.
For the Lord has founded it upon the seas
And established it upon the rivers.
Who may ascend the mountain of the Lord,
And who may stand in God's holy place?
Those of innocent hands and purity of heart,
Who do not swear on God's being
Nor do they pledge by what is false.
They shall receive blessing from the Lord
And righteousness from the God of their salvation.
Such is the generation of those who seek you, O Lord,
Of those who seek your face, O God of Jacob.]

CHORUS & REFRAINS (sung) Lift up your heads, O gates
And be lifted up, O everlasting doors,
That the King of Glory may come in.
Who is this King of Glory?
The Lord, strong and mighty,
The Lord, mighty in battle.
Lift up your heads, O gates
And be lifted up, O everlasting doors,
That the King of Glory may come in.
Who is this King of Glory?
Truly, the Lord of Hosts
Is the King of Glory.
Alleluia! Alleluia! Alleluia!

The second Byzantine Eucharist Procession hymn was composed as a longer choir chorus upon Psalm 24. In practice the congregation joined in the old triple Alleluia refrain as before. Sung today on more Sundays than all the rest, this lyric expands the royal Preface that follows next, by evoking Isaiah, who saw God enthroned in the empty space above the Ark like a traditional Middle Eastern deity, and heard the surrounding divine court's *Sanctus* hymn. Most Eastern churches have added their own melodies:

> Now let us, who mystically represent the Cherubim,
> Let us lay aside every earthly care
> While we sing the thrice-holy hymn
> To the Life-giving Trinity,
> That we may receive the King of All
> Who comes escorted invisibly by angelic hosts.
> Alleluia, Alleluia, Alleluia!

The third and most elaborate Preface Procession hymn was composed last. Anglophone congregations know it from Gerald Moultrie's verse paraphrase, sung to a beloved French tune. It expands the same themes as the first three:

> Let all mortal flesh keep silence
> And with fear and trembling stand.
> Ponder nothing earthly-minded,
> For with blessing in his hand
> Christ our God to earth descendeth
> Our full homage to command.
> > King of kings, yet born of Mary
> > As of old on earth he stood,
> > Lord of lords in human vesture,
> > In the Body and the Blood.
> > He will give to all the faithful
> > His own self for heavenly food.
> Rank on rank the host of heaven
> Spreads its vanguard on the way
> As the light of lights descendeth
> From the realms of endless day,
> That the powers of hell may vanish
> As the darkness clears away.
> > At his feet the six-winged seraphs,
> > Cherubim with sleepless eye,
> > Veil their faces to the Presence,
> > As with ceaseless voice they cry:
> > > Alleluia, Alleluia,
> > > Alleluia, Lord most high!

A fourth Procession lyric fits the liturgy of Pre-Sanctified Gifts, for Communion from bread and wine reserved at Sunday's Eucharist, and consumed after Vespers on fasting Lenten Wednesdays. (Note that Eastern Christians sing Alleluias all year.) The third and fourth lyrics alone mention the Eucharistic gifts.

Now the powers of heaven stand
to serve with us unseen,
As the sacrifice is borne on high,
fulfilled.
Let us draw near with faith and love,
And share the taste of life eternal.
Alleluia, Alleluia, Alleluia!

Finally, the hymn sung on the Thursday of Passion Week, commemorating Jesus's Last Supper:

Lord, receive me as a guest at your mystical supper.
I will not betray you with a kiss [like Judas]
But with the penitent thief I say:
Lord, remember me when you come into your kingdom!

In place of YHWH'S royal court, this last hymn evokes Jesus's crucifixion the following day, and a dying sinner's prayer for salvation when Christ's kingdom appears. It links both to this supper ritual here today. Eastern sanctuaries often place an icon of the Last Supper above the doorway where people take Communion: there as communicants look upward and open their mouths, they can feel themselves dining even now at Jesus's banquet. Another Eastern Communion icon shows Jesus giving his sacramental body and blood to his disciples from this very church altar. In the West, similar imagination of Bible scenes eventually produced Ignatian meditation, Passion plays, and Protestant musical Passions.

B.   TRADITIONAL WESTERN HYMNS FOR THE EUCHARIST PROCESSION

Chapter 2 ends with a hymn by Charles Wesley, one example of 222 traditional Western hymns listed for free download at *www.churchpublishing.org/signsoflife*. Readers will find this publication method most practical for searching and sorting hymns, as well as printing them.

Drawn from official ELCA Lutheran and American Episcopal hymnals, these 222 hymns evoke Christ's arrival in this liturgy here and now, with authority to make justice and peace, in parallel with Eastern hymns for the Eucharist Procession. Some are already officially published for Advent season but will serve any occasion when they fit lectionary readings. Western lyrics setting the classic Eastern Procession Hymns into rhythm appear here in **BOLDFACE**.

The Easter and Christmas cycles also provide seasonal hymns that are not cited here. In keeping with Jesus's immanent "realized" eschatology, apocalyptic lyrics and penitential lyrics do not appear. Only one hymn in the Episcopal version (alone) requires a small edit. Congregations can reform gender language by their own preferred standards.